Samsung
Galaxy Tab™
FOR
DUMMIES®

Samsung Galaxy Tab™

FOR

DUMMIES®

by Dan Gookin

WILEY

Wiley Publishing, Inc.

Samsung Galaxy Tab™ For Dummies®

Published by
Wiley Publishing, Inc.
111 River Street
Hoboken, NJ 07030-5774

www.wiley.com

Copyright © 2011 by Wiley Publishing, Inc., Indianapolis, Indiana

Published by Wiley Publishing, Inc., Indianapolis, Indiana

Published simultaneously in Canada

For general information on our other products and services, please contact our Customer Care Department within the U.S. at 877-762-2974, outside the U.S. at 317-572-3993, or fax 317-572-4002.

For technical support, please visit www.wiley.com/techsupport.

Wiley also publishes its books in a variety of electronic formats. Some content that appears in print may not be available in electronic books.

Library of Congress Control Number: 2011923433

ISBN: 978-1-118-02445-4

Manufactured in the United States of America

10 9 8 7 6 5 4 3 2 1

WILEY

About the Author

Dan Gookin has written more than 120 books about technology, many of them accurate. He is most famously known as the author of the original *For Dummies* book, *DOS For Dummies*, published in 1991. Additionally, Dan has achieved fame as one of the first computer radio talk show hosts, the editor of a computer magazine, a national technology spokesman, and an occasional actor on the community theater stage.

Dan still considers himself a writer and technology "guru" whose job it is to remind everyone that our electronics are not to be taken too seriously. His approach is light and humorous yet very informative. He knows that modern gizmos can be complex and intimidating but necessary to help people become productive and successful. Dan mixes his vast knowledge of all things high-tech with a unique, dry sense of humor that keeps everyone informed — and awake.

Dan's most recent books are *Word 2010 For Dummies, PCs For Dummies,* Windows 7 Edition, and *Laptops For Dummies*, 4th Edition. He holds a degree in communications/visual arts from the University of California, San Diego. Dan dwells in North Idaho, where he enjoys woodworking, music, theater, riding his bicycle, being with his boys, and fighting local government corruption.

Author's Acknowledgments

I would like to thank Kim Titus and Libertie Bridges, of Samsung, for their kind assistance with this project.

Publisher's Acknowledgments

We're proud of this book; please send us your comments through our online registration form located at http://dummies.custhelp.com. For other comments, please contact our Customer Care Department within the U.S. at 877-762-2974, outside the U.S. at 317-572-3993, or fax 317-572-4002.

Some of the people who helped bring this book to market include the following:

Acquisitions and Editorial

Senior Project Editor: Mark Enochs

Acquisitions Editor: Katie Mohr

Copy Editor: Rebecca Whitney

Editorial Manager: Leah Cameron

Editorial Assistant: Amanda Graham

Sr. Editorial Assistant: Cherie Case

Cartoons: Rich Tennant
(www.the5thwave.com)

Composition Services

Project Coordinator: Sheree Montgomery

Layout and Graphics: Claudia Bell, Samantha K. Cherolis, Joyce Haughey

Proofreaders: Amanda Graham, Leslie Saxman

Indexer: Potomac Indexing, LLC

Publishing and Editorial for Technology Dummies

Richard Swadley, Vice President and Executive Group Publisher

Andy Cummings, Vice President and Publisher

Mary Bednarek, Executive Acquisitions Director

Mary C. Corder, Editorial Director

Publishing for Consumer Dummies

Diane Graves Steele, Vice President and Publisher

Composition Services

Debbie Stailey, Director of Composition Services

Contents at a Glance

Table of Contents

Introduction

*I*t's not a cell phone. It's not a computer. It's the latest craze: the tablet. It exists somewhere between the traditional computer and the newfangled smart phone. That makes the tablet kind of an oddball, but quite a popular oddball.

The Galaxy Tab is Samsung's solution to your mobile, wireless, communications, information, and entertainment needs. Oh, I could blather on and on about how wonderful it is, but my point is simple: The Galaxy Tab does so much, but it comes with such scant documentation that you would merely have to sneeze into the obligatory *Getting Started* pamphlet and the thing would be ruined.

Anyone wanting more information about how to get the most from the Galaxy Tab will need another source. This book is that source.

About This Book

This book was written to help you get the most from the Galaxy Tab's massive potential. It's a reference. Each chapter covers a specific topic, and the sections within each chapter address an issue related to the topic. The overall idea is to show how things are done on the Galaxy Tab and to help you get the most from the Tab without overwhelming you with information or intimidating you into despair.

Sample sections in this book include:

- Making a home for the Tab
- Attaching your Google account to the Galaxy Tab
- Importing contacts from your computer
- Reading an email message
- Running Facebook on your Galaxy Tab
- Making a Skype phone call
- Video phone calls with Tango
- Doing a panoramic shot
- Galaxy Tab travel tips

You have nothing to memorize, no sacred utterances or animal sacrifices, and definitely no PowerPoint presentations. Instead, every section explains a topic as though it's the first thing you read in this book. Nothing is assumed, and everything is cross-referenced. Technical terms and topics, when they come up, are neatly shoved to the side, where they're easily avoided. The idea here isn't to learn anything. This book's philosophy is to help you look it up, figure it out, and get on with your life.

How to Use This Book

This book follows a few conventions for using the Galaxy Tab. First of all, the Galaxy Tab is referred to as the *Galaxy Tab* throughout the book. I might also break down and call it the *Tab* for short, just because, for some reason, typing the word *Galaxy* isn't the easiest thing for me. I might also simply call the Galaxy Tab a *device*, which is how the Tab refers to itself.

The way you interact with the Galax Tab is by using its *touchscreen,* the glassy part of the device as it's facing you. Some physical buttons are also on the device, as well as four buttons along the bottom of the screen. All those buttons are described in Chapter 1.

There are various ways to touch the screen, which are explained and named in Chapter 3.

Chapter 4 discusses text input on the Galaxy Tab, which involves using an onscreen keyboard. The Galaxy Tab comes preconfigured with the Swype onscreen keyboard, which presents a new, fast way to input text. Also, you can input text by speaking to the Galaxy Tab, which is also covered in Chapter 4.

This book directs you to do things by following numbered steps. Each step involves a specific activity, such as touching something on the screen; for example:

3. Choose Downloads.

This step directs you to touch the text or item labeled *Downloads* on the screen. You might also be told to do this:

3. Touch Downloads.

 Some options can be turned off or on, as indicated by a gray box with a green check mark in it, as shown in the margin. By touching the box on the screen, you add or remove the green check mark. When the green check mark appears, the option is on; otherwise, it's off.

The barcodes in the margins are there to help you install recommended apps. To install the app, scan the barcode using barcode reader software you install on the Galaxy Tab. Chapter 17 discusses how to add software, or *apps,* on the Tab. One of the first apps to get should be a barcode reader. I use the Barcode Scanner app.

Foolish Assumptions

Even though this book is written with the gentle handholding required by anyone who is just starting out, or who is easily intimidated, I have made a few assumptions. For example, I assume that you're a human being and not the emperor of Jupiter.

My biggest assumption: You have a Samsung Galaxy Tab of your own. Though you could use this book without owning a Galaxy Tab, I think the people in the phone store would grow tired of you reading it while standing in front of the demo model.

The Galaxy Tab can be purchased from one of several major U.S. cellular carriers. You can get yours from AT&T, Sprint, T-Mobile, US Cellular, or Verizon. Each of these carriers enhances the Galaxy Tab with specific software, though this book doesn't go into detail on the specific software preinstalled by those services.

I also assume that you have a computer, either a desktop or laptop. The computer can be a PC or Windows computer or a Macintosh. Oh, I suppose it could also be a Linux computer. In any event, I refer to your computer as "your computer" throughout this book. When directions are specific to a PC or Mac, the book says so.

Programs that run on the Galaxy Tab are *apps,* which is short for *applications.* A single program is an app.

Finally, this book doesn't assume that you have a Google account, but already having one helps. Information is provided in Chapter 2 about setting up a Google account — an extremely important part of using the Galaxy Tab. Having a Google account opens up a slew of useful features, information, and programs that make using your Tab more productive.

How This Book Is Organized

This book is divided into six parts, each of which covers a certain aspect of the Galaxy Tab or how it's used.

Part I: The Galaxy in Your Hands

This part of the book is an introduction to the Galaxy Tab. Chapters cover setup and orientation to familiarize you with how the device works. It's a good place to start if you're completely new to the concept of tablet computing, mobile devices, or the Android operating system.

Part II: The Communications Tab

In this part of the book, you'll read about various ways that the Galaxy Tab can electronically communicate with your online friends. There's texting, email, the Web, social networking, and even the much-wanted trick of using the nonphone Galaxy Tab to make phone calls and do video chat.

Part III: The Everything Else Tab

The Galaxy Tab is pretty much a limitless gizmo. To prove it, the chapters in this part of the book cover all the various and wonderful things the Tab does: It's an eBook reader, a map, a navigator, a camera, a video recorder, a picture book, a portable music player, a calendar, and potentially so much more.

Part IV: A Well-Connected Tab

Part IV of this book covers how to connect the Galaxy Tab wirelessly to the Internet as well as to other gizmos, such as a Bluetooth speaker or printer. It covers the necessary job of connecting the Tab to your computer for sharing and exchanging files, plus connecting the Galaxy Tab to a high-definition (HD) television for watching the Tab on the "big" screen.

Part V: Your Personal Galaxy

You can do a lot of things to customize the Galaxy Tab, and those things are covered in this part of the book. Chapters here also touch upon taking the Tab with you, preparing for a trip, and using the Tab overseas, plus the necessary topics of Galaxy Tab maintenance, updating, and troubleshooting.

Part VI: The Part of Tens

Things are wrapped up in this book with the traditional *For Dummies* Part of Tens. Each chapter in this part lists ten items or topics. The chapters include tips, tricks, shortcuts, things to remember, and things not to forget, plus a smattering of useful apps that no Galaxy Tab should be without.

Icons Used in This Book

This icon flags useful, helpful tips or shortcuts.

This icon marks a friendly reminder to do something.

This icon marks a friendly reminder not to do something.

This icon alerts you to overly nerdy information and technical discussions of the topic at hand. Reading the information is optional, though it may win you a pie slice in *Trivial Pursuit.*

Where to Go from Here

Start reading! Observe the table of contents and find something that interests you. Or, look up your puzzle in the index. When those suggestions don't cut it, just start reading Chapter 1.

My email address is dgookin@wambooli.com. Yes, that's my real address. I reply to all email I get, and you'll get a quick reply if you keep your question short and specific to this book. Although I do enjoy saying Hi, I cannot answer technical support questions, resolve billing issues, or help you troubleshoot your Galaxy Tab. Thanks for understanding.

You can also visit my Web page for more information or as a diversion: www.wambooli.com.

Enjoy this book and your Galaxy Tab!

Part I
The Galaxy in Your Hands

The 5th Wave   By Rich Tennant

©RICHTENNANT

"What I'm doing should clear your sinuses, take away your headache, and charge your Tab."

In this part . . .

Tablets are nothing new. Moses had a pair of them up on Mount Sinai. Back then, their capacity was small, seeing how they were text-only devices. But their contents were everlasting. Lamentably, Moses broke his tablets in a fit of rage. It would be another few thousand years before tablets would once again become popular, albeit in a different sort of rage.

The Galaxy Tab is probably your introduction to the world of mobile computing devices, commonly called *tablets.* A tablet is not a cell phone. It's not a computer. It's not a gaming device. No, it's more a combination of the best parts of all of them. This part of the book is your introduction to your new gizmo.

Welcome to Tablet Land

In This Chapter
- Unboxing your Galaxy Tab
- Charging the battery
- Locating important things
- Getting optional accessories
- Storing the Tab

There's nothing like getting a new gizmo, opening its box, letting your expectations build, and then experiencing the gnawing frustration of not knowing what to do next. I'm certain that you're eager to get going with your Galaxy Tab, or perhaps you've already torn through the box. Either way, you've discovered nary a hint of what to do next. Fret not, gentle reader.

Whether your Galaxy Tab has been liberated from its box or you've yet to lift the box's lid with quivering anticipation, this chapter helps you get oriented, organized, and off to a good start with the latest craze in mobile devices: the Samsung Galaxy Tab.

Set Up Your Galaxy Tab

Odds are good that the folks who sold you the Galaxy Tab have already done some preconfiguration. In the United States, the Tab is available primarily from cellular phone providers and getting digital cellular service is a usual part of purchasing the Tab.

Most likely, your Tab has already been unboxed and completely manhandled by the cell phone company — maybe even in front of your own eyes!

That's a necessary step, and even though it might have broken your heart (as it did mine), you need the initial setup done by the cell phone company before you can unbox and set up the Galaxy Tab for yourself.

- ✒ If you ordered your Galaxy Tab online, the setup may have been done before the Tab shipped. If not, see Chapter 2.

- ✒ The initial setup identifies the Tab with the cellular network, giving it a network ID and associating the ID with your cellular bill.

- ✒ Additional software setup is required for the Tab, primarily to link it with your Gmail and other Google accounts on the Internet. See Chapter 2 for the details.

- ✒ See the later sidebar "Here a Tab, there a Tab" for more information about the various cellular service providers that offer the Galaxy Tab in the United States.

- ✒ A version of the Galaxy Tab is available that uses only Wi-Fi access. It requires no cellular activation when it's purchased or as part of the initial setup, though you will want to connect to a Wi-Fi network to get the most from the Tab. See Chapter 18.

Opening the box

You gotta hand it to Samsung: No space is wasted in the Galaxy Tab box. The Tab itself fits snugly on top.

Remove the Galaxy Tab by locating the tiny thumb tab of plastic at its top end. Lift, and the Tab is free from the box.

You can remove the plastic sheeting that's clinging to the Tab's front and back.

In the box's bottom compartment, you find

- ✒ **A USB cable:** You can use it to connect the Tab to a computer or a wall charger.

- ✒ **A wall charger:** It comes in two pieces. The larger piece has the USB connector, and the smaller piece is customized for your locality's wall sockets.

- ✒ **Pamphlets with warnings and warranty information:** You also receive a useless *Tips, Hints, and Shortcuts* booklet, which you're free to ignore because, honestly, this book puts that thing to shame.

Go ahead and free the USB cable and power charger from their clear plastic cocoons. Assemble the power charger's two pieces, which fit so snugly together that you'll probably never be able to pry them apart.

Keep the box for as long as you own your Galaxy Tab. If you ever need to return the thing, or ship it somewhere, the original box is the ideal container. You can shove all those useless pamphlets and papers back into the box as well.

Charging the battery

The first thing that I recommend you do with your Galaxy Tab is give it a full charge. Obey these steps:

1. **Assemble the plug-thing that came with the Tab.**

   Put the two pieces together, if you haven't already: the USB part and the part that contains the plug that sticks into a wall socket.

2. **Attach the USB cable to the Galaxy Tab.**

   The side of the cable end that says Samsung faces you as you're looking at the front of the Tab.

3. **Attach the other end of the USB cable to the plug-thing.**

4. **Plug the plug-thing into the wall.**

Upon success, you may see a large Battery icon appear on the Galaxy Tab touchscreen. The icon gives you an idea of the current battery-power level and lets you know that the Galaxy Tab is functioning properly, thought you shouldn't be alarmed if the Battery icon fails to appear.

- ✏ Your Galaxy Tab most likely came fully charged from the factory, though I still recommend giving it an initial charge just in case, as well as to familiarize yourself with the process.

- ✏ The USB cable is used for charging the Galaxy Tab and for connecting it to a computer to share information or exchange files or use the Galaxy Tab as a computer modem. (This *tethering* process is covered in Chapter 18.)

- ✏ You can also charge the Tab by connecting it to a computer's USB port. As long as the computer is on, the Tab charges.

- ✏ The battery charges more efficiently if you plug it into a wall rather than charge it from a computer's USB port.

- ✏ The Galaxy Tab does not feature a removable battery.

Here a Tab, there a Tab

There's only one Galaxy Tab, which is the device I cover in this book. Yet several different cell providers retail the Tab in the United States: AT&T, Sprint, T-Mobile, U.S. Cellular, and Verizon. As far as the hardware goes, other than some color and cosmetic differences, every Tab is pretty much identical. (The cell provider's name appears on the back of the Tab.)

Beyond the hardware, every Tab comes with the same basic apps — software or programs that let you do interesting things. The cell providers include their own, customized apps with their Tabs. For example, Verizon features V CAST and My Verizon apps on its Tab, Sprint offers Sprint Music, and other providers probably toss in other software as well. But, for basic operations, the Galaxy Tab is considered the same gizmo no matter which cell provider you're using.

Know Your Way Around the Galaxy

"Second star to the right and straight on till morning" may get Peter Pan to Neverland, but for navigating your way around the Galaxy Tab, you need more-specific directions.

Finding things on the Tab

Take heed of Figure 1-1, which is my attempt at illustrating the basic Galaxy Tab hardware features. Follow along on your own Tab as you find key features, described in this section.

On the front of the Galaxy Tab, locate these goodies:

Touchscreen display: The biggest part of the Tab is its touchscreen display, which occupies almost all the territory on the front of the device. The touchscreen display is a touch-see thing: You look at it and also touch it with your fingers to control the Tab.

Soft buttons: At the bottom of the touchscreen display are four icons. These *soft buttons* are controls you use to work the Tab's software, programs, and apps. You can read more about the soft buttons in Chapter 3.

Front camera: The Galaxy Tab's front-facing camera is found above the top-right corner of the touchscreen. The camera is used for taking self-portraits as well as for video conferencing.

Light sensor: Though it's difficult to see, just to the left of the front camera is a teensy light sensor. It's used to help adjust the brightness level of the touchscreen.

Figure 1-1: Things on the Galaxy Tab.

Around the Galaxy Tab, you find a variety of buttons, holes, connectors, and other doodads, all carefully explained here:

Headphone jack: Atop the Tab case, you see a hole where you can connect standard headphones.

Microphone: A tiny hole on the left side of the Tab (see Figure 1-1) is used as the device's microphone.

Power/Lock: The power/lock button is labeled with the universal power icon, shown in the margin. Press this button to turn on the Tab, to lock it (put it to sleep), to wake it up, and to turn it off. Directions for performing these activities are found in Chapter 2.

Volume Up/Volume Down: The Tab's volume control is found on the right side of the unit, just below the power/lock button. The button toward the top of the unit is Volume Up, and the other button is Volume Down.

Memory slot: The memory slot is where you find the Galaxy Tab's MicroSD card, a media card on which information is stored. See the next section.

Speaker(s): Stereo speakers are found at the bottom of the Tab — one to the left and the other to the right of the USB connector.

Dock/USB power connector: The Galaxy Tab has a slot on the bottom where you connect the USB cable, which is used to charge the battery and connect your Tab to a computer. The slot is also where the Tab connects to the dock, if you have one. See the later section "Getting optional accessories."

Not shown in Figure 1-1 is the back of the Galaxy Tab. That's because the back is boring: On it, you find the Tab's main camera and LED flash. That's it, which explains why you don't see a lovely-but-pricey illustration of the back of the Galaxy Tab in this book.

> ✔ The back of the Verizon Galaxy Tab is black with a polka dot or stippled design. The back of the Sprint Galaxy Tab is white. All other Galaxy Tabs feature a plain black rump.

> ✔ Don't stick anything into the microphone hole. The only things you need to stick into the Tab are the USB cable (or the connector on the dock) or headphones.

Removing and inserting the MicroSD card

The Galaxy Tab comes with a media card — a *MicroSD card.* It's used to store your stuff, similar to the way a media card stores images in a digital camera. The MicroSD card is basically a tiny (thumbnail-size) storage device.

Yes, it's teensy.

The MicroSD card is preinstalled at the factory; you don't have to insert the card when you first configure the Galaxy Tab. The only time you need to remove the card is when you want to replace it with a higher-capacity card or when you need to remove the card to use it in another device. When that urge hits you, follow these steps:

1. **Turn off your Galaxy Tab.**

   Specific directions are offered in Chapter 2, but for now, press and hold the Power button (see Figure 1-1) and choose the Power Off command from the Device Options menu.

   The MicroSD card can be damaged if it's improperly removed. By turning off the Tab, you ensure that the card can be removed safely.

   To confirm that the Tab is turned off, press and release the Power button quickly. The Tab shouldn't come back to life. If it does, repeat Step 1.

2. **Insert your fingernail at the bottom of the teensy hatch that covers the MicroSD slot and then pry the hatch upward.**

   A fingernail-size indentation lives at the bottom of the slot, as shown in Figure 1-2. When pressure is applied, the hatch that covers the slot pops up and kind of flops over to the side. The slot cover doesn't come off completely.

Right side of the Galaxy Tab

Lift here.

Figure 1-2: Opening the memory card hatch.

3. **Using the same fingernail again, press the MicroSD card inward a tad.**

   The MicroSD card is spring-loaded, so pressing it in pops it outward.

4. **Pinch the MicroSD card between your fingers and remove it completely.**

The MicroSD card is truly an itty-bitty thing, much smaller than your typical media card.

The Galaxy Tab still works without the MicroSD card installed. You can't access any information that was stored on the card, which includes your contacts, pictures, videos, music, and other items necessary to use the Tab. So my advice is to keep the MicroSD card installed.

To insert a MicroSD card into your Galaxy Tab, follow these steps:

1. **Ensure that the Galaxy Tab is turned off.**

   It may also work if the Tab's turned on, but it's safer to turn the Tab off.

2. **Open the little hatch covering the MicroSD card slot.**

3. **Orient the MicroSD card so that the printed side faces up and the teeny triangle on the card points toward the Galaxy Tab.**

4. **Use your fingernail or a paperclip to gently shove the card all the way into the slot.**

   The card makes a faint clicking sound when it's fully inserted.

5. **Close the hatch covering the MicroSD card slot.**

After the MicroSD card is installed, turn on your Galaxy Tab. See Chapter 2 for details, though you basically just press and hold the Power button until the touchscreen comes to life. (You see the text *Samsung.*)

- ✔ You can buy an SD card adapter, into which you can insert a MicroSD card. The SD card adapter can then be used in any computer or digital device that reads SD cards.

- ✔ SD, which stands for Secure Digital, is but one of about a zillion different media card standards.

- ✔ MicroSD cards come in a smattering of capacities. The Galaxy Tab ships with a 16GB MicroSD card, though you can buy one with a larger capacity if you and your credit card are willing.

- ✔ In addition to the MicroSD card, the Galaxy Tab features internal storage. This storage is used for the programs you install on the Tab as well as for the Tab's operating system and other control programs. The internal storage isn't used for your personal information, media, and other items, which is why you must keep the MicroSD card inside your Galaxy Tab.

Getting optional accessories

You can buy an assortment of handy Galaxy Tab accessories, and I'm sure that the pleasant people at the phone store showed you the variety when you bought your Tab. Here are just a few of the items that are available or that you can consider getting in order to complete your Tab experience:

Earphones: You can use any standard cell phone or portable media player earphones with the Galaxy Tab. Simply plug the earphones into the headphone jack at the top of the Tab and you're ready to go.

HDMI cable: You can use the HDMI cable with the multimedia dock to view the Tab's output on an HDMI-compatible monitor or television.

Keyboard dock: When you tire of touchscreen typing, try the keyboard dock. It props up the Tab for easy viewing and provides a laptop-style keyboard. Unlike the multimedia dock, the keyboard dock has no HDMI connector.

Leather sleeve: A handy accessory to have, the leather sleeve is a form-fitting pouch that holds the Galaxy Tab when you aren't using it. Though you may not need a leather sleeve, I highly recommend getting a pouch, kangaroo, or a similar item in which to store your Tab when you aren't using it.

Multimedia dock: Another good accessory, the multimedia dock is a place to store your Tab in a handy, upright position. Further, you can use the multimedia dock to connect the tab to a computer or an HDMI-capable television or monitor.

Screen protectors: These plastic, clingy things are affixed to the front of the Tab, right over the touchscreen. They help protect the touchscreen glass from finger smudges and sneeze globs while still allowing you to use the touchscreen.

Vehicle charger: You can charge the Galaxy Tab in your car when you buy the vehicle charger. This adapter plugs into your car's 12-volt power supply, in the receptacle once known as a cigarette lighter. The vehicle charger is a must-have if you plan to use the Galaxy Tab navigation features in your auto or you need a charge on the road.

Additional accessories may be available. Check the location where your Galaxy Tab was sold to inquire about new items.

✔ None of this extra stuff is essential to using the Tab.

✔ Beyond the multimedia dock, you can buy other types of stands for propping up the Tab for better access (viewing, typing, and touching), some of which may also double as carrying pouches.

✔ You must have the multimedia dock to use the HDMI cable.

✔ You can also use Bluetooth earphones, or a cell phone Bluetooth headset, with the Galaxy Tab.

✔ If the earphones feature a microphone, you can use it for dictation and recording on the Tab.

✔ If the earphones feature a button, you can use the button to pause and play music. Press the button once to pause, and again to play.

✔ The Galaxy Tab doesn't recognize more than one earphone button. For example, if you use earphones that feature a Volume or Mute button, pressing the extra button does nothing on the Tab.

✔ The set of screen protectors I purchased also came with a microfiber cloth to help clean the Tab's screen, plus a special cleaning-solution wipe. See Chapter 22 for more information about cleaning the Galaxy Tab screen.

Where to Keep Your Tab

Like your car keys, glasses, wallet, and light saber, you'll want to keep your Galaxy Tab in a place where it's safe, easy to find, and always handy whether you're at home, at work, on the road, or in a galaxy far, far away.

Making a home for the Tab

I recommend keeping the Galaxy Tab in the same spot when you're done using it. My first suggestion is to make a spot next to your computer. Keep the charging cord handy, or just plug the cord into the computer's USB port so that you can synchronize information with your computer regularly and keep the Tab charged.

If you have a docking stand, plug your Tab into it when you're not toting it about.

Above all, avoid keeping the Tab in a place where someone might sit on it, step on it, or damage it. For example, don't leave the Tab under a stack of newspapers on a table or counter, where it might get accidentally tossed out or put in the recycle bin.

As long as you remember to return the Tab to the same spot when you're done with it, you'll always know where it is.

Taking the Galaxy Tab with you

If you're like me, you probably carry the Galaxy Tab around with you, around the house, around the office, at the airport, in the air, or while you're in the car. I hope you're not using the Tab while you're driving! Regardless, have a portable place to store your Tab while you're on the road.

The ideal storage spot for the Tab is a specially designed Galaxy Tab pouch, such as the leather sleeve I describe earlier in this chapter. That pouch keeps the Tab from being dinged, scratched, or even unexpectedly turned on while it's in your backpack, purse, carry-on luggage, or wherever you put the Tab when you aren't using it.

Also see Chapter 20 for information on using the Galaxy Tab on the road.

2

Galaxy Tab On and Off

The bestseller *Pencils For Dummies* (Wiley) has no chapter describing how to turn on a pencil. There's a chapter titled "Enabling the Pen to Write" in *Pens For Dummies* (also from Wiley), but that isn't an On-Off thing, and the author of that book describes in great detail how awkward an On-Off switch or Power button would be on a pen. Aren't we all lucky that we live in an age when such things are carefully described for us?

The Galaxy Tab is far more complex than a pen or pencil, and often it's more useful. As an advanced piece of technology, the Tab features not an On-Off button, but, rather, a Power button. This button does more than just turn the Galaxy Tab on or off, which is why this book has an entire chapter devoted to the subject.

Hello, Tab

In all the effort made by engineers and wizards to make technology easier, one area where they fail is in the basic way you turn on a gizmo.

Take the Galaxy Tab: There are two different ways to turn it on, plus special bonus goodies that happen the *first* time you turn on the Tab. This section discusses the details.

✔ Initial setup of the Galaxy Tab works best when you already have a Google, or Gmail, account on the Internet. If you lack a Google account, see the section "Setting up a Google account," later in this chapter, for details.

✔ Setup works differently depending on whether you have a cellular Tab or Wi-Fi only. When you have a Wi-Fi only tab, the cellular network activation stage is skipped during setup.

✔ See Chapter 18 for information on connecting your Galaxy Tab to a Wi-Fi network.

✔ The Tab doesn't start unless the battery is charged. See Chapter 1.

Turning on your Galaxy Tab (for the first time)

The very, very first time your Galaxy Tab was turned on was most likely at the phone store or at a factory if you ordered your Tab online. That session involved hooking up the Tab to the phone company's digital network, but that was the extent of the operation.

If the phone company hasn't configured your Tab, you have to do it. See the next section "Activate your Galaxy Tab." Otherwise, skip ahead to the section "Your Google account."

Activate your Galaxy Tab

Follow these steps to turn on your Galaxy Tab for the first time and activate your cellular service:

1. **Press the Power button.**

   You may have to press it longer than you think; when you see the text *Samsung* on the screen, the Tab has started.

2. **Unlock the Tab by sliding the Lock tab to the right, as shown in Figure 2-1.**

3. **Choose English.**

   Yes, if you're reading this in English, you choose English as the language for your Tab. Если ты говоришь руский, выбрать Русский язык.

4. **Touch the Activate button.**

   The Tab contacts your cellular provider to confirm that you have an active account.

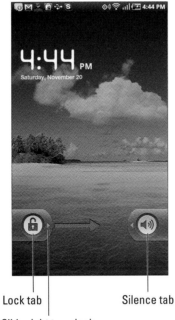

Lock tab   Silence tab

Slide right to unlock.

Figure 2-1: The main Galaxy Tab unlock screen.

5. **Obey the directions of your cellular provider.**

   The specifics of what happens next depend on your cellular provider.

6. **Touch the Next button when you see the text *Device Is Activated*.**

   The Galaxy Tab restarts.

 If you have trouble activating the Tab, contact your cellular provider. You need to read information from the Galaxy Tab's box, which has activation information printed on a label.

Continue reading in the next section.

Your Google account

After your Galaxy Tab has been activated, the next step in configuring it is to synchronize the device with your Google account. Obey:

1. **Start the Galaxy Tab, if you haven't already.**

   Press the Power button until you see the word *Samsung* on the screen.

2. **Unlock the screen as described in the preceding section.**

   Because you haven't yet identified your Google account on the Tab, a special program — the Setup Wizard — runs automatically.

3. **Ignore the text on the Google Service Login screen and touch the Next button.**

   If you chicken out and elect to touch the Skip button, the Tab isn't synchronized with your Google account on the Internet. You can choose to complete the setup operation later; see the section "Attaching your Google account to the Galaxy Tab," later in this chapter.

4. **Ignore the information about adding a Google account and touch the Next button.**

5. **Because you read the Tip icon at the start of this chapter, you can touch the Sign In button to sign into your Google account.**

6. **Touch the Username text box and type your Google account name.**

   The Swype keyboard appears, which features a special way to input text — if you know how it works. If you don't, touch the character buttons or keys on the touchscreen to work the keyboard. See Chapter 4 for more information about typing text on your Galaxy Tab.

7. **Touch the Password field and type your Google account password.**

8. **Touch the Sign In button.**

    If you can't see the Sign In button, press the Back soft button below the touchscreen; the Back button's icon is shown in the margin.

9. **Type the text shown in the Captcha window, if prompted.**

   The *captcha* security feature is designed to foil robots and other artificial life forms from signing into your Google account. The prompt may not appear on your Tab. If so, great.

10. **Ignore the information on the Back Up Data screen and touch the Next button.**

11. **Touch the Finish Setup button.**

    Sorry, but you're not quite done yet. Instead, you see the Account Setup screen. You can choose to add more accounts, though that topic is covered in Chapters 5 and 9. Instead:

12. **Touch the Next button.**

13. **Ensure that check marks appear next to each item on the next screen.**

    You might see three items, though the name of each one may change depending on which cellular provider you're using:

Location Services: Enable your cellular data provider to access location information, which aids in running Maps and other location apps.

Standalone GPS Services: Allow location information to be accessed by the Tab's apps as well as the Internet.

Google Location Services: Allow Google to collect your location data anonymously.

After touching the square to place a check mark, touch the Agree button.

14. **Touch the Next button.**

15. **If you see the Backup Assistant screen, touch the Skip button.**

    I believe that the Backup Assistant option is specific to the Verizon Tab, and it's something you don't have to use.

16. **Touch the Begin button to start using your Galaxy Tab.**

The good news is that you're done. The better news is that you need to complete this setup only once on your Galaxy Tab. From this point on, starting the Galaxy Tab works as described in the next few sections.

- Information on your Galaxy Tab is synchronized with the information from your Google account on the Internet. Your contact list, Gmail messages, calendar appointments, and other "Googly" things are all updated between the Tab and the Internet nearly instantaneously.

- One of the first things you may notice to be synchronized between your Tab and Google is your Gmail inbox. See Chapter 7 for more information on Gmail.

- See the later sidebar "Who is this Android person?" for more information about the Android operating system.

- You can manually activate your Galaxy Tab on a cellular network. To do so while viewing the Home screen, press the Menu soft button and choose Settings. Choose Wireless and Networks and then choose Roaming Capability Update. Follow the directions on the screen.

Turning on your Galaxy Tab

To turn on your Galaxy Tab, press and hold the Power button. After a few seconds, you see the word *Samsung* and then maybe an animation or a logo from the phone company. The Tab is starting.

Eventually, you see the main unlock screen, shown earlier, in Figure 2-1. Use your finger to slide the Lock tab to the right, as indicated in the figure. After your Galaxy Tab is unlocked, you can start using it — and, unlike the first time you turned the thing on, you aren't prompted to complete the setup routine. (well, unless you skipped setup the first time).

✏ The Power button is found on the upper right side of the Tab. Refer to Figure 1-1, in Chapter 1, for the specific location.

✏ You probably won't turn on your Galaxy Tab much in the future. Mostly, you'll wake the gizmo from an electronic snooze. See the later section "Waking up the Tab."

Working the various lock screens

The unlock screen you see when you turn on (or wake up) the Tab isn't a tough lock to pick. In fact, it's known as the None option in the Screen Unlock Settings window. If you've added more security, you might see any one of three different lock screens.

The pattern lock, shown in Figure 2-2, requires that you trace your finger along a pattern that includes as many as nine dots on the screen. After you match the pattern, the Tab is unlocked and you can start using it.

Trace your finger over the dots.

Continue tracing the pattern.

Figure 2-2: The Pattern Lock screen.

The PIN lock is shown in Figure 2-3. It requires that you input a secret number to unlock the Tab. Touch the OK button to accept input, and use the Del button to back up and erase.

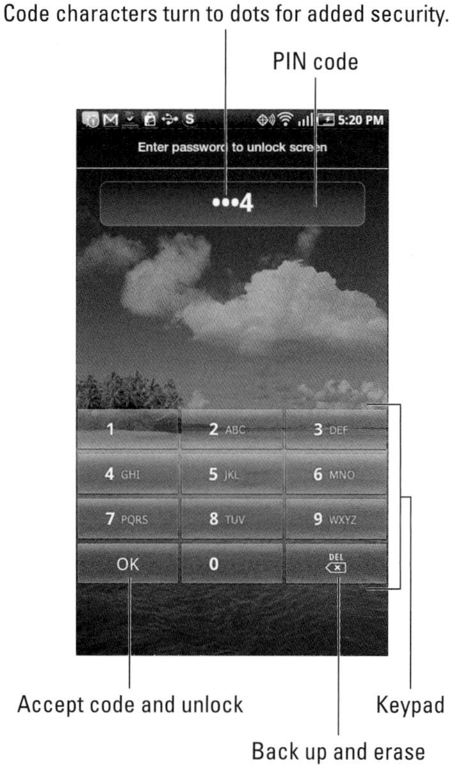

Code characters turn to dots for added security.

PIN code

Accept code and unlock   Keypad

Back up and erase

Figure 2-3: The PIN Lock screen.

Finally, the password lock requires that you type a multicharacter password on the screen before the Tab is unlocked. Use the keyboard, as shown in Figure 2-4, to type the password. Touch the OK button to accept the password and unlock the Galaxy Tab.

Password

Onscreen keyboard   Back up and erase

Accept password and unlock

Figure 2-4: The Password Lock screen.

Whether or not you see these various lock screens depends on how you've configured the Galaxy Tab's security. Specific directions for setting the locks, or for removing them and returning to the standard screen lock, are found in Chapter 21.

- The Galaxy Tab always has a lock screen. When no specific lock is chosen, the standard locking screen, shown in Figure 2-1, is used.

- The pattern lock can start at any dot, not necessarily the upper left dot, as shown in Figure 2-2.

- The password lock must contain at least one letter and number, though it can also include a smattering of symbols and other characters.

- For additional information on working the onscreen keyboard, see Chapter 4.

Who is this Android person?

Just like your computer, your Galaxy Tab has an operating system. It's the main program in charge of all the software (other programs) inside your Tab. Unlike on your computer, however, Android is a mobile device operating system, designed primarily for use in cell phones but also in the Galaxy Tab. (For that reason, you often see the Tab referred to as a *phone* in various apps.)

You find the Android operating system used on many of today's most popular smartphones, including the Droid X, HTC Incredible, and Samsung Galaxy. By using Android, the Tab has access to all the Android software — the *apps* or programs — available to Android phones and other mobile devices. You can read how to add those apps to your Tab in Chapter 17.

Android is based on the Linux operating system, which is also a computer operating system, though it's much more stable and bug-free than Windows, so it's not as popular. Google owns, maintains, and develops Android, which is why your online Google information is synced with the Galaxy Tab.

The Android mascot, shown here, often appears on Android apps or hardware. He has no official name, though most folks call him Andy.

Waking up the Tab

You'll probably leave your Galaxy Tab on all the time. It was designed that way. The battery lasts quite a while, so when the Tab is bored or when you've ignored it for a while, it falls asleep. Well, it's technically named *Sleep mode*, a special low-power, energy-saving state where the Tab's screen goes blank.

When the Galaxy Tab is sleeping, you wake it up by pressing the Power button. Unlike turning the Tab on, a quick press of the Power button is all that's needed.

After waking the Tab, you see the unlock screen, shown in Figure 2-1. Or, if you've configured the Tab for more security, you see one of the unlocking screens shown in Figures 2-2 through 2-4. Simply unlock the screen and you can start using the Tab.

- The Galaxy Tab continues to run while it's sleeping. Mail is received, as are text messages. The Tab also continues to play music while it's sleeping and the display is off.

✔ Touching the touchscreen when it's off doesn't wake up the Tab.

✔ Loud noises don't wake up the Tab.

✔ The Tab doesn't snore while it's sleeping.

✔ See the section "Putting the Tab to sleep," later in this chapter, for information on manually snoozing the Galaxy Tab.

Account Creation and Configuration

After you've done the initial configuration as described earlier in this chapter, there's nothing else you need to do to set up the Galaxy Tab. If you've skipped that step or you need to create a Google account, follow the directions in this section to complete the setup process.

Setting up a Google account

To get the most from your Galaxy Tab, you must have a Google account. If you don't already have one, drop everything (but not this book) and follow these steps to obtain one:

1. **Open your computer's Web browser program.**

   Yes, it works best if you use your computer, not the Tab, to complete these steps.

2. **Visit the main Google page at www.google.com.**

   Type **www.google.com** into the Web browser's address bar.

3. **Click the Sign In link.**

   Another page opens, where you can log in to your Google account, but you don't have a Google account, so:

4. **Click the link to create a new account.**

   The link is typically found beneath the text boxes where you would log in to your Google account. As I write this chapter, the link is titled Create an Account Now.

5. **Continue heeding the directions until you've created your own Google account.**

Eventually, your account is set up and configured.

To try things out, log off from Google and then log back in. That way, you ensure that you've done everything properly — and remembered your password. (Your Web browser may even prompt you to let it remember the password for you.)

I also recommend creating a bookmark for your account's Google page: The Ctrl+D or Command+D keyboard shortcut is used to create a bookmark in just about any Web browser.

Continue reading in the next section for information on synchronizing your new Google account with the Galaxy Tab.

Attaching your Google account to the Galaxy Tab

Don't fret if you've failed to obey the prompts and neglected to sign in to your Google account when first configuring the Galaxy Tab. You can rerun the configuration setup at any time. Just follow these steps:

1. **Turn on or wake up the Galaxy Tab, if it's not already on and eagerly awaiting your** next move.

2. **Unlock the Tab, if necessary.**

   Directions are found earlier in this chapter.

 3. **Press the Menu soft button.**

   The Menu soft button is found beneath the touchscreen. Its icon is shown in the margin.

4. **Choose the Settings command.**

   The Settings screen appears, which contains commands for configuring and setting options for the Galaxy Tab.

5. **Scroll to the bottom of the list.**

   Swipe or flick your finger across the touchscreen in an upward motion. (See Chapter 3 for specifics on how to manipulate the touchscreen using your fingers.)

6. **Choose the Setup Wizard option.**

   It's the last item in the list.

7. **Work through the wizard as described earlier in this chapter.**

   Follow the steps listed in the section "Turning on your Galaxy Tab (for the first time)."

Your goal is to synchronize your Google account information on the Internet with the information on your Galaxy Tab. It all happens in a few seconds after you complete the Setup Wizard.

Adding your personal email account to the Tab, as well as other free online email accounts, is covered in Chapter 7. Refer to Chapter 9 for information on adding social networking accounts, such as Facebook and Twitter.

Resetting your Google password

You should change your password every so often. Despite its being a good idea, few people bother. If the mood hits you, or a security breach makes it necessary, you can change your Google password. Doing so requires updating the Galaxy Tab with the new password information. Rather than make that task an ordeal, heed these steps:

1. **On your computer, direct the Web browser to go to the main Google page,** `www.google.com`

2. **From the top of the page, click the Settings link.**

   As I write this chapter, the link is found in the upper right part of the page.

3. **Choose Google Account Settings from the Settings link menu.**

4. **By the Security heading, click the Change Password link.**

5. **Obey the directions on the screen for setting a new password.**

   For example, type the current password and then type your new password twice. Click the Save button.

   After your password has been reset, update the Galaxy Tab with the new password. If you don't, you see incessant error messages and the device pesters you until you want to hurl it out a window. Continue with these steps:

6. **Wake up or turn on your Tab.**

    In a few moments, you see an Alert icon appear on top of the touchscreen display, in the notification area.

7. **Slide the notification area down by using swiping it with your finger.**

   The specifics for performing this action are covered in Chapter 3.

8. **From the list of notifications, choose Alert.**

   The Alert message says Sign-In Error or Sign into Your Account.

9. **Type your new Google password into the box that appears on the touchscreen display.**

After you enter the new password, the Galaxy Tab instantly becomes happy and continues to sync your Google account information.

Press the Home soft button to return to the Home screen.

Goodbye, Tab

I know of three ways to say goodbye your Galaxy Tab, and only one of them involves renting a steamroller. The other two methods are documented in this section.

Putting the Tab to sleep

To sleep the Tab, simply press its Power button. The display goes dark; the Tab is asleep.

- ✔ In Sleep mode, the Galaxy Tab still works, still receives email, and can still play music. But it's not using as much power as it would with the display on.

- ✔ The Galaxy Tab will probably spend most of its time in Snooze mode.

- ✔ Snoozing doesn't turn off the Tab.

- ✔ Any timers or alarms you set still activate when the Tab is in Sleep mode. See Chapter 16 for information on setting timers and alarms.

- ✔ To wake up the Tab, press and release the Power button. See the section "Waking up the Tab," earlier in this chapter.

Controlling the sleep timeout

You can manually snooze the Galaxy Tab at any time by pressing the Power button. In fact, some documentation calls it the Power *Lock* button because snoozing the Tab is the same as locking it. When you don't manually snooze the tab, it automatically goes into Sleep mode after a given period of inactivity, just like Uncle Tony does during family gatherings.

You have control over the snooze timeout value, which can be set anywhere from 15 seconds to one hour. Obey these steps:

1. **From the Home screen, press the Menu soft button.**

2. **Choose Settings.**

3. **Choose Display Settings**

4. **Choose Screen Timeout.**

5. **Choose a timeout value from the list.**

   I prefer 1 minute; the standard value is 30 seconds.

6. **Press the Home soft button to return to the Home screen.**

The sleep timer begins after a period of inactivity; when you don't touch the screen or press a soft button, the timer starts ticking. About 5 seconds before the timeout value you set (refer to Step 5), the touchscreen dims. Then it turns off and the Tab goes to sleep. If you touch the screen before then, the timer is reset.

Turning off the Galaxy Tab

To turn off the Tab, heed these steps:

1. **Press and hold the Power button.**

   You see the Device Options menu, shown in Figure 2-5.

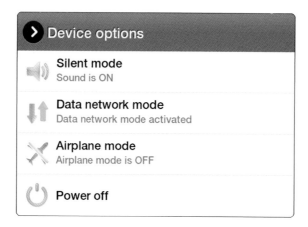

Figure 2-5: The Device Options menu.

 If you chicken out and don't want to turn off the Tab, press the Back soft button.

2. **Touch the Power Off item.**

   The Galaxy Tab turns itself off.

The Tab doesn't run when it's off, so it doesn't remind you of appointments, collect email, or let you hear any alarms you've set. The Tab also isn't angry with you for turning it off, though you may sense some resentment when you turn it on again.

Be sure to keep the Tab in a safe place while it's turned off. See the section "Where to Keep Your Tab" in Chapter 1.

Find Your Way Around the Galaxy

In This Chapter

▷ Working the soft buttons
▷ Using the touchscreen
▷ Changing the volume
▷ Getting around the Home screen
▷ Checking notifications
▷ Running apps (programs)
▷ Searching for applications
▷ Accessing recently used apps

*O*nce upon a time, you could tell how sophisticated a device was by the number of buttons it had. Those computers in the Batcave, for example, have lots of buttons, switches, and lights because they're very powerful and, well, Bruce Wayne has enough money to buy the top-of-the-line Dell Batcave PCs. But buttons alone are no measure for how complex something can be.

The Galaxy Tab has two buttons: Power Lock and Volume. Well, it's three buttons if you count Volume Up and Volume Down as separate buttons (though they're on the same physical button). Despite its dearth of buttons, the Galaxy Tab is one powerful gizmo. Obviously, there's more to using the thing than its buttons.

Basic Operations

It's not a computer. It's not a phone. The Galaxy Tab is truly something different, unlike anything you've ever used. To use this unique gizmo, you have to familiarize yourself with some basic tablet operations, as covered in this section.

Future versions of the Galaxy Tab may offer phone service. Presently, the version of the Tab being sold overseas can be used as a phone. The hardware is available to make phone calls, but US cellular providers don't offer this service because the Galaxy Tab hasn't been licensed by the FCC for use as a phone.

Introducing the soft buttons

Below the touchscreen, you find four icons. These icons represent the four *soft buttons,* which perform specific functions no matter what you're doing with your Galaxy Tab. Table 3-1 lists the soft buttons' names and functions.

Table 3-1		Galaxy Tab Soft Buttons		
Button	*Name*	*Press Once*	*Press Twice*	*Press and Hold*
⬜	Menu	Display the menu	Dismiss the menu	Do nothing
⌂	Home	Go to the Home screen	Do nothing	Show recent applications
◀	Back	Go back close, or dismiss the keyboard	Do nothing	Do nothing
🔍	Search	Open Tab and Web search	Do nothing	Run the Voice Search app

Not every button always performs the actions listed in Table 3-1. For example, if there's no menu to open, pressing the Menu button does nothing.

- Various sections throughout this book give examples of using the soft buttons. Their images appear in the book's margins wherever relevant.

- The Galaxy Tab documentation refers to the soft buttons as *command keys.*

Touching the touchscreen

Bereft of buttons and knobs, the way you control the Galaxy Tab is for the most part by manipulating things on the touchscreen with one or two fingers. It doesn't matter which fingers you use, and feel free to experiment with other body parts as well, though I find fingers to be handy.

You have specific ways to touch the touchscreen, and those specific ways have names. Here's the list:

Touch: The simplest way to manipulate the touchscreen is to touch it. You touch an object, an icon, a control, a menu item, a doodad, and so on. The touch operation is similar to a mouse click on a computer.

Double-tap: Touch the screen twice in the same location. Double-tapping can be used to zoom in on an image or a map, but it can also zoom out. Because of the double-tap's dual nature, I recommend using the pinch or spread operation instead when you want to zoom.

Long-press: A long-press occurs when you touch part of the screen and keep your finger down. Depending on what you're doing, you may see a pop-up menu appear, or the item you're long-pressing may get "picked up" and you can move it around after a long-press. *Long-press* might also be referred to as *touch and hold* in some documentation.

Swipe: To swipe, you touch your finger on one spot and then drag it to another spot. Swipes can go up, down, left, or right, which moves the touchscreen content in the direction you swipe your finger. A swipe can be fast or slow. It's also called a *flick* or *slide*.

Pinch: A pinch involves two fingers, which start out separated and then are brought together. The effect is used to zoom out, to reduce the size of an image or see more of a map.

Spread: The opposite of pinch is spread. You start out with your fingers together and then spread them. The spread is used to zoom in, to enlarge an image or see more detail on a map.

Rotate: A few apps let you rotate an image on the screen by touching with two fingers and twisting them around a center point. Think of turning a combination lock on a safe and you get the rotate operation.

You cannot manipulate the touchscreen while wearing gloves, unless they're gloves specially designed for using electronic touchscreens, such as the gloves that Batman wears.

Changing your orientation

The Galaxy Tab features a gizmo called an *accelerometer*. It determines in which direction the Tab is pointed, or whether you've reoriented the device from an upright to a horizontal position, or even upside down. That way, the information on the Tab always appears upright, no matter how you hold it.

To demonstrate how the Galaxy Tab orients itself, rotate the Tab to the left, horizontally. You see the Home screen change, as shown in Figure 3-1.

Figure 3-1: Galaxy Tab, horizontal orientation.

Turn the Tab upside down and the Home screen reorients itself vertically. No matter how you turn the Tab, up is always up.

✐ This book shows the Home screen, as well as most other apps, in a verti-cal orientation. See the later section "Behold the Home Screen" for more information on the Home screen.

✐ Not every app switches between horizontal and vertical orientations. Some apps, such as most games, are fixed and don't reorient themselves.

✐ The YouTube app is fixed in a horizontal orientation with the Tab turned to the left. See Chapter 16 for more information about YouTube.

✐ If the screen doesn't rotate, check to ensure that the orientation lock isn't set. Or, if you don't want the screen to reorient itself, turn Orientation Lock on. See the section "Changing a setting with a quick action," later in this chapter.

✐ A great application for demonstrating the Galaxy Tab accelerometer is the game *Labyrinth*. It can be purchased at the Android Market, or the free version, *Labyrinth Lite,* can be downloaded. See Chapter 17 for more information about the Android Market.

Controlling the volume

There are times when the sound level is too loud. There are times when it's too soft. And, there are those rare times when it's just right. Finding that just-right level is the job of the volume control buttons that cling to the right side of the Galaxy Tab.

Pressing the top part of the Volume button makes the volume louder; pressing the bottom part makes the volume softer. As you press the button, a graphic appears on the touchscreen to illustrate the relative volume level, as shown in Figure 3-2.

Softer   Louder

Figure 3-2: Setting the volume.

When you press the Volume button and see the control shown in Figure 3-2, you hear a beep. That's your aural gauge of how loud the volume is set.

✔ When the volume is set all the way down, the Tab is silenced.

✔ Silencing the Tab by sliding down the volume level doesn't place it into Vibration mode.

✔ The Volume button works even when the Tab is snoozing (in Sleep mode or when the touchscreen display is off). That means you don't need to wake the Tab if you're playing music and need to adjust the volume.

✔ To quickly silence the Tab when it's snoozing, press the Power button and slide the Silence tab to the left. (Refer to Figure 2-1, in Chapter 2.) By sliding the Power button to the left, you place the Tab into Vibration mode. Sliding the Silence tab to the left again restores the volume level.

✔ Refer to Chapter 21 for information on setting individual volume levels for the various apps, chimes, and activities on the Galaxy Tab.

✔ Also see Chapter 21 for information on placing the Tab into Vibration mode.

Behold the Home Screen

The main base from which you begin exploration of the Galaxy Tab is the *Home* screen. It's the first thing you see after unlocking the Tab, and the place you go to whenever you quit an application.

Touring the Home screen

The main Home screen for the Galaxy Tab is illustrated in Figure 3-3.

Figure 3-3: The Home screen.

There are several fun and interesting things to notice on the Home screen:

Status bar: The top of the Home screen is a thin, informative strip that I call the *status bar.* It contains notification icons and status icons, plus the current time.

Notification icons: These icons come and go, depending on what happens in your digital life. For example, new icons appear whenever you receive a new email message or have a pending appointment. The section "Reviewing notifications," later in this chapter, describes how to deal with notifications.

Status icons: These icons represent the Tab's current condition, such as the type of network it's connected to, signal strength, and battery status, as well as whether the Tab is in Vibration mode or a Wi-Fi network is connected, for example.

Panel indicator: Your Tab has more than one Home screen, and it's the job of the Panel indicator to tell you which Home screen you're viewing. See the next section for details.

Widgets: A widget is a teensy program that can display information, let you control the Tab, access features, or do something purely amusing. You can read more about widgets in Chapter 21.

Application icons: The meat of the meal on the Home screen plate are the application icons. Touching an icon runs its program.

Primary shortcuts: Two application icons appear at the bottom of every Home screen. In Figure 3-3, they're the Browser and Email programs. Those are the primary shortcuts, which should be for programs you plan to access most frequently. The primary shortcuts can be changed, a topic I cover in Chapter 21.

Applications button: Touching the Applications button displays the Applications screen, a multipage list of all applications installed on your Galaxy Tab. The section "The Applications Screen," later in this chapter, describes how it works.

Ensure that you recognize the names of the various parts of the Home screen, because the terms are used throughout this book and in whatever other scant Galaxy Tab documentation exists. Directions for using the Home screen gizmos are found throughout this chapter.

  ✒ The Home screen is entirely customizable. You can add and remove icons from the Home screen, add widgets and shortcuts, and even change wallpaper images. See Chapter 21 for more information.

  ✒ When you rotate the Galaxy Tab, the Home screen changes its orientation to match (refer to Figure 3-1). The horizontal Home screen features all the same gizmos as the vertical Home screen, but the primary shortcuts are located to the right rather than at the bottom.

✔ Touching a part of the Home screen that doesn't feature an icon or a control does nothing. That is, unless you're using the *live wallpaper* feature. In that case, touching the screen changes the wallpaper in some way, depending on the wallpaper that's selected. You can read more about live wallpaper in Chapter 21.

✔ The variety of notification and status icons is fairly broad. You see the icons referenced in appropriate sections throughout this book. For example:

 ✔ The status icon shown in the margin indicates that the Galaxy Tab location services are on. It has two location services: standalone GPS services and Google Location Service. Additionally, your cellular provider may have location services. These services can be turned on or off by running the Settings app and choosing Location and Security.

Accessing multiple Home screens

The Galaxy Tab features a whole subdivision of Home screens. Out of the box, the Tab is configured with five Home screens, and the main Home screen is number 3, the center screen. Figure 3-4 illustrates the Home screen neighborhood.

Panel indicator displays Home screen number.   Main Home screen   Touch Panel Indicator button to switch Home screens.

Application icons   Widgets

Swipe to switch Home screens.

Figure 3-4: All the Home screens.

The panel indicator, located at the top of each Home screen, shows you which Home screen you're viewing.

To switch to another Home screen, swipe your finger to the left or right. As you swipe, another Home screen pulls into view. The background wallpaper image may even shift a tad.

You can also switch Home screens by touching a dot on the panel indicator: Touch the first dot to zoom instantly to the first Home screen, for example.

Every Home screen features its own set of app icons and widgets, though the primary shortcuts (refer to Figure 3-3) remain the same on all Home screens.

- ✏ No matter which part of the Home screen you're viewing, the top part of the touchscreen stays the same, displaying notification and status icons and the time.

- ✏ You always swipe the Home screen left or right to see additional screens, even when the Tab is in a horizontal orientation.

- ✏ The panel indicator appears when the Tab is in horizontal orientation, but only when you swipe from one screen to another.

- ✏ To return to the Home screen at any time, press the Home soft button.

- ✏ You can set the number of Home screens to any odd value between 3 and 9. See Chapter 21 for instructions on adding or removing Home screens, as well as specifying which Home screen is the main screen.

Home Screen Duties

To become a cat, you must know how to perform several duties: Sleep, eat, catch critters, and cause mischief. A cat's life isn't difficult, and neither is your Galaxy Tab life, as long as you know how to do some basic duties on the Home screen. As with the cat, you have only a few duties to know about.

Reviewing notifications

Notifications appear as icons at the top of the Home screen, as illustrated earlier, in Figure 3-3. To see the notifications themselves, you peel down the top part of the screen (see Figure 3-5).

Notification icons

Touch here.

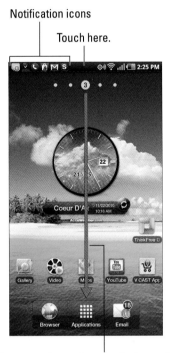

Drag your finger down to display notifications.

Figure 3-5: Accessing notifications.

The operation works like this:

1. **Touch the status bar at the top of the Home screen.**

2. **Swipe your finger all the way down the touchscreen.**

    Think of it like controlling a roll-down blind: You grab the top part of the touchscreen and drag it downward all the way. The notifications appear in a list, as shown in Figure 3-6.

    You need to drag the notification list all the way to the bottom of the touchscreen to prevent it from rolling back up again. Use the notification window control to pull the list all the way down, as shown in Figure 3-6.

3. **Touch a notification to see what's up.**

Touching an item in the list takes you to the program that generated the notification. For example, touching a Gmail notification opens a new message or your inbox.

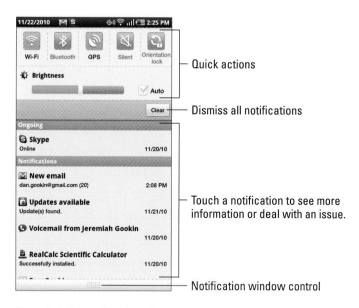

Quick actions

Dismiss all notifications

Touch a notification to see more information or deal with an issue.

Notification window control

Figure 3-6: The notifications list.

If you choose not to touch a notification, you can "roll up" the notification list by sliding the window control back up to the top of the touchscreen, or just press the Back soft button.

✔ If you don't deal with the notifications, they can stack up!

✔ Notification icons disappear after they've been chosen.

✔ To dismiss all notification icons, touch the Clear button, shown in Figure 3-6.

✔ When more notification icons are available than can appear on the status bar, you see the More Notifications icon, shown in the margin. The number in the circle indicates the number of notification icons you can't see.

✔ You can turn the Tab to its horizontal orientation to see additional notification icons, or just display the list of notifications as described in this section; scroll the list up and down by swiping your finger.

✔ Dismissing notifications doesn't prevent them from appearing again in the future. For example, notifications to update your programs continue to appear, as do calendar reminders.

✔ Some programs, such as Facebook and the various Twitter apps, don't display notifications unless you're logged in. See Chapter 9.

✔ The Galaxy Tab plays a sound, or *ringtone*, when a new notification floats in. You can choose which sound plays; see Chapter 21 for more information.

✔ See Chapter 16 for information on dismissing calendar reminders.

> ✔ Notification icons appear on the screen when the Galaxy Tab is locked. Remember that you must unlock the Tab before you can drag down the status bar to display notifications.

Changing a setting with a quick action

The top of the notification list contains a smattering of handy switches that control certain key items on your Galaxy Tab. I call them *quick actions*, and they're shown in Figure 3-6. Here's the list:

Wi-Fi: Turns the Tab's Wi-Fi on or off. See Chapter 18 for information on accessing wireless networks.

Bluetooth: Turns the Bluetooth radio on or off. See Chapter 18 for details on how to connect Bluetooth gizmos to the Galaxy Tab.

GPS: Turns the global positioning system (GPS) on or off, which enables some applications (Maps, Browser) to determine the Galaxy Tab's location.

Silent: Switches the Galaxy Tab into Silent mode. The Tab's speakers go mute, and Vibration mode is activated.

Orientation lock: Prevents the touchscreen from reorienting itself based on which way you're holding the Galaxy Tab. See the section "Changing your orientation," earlier in this chapter.

Brightness: Specifies how bright the touchscreen appears. Adjust brightness by moving the slider around with your finger, or touch the Auto button to have the Tab adjust brightness based on the amount of ambient light.

 When the Tab is in Vibration mode, the Vibration Mode icon appears on the status bar, as shown in the margin.

The Galaxy Tab Volume buttons don't work when Vibration mode is active.

Starting an application

It's blissfully simple to run an application on the Home screen: Touch its icon. The application starts.

> ✔ Not all applications appear on the Home screen, but all of them appear when you display the Applications screen. See the section "The Applications Screen," later in this chapter.

> ✔ When an application closes or you quit the application, you're returned to the Home screen.

> ✔ Application is abbreviated as *app*.

Accessing a widget

Like application icons, widgets appear on the Home screen. To use a widget, touch it. What happens next, of course, depends on the widget and what it does.

For example, touching the big clock widget on the main Home screen displays the AccuWeather Clock app. Touching the Google widget displays the onscreen keyboard and lets you type, or dictate, something to search for on the Internet. Other widgets do similar things, and some widgets merely display information or let you interact with them in an amusing manner.

Information about these and other widgets appears elsewhere in this book. See Chapter 21 for information on working with widgets.

Using the Digital Frame

The Digital Frame app is perfect for those times when you shove the Galaxy Tab into the multimedia dock. The Digital Frame app displays a large clock, as shown in Figure 3-7, or you can view a slide show or listen to music. Touch the screen to see the control appear, as shown in Figure 3-7.

Figure 3-7: The Digital Frame app.

To exit the Digital Frame app, press the Home soft button.

The Applications Screen

The application icons you see on the Home screen don't represent all the apps in your Galaxy Tab. Those icons aren't even applications themselves; they're shortcuts. To see all applications installed on your Galaxy Tab, you must visit the Applications screen.

Accessing all apps in the Galaxy Tab

To start a program — an *app* — on your Tab, heed these steps:

1. Touch the Applications button at the bottom of the Home screen.

The Applications screen appears, as shown in Figure 3-8. App icons are listed alphabetically. The apps preinstalled on your Galaxy Tab appear first, in alphabetical order. After that, you find the apps you've installed yourself, listed in the order in which they were installed.

2. Scroll the list of app icons by swiping your finger left or right.

The apps are organized into pages or panels, just like the layout of the Home screen. An indicator, similar to the panel indicator on the Home screen, appears atop the Applications screen (see Figure 3-8).

3. Touch an icon to start its app.

Or, you can touch the Home button to return to the Home screen.

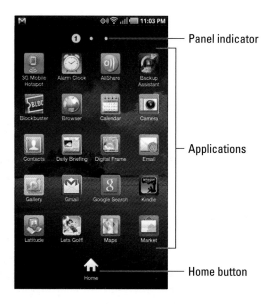

Figure 3-8: The Applications screen.

The app that starts takes over the screen and does whatever good thing that program does.

- On my Tab, the apps I've installed myself start appearing on panel 3 of the Applications screen.
- You can edit the Applications screen, by adding more panels or moving the icons around. See Chapter 17.
- The terms _program_, _application_ and _app_ all mean the same thing.

Locating lost apps

It may happen. Someday, you may have so many apps installed on your Galaxy Tab that you can't even find the app you're looking for. Or, maybe you believe the app to be named Translator when, in fact, it's named Language Translation. Rather than strain your eyes by looking at page after page of apps on the Applications screen, you can use the Tab's powerful Search command to quickly locate any app. Here's how:

1. **Press the Search soft button.**

   The Search screen appears. A Search text box appears atop the screen, and the onscreen keyboard appears at the bottom.

2. **Use your finger to type all or part of the app's name.**

   See Chapter 4 for more information on using the onscreen keyboard.

   As you type, items matching what you've typed appear in the list. The text _Application_ appears beneath the program name of any application in the list.

3. **Scroll the list to explore the apps that have been found.**

   Use your finger to swipe the list up and down.

4. **Touch the name of the app you're looking for.**

   The app starts.

Searching for apps is a small part of searching for all kinds of information on the Galaxy Tab, such as contact information, appointments, and email. Various chapters throughout this book describe other ways you can use the Search function.

You can search for apps at any time you're using the Galaxy Tab. You don't have to be at the Home screen or Applications screen for the Search command to find missing apps.

See Chapter 17 for information on how to use the Android Market to get more apps for your Galaxy Tab.

Reviewing recent apps

If you're like me, you probably use the same apps over and over on your Galaxy Tab. You can easily access that list of recent apps by pressing and holding the Home soft button. When you do, you see the eight most recently accessed programs, similar to the ones shown in Figure 3-9.

Figure 3-9: Recently used apps.

To exit the recently used apps list, press the Back soft button.

You can press and hold the Home soft button in any application at any time to see the recently used apps list.

For the programs you use all the time, consider creating shortcuts on the Home screen. Chapter 21 describes how to create shortcuts for apps, as well as shortcuts to people and shortcuts for instant messaging and all sorts of fun stuff.

4

Rule the Galaxy Interface

In This Chapter

▷ Using the onscreen keyboard

▷ Typing on the Samsung keypad

▷ Accessing special characters

▷ Using Swype to enter text

▷ Editing text

▷ Selecting, cutting, copying, and pasting text

▷ Dictating text with voice input

*E*mperor Tazrog never conquered the Goongas. That's because he couldn't communicate with them. He tried, but all his efforts failed: speech, writing, television, pelting the planet with meteors — nothing worked. Not being able to claim the Goonga home world was one of the great disappointments of what was otherwise a stellar career of slaughter and subjugation.

If you're going to rule the Galaxy — specifically, your Galaxy Tab —you need to be able to communicate with the indigenous population. That means being able to express your thoughts. Unlike the Goongas, the Galaxy Tab understands the simple concept of typing. As a bonus, the Galaxy Tab also speaks English, and appreciates your words, in the form of dictation. Conquering the Galaxy Tab has never been easier.

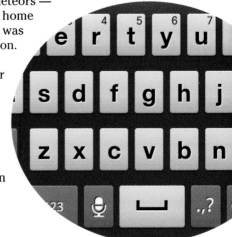

Ode to the Keyboard

The primary way you express yourself on the Galaxy Tab is to touch the screen. For text communications, you touch an onscreen keyboard. The Tab has two types of onscreen keyboard.

In Figure 4-1, you see the Samsung keypad, which is more of a traditional, typewriter-like keyboard.

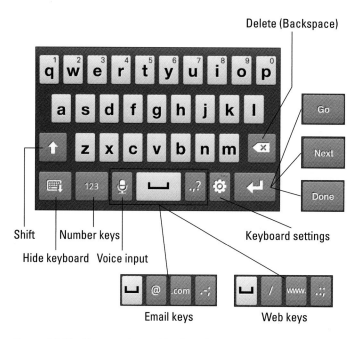

Figure 4-1: The Samsung keypad keyboard.

Figure 4-2 shows the Swype keyboard, which offers a new, faster way to type text.

You can switch between the Samsung and Swype keyboards by following these steps:

1. **At the Home screen, press the Menu soft button.**

2. **Choose Settings.**

3. **Choose Language and Keyboard.**

4. **Choose Set Input Method.**

5. **From the list, choose the keyboard you want to use.**

   Two options are available: Swype and Samsung Keypad.

6. **Press the Home soft button to return to the Home screen.**

Press and hold to produce symbols.

Shift

Delete (Backspace)

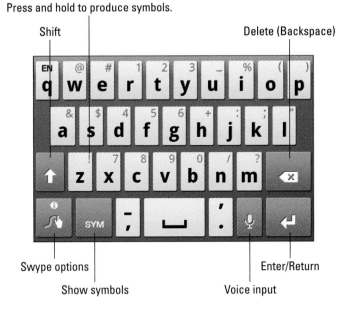

Swype options

Show symbols

Enter/Return

Voice input

Figure 4-2: The Swype keyboard.

The keyboard you've selected shows up anytime text needs to be typed, such as when you touch a text field on a Web site, search the Internet, type a message, or jot down a note.

The following sections detail how to work each keyboard.

> ✔ The Galaxy Tab ships with the Swype keyboard activated.

> ✔ Both keyboards can reorient themselves when you turn the Tab to a horizontal position. The onscreen keyboard becomes larger in that orientation, which makes typing easier.

> ✔ Additional keyboard options may be available for the Tab, and they would show up in Step 5. You can download alternative keyboards from the Android Market. See Chapter 17.

> ✔ If you obtain the optional keyboard dock, you can experience the thrill of using an actual — albeit laptop-size — keyboard with your Galaxy Tab. That's about your best option for "real" typing. See the nearby sidebar, "The keyboard dock."

> ✔ I've tried to connect a Bluetooth keyboard to the Galaxy Tab and haven't gotten it to work.

The keyboard dock

If typing is your thing and the onscreen keyboards don't do it for you, consider getting the Galaxy Tab *keyboard dock:* This docking stand props up the Tab at a good viewing angle but, unlike the multimedia dock, features a laptop-size keyboard.

In addition to the standard typewriter keys, adorning the keyboard dock are many special function keys that make using the Galaxy Tab a lot easier. You can find keys to launch the Browser or Music Player and to view videos.

Use the control keys to set the brightness or volume level or to play music or videos. A blank key, when pressed, even implodes your enemies, or so I believe.

The keyboard dock features a speaker output, but unlike the multimedia dock, it doesn't have an HDMI jack. Also, you need to configure the Galaxy Tab to use the Samsung keypad keyboard and not Skype; otherwise, the keyboard dock won't work properly.

Swype Your Text

The Swype keyboard, shown in Figure 4-2, is designed to drastically improve your typing speed when using an onscreen keyboard. The secret is that Swype allows you to type without lifting your finger; you literally swipe your finger over the touchscreen to rapidly type words.

Typing with Swype the old-fashioned way

It's entirely possible to hunt-and-peck on the Skype keyboard: Touch a key and that key's character appears on the screen. It's simple and logical, but it's not the best way to use Skype. In fact, if you type your text that way, you might as well be using the Samsung onscreen keyboard instead.

 The one-time that the hunt-and-peck works on the Skype keyboard is when you need to access special character keys. For example, in Figure 4-2, you see that the exclamation point symbol shares the Z key. To produce that character, press and hold the Z key. You may hear a little "pop" sound, and then the exclamation point character appears.

You see lots of handy symbols on the Skype keyboard, as illustrated in Figure 4-2.

When you hunt-and-peck with the Skype keyboard, you can use the Shift key to produce a capital letter. Pressing the Shift key twice turns on Caps Lock. Press the Shift key again to return to normal (lowercase) letters.

Typing with Swype without lifting a finger

The key to using Swype isn't to lift your finger from the keyboard: Start slowly; don't worry that the teenager sitting next to you is "swyping" so fast that it looks like he's drawing Chinese characters.

Your first task in Swype is to learn how to type simple, short words: Keep your finger on the touchscreen and drag it over the letters in the word, such as the word *tab*, shown in Figure 4-3. Lift your finger when you've completed the word, and the word appears in whichever app you're using.

Figure 4-3: Swype the word *tab*.

Type capital letters by dragging your finger above the keyboard after touching the letter, as shown in Figure 4-4, where *Utah* is typed.

To get a double letter, such as the *oo* in *book*, you need to do a little loop on that key. In Figure 4-5, the word *Goober* is typed, which uses both the capital-letter trick and the double-letter trick.

Figure 4-4: Swyping a capital letter.

Rise above the
keyboard to
capitalize

Little circle makes
a double letter

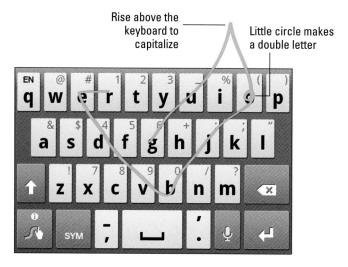

Figure 4-5: Swyping double letters.

When Swype is confused about what you've typed, a pop-up window appears with word suggestions, as shown in Figure 4-6.

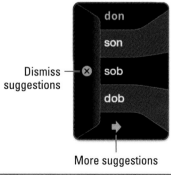

Dismiss suggestions

More suggestions

Figure 4-6: Choose the right word.

Choose a suggestion from the list or switch to the alternative suggestions, as illustrated in Figure 4-6.

- ✓ See the earlier section "Ode to the Keyboard" for information on activating the Swype keyboard, if it's not currently the onscreen keyboard.

- ✓ To view the Swype tutorial, press the Swype Options button on the keyboard (refer to Figure 4-2) and then touch the Tutorial button.

- ✓ When the space key grows a "no" icon, as shown in the margin, it means that the Auto Spacing feature has been disabled. Auto Spacing normally adds a space after each word you create with Skype. Auto Spacing is disabled for typing email addresses, passwords, and other text where spaces aren't appreciated.

- ✓ Even though Swype is fast, dictation can be faster: Touch the Microphone button to enter Dictation mode. See the section "Galaxy Tab Dictation," later in this chapter.

✔ The Microphone button becomes disabled when voice input isn't allowed or wanted, such as when typing a password.

✔ The Swype software interprets your intent as much as it does your accuracy. Even being close to the target letter is good enough; as long as you get the pattern over the keyboard correct, Swype usually displays the right word.

✔ The Swype keyboard doesn't have a Hide key. To dismiss the Swype keyboard, press the Back soft button.

✔ Don't confuse Swype with Skype, which is a utility you can use to place free phone calls and send instant text messages over the Internet. Skype is covered in Chapter 10.

✔ Slow down and you'll get the hang of it.

Accessing Swype keyboard variations

The Swype keyboard has several different versions, each with a smattering of different characters. Getting at those different keyboard layouts isn't obvious — unless you read this section!

The first keyboard variation is the Symbol keyboard, shown in Figure 4-7. It's accessed by touching the SYM key.

Figure 4-7: The Swype Symbol keyboard.

The second keyboard variation makes available even more symbols, shown in Figure 4-8. To display the keyboard, touch the Shift key after touching the SYM key.

Figure 4-8: The Swype Shift Symbol keyboard.

A numeric keypad is available by touching SYM, Shift, and then 123. It's shown in Figure 4-9.

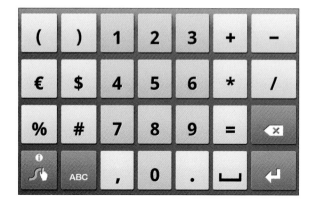

Figure 4-9: The Swype numeric keypad keyboard.

Finally, you can use the handy text-editing keyboard layout, shown in Figure 4-10. To see that layout, use your finger to drag the Swype key (lower left corner) to the SYM key.

No matter which variation of the Swype keyboard you're using, you can press the ABC key to return to the standard alphabetic keyboard layout.

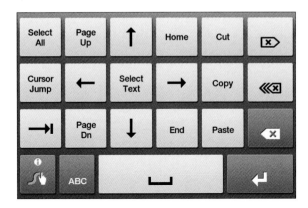

Figure 4-10: The Swype text-editing keyboard.

The Old Hunt-and-Peck

The old mechanical typewriters required a lot of effort to press their keys. It was forceful: clackity-clack-clack. Electronic typewriters made typing easier. And, of course, the computer is the easiest thing to type on. A tablet? That device takes some getting used to because its keys are merely flat rectangles on a touchscreen. If this concept doesn't drive you nuts, typing on a tablet is something you should master with relative ease.

Working the Samsung keypad

You can easily type on the Galaxy Tab onscreen keyboard: Just press a letter to produce the character. It works just like a computer keyboard in that respect. Unlike on a computer keyboard, you'll notice that some of your favorite keys are probably missing. The challenge is to get the onscreen keyboard to produce those characters.

Figure 4-1 illustrates the standard Samsung keypad in Alphabetic mode. You see keys from A through Z in lowercase, arranged just like on a computer keyboard. You also see a Shift key for producing capital letters, and a Delete key, which works to backspace and erase.

The large U key at the bottom center of the onscreen keypad is the Space key. To its left and right are useful keys, as illustrated in Figure 4-1: Hide Keyboard makes the keyboard disappear when you don't need it; 123 displays the numeric keyboard; the Microphone key, used for dictation; and the Gear key, which opens up the Samsung Keypad Settings screen.

The key in the lower right corner changes its look depending on what you're typing. Four variations are shown in Figure 4-1.

Here's what each one does:

> **Enter/Return:** Just like the Enter or Return key on your computer keyboard, this key ends a paragraph of text. It's used mostly when filling in long stretches of text or when multiline input is available.
>
> **Go:** This action key directs the app to proceed with a search, accept input, or perform another action.
>
> **Search:** You see the Search key appear when you're searching for something on the Tab. Touching the key starts the search.
>
> **Next:** This key appears when you're typing information into multiple fields. Touching this key switches from one field to the next, such as when typing a username and password.
>
> **Done:** Use this key to dismiss the onscreen keyboard and view the app in Full-Screen mode. Normally, this key appears whenever you've finished typing text in the final field of a screen that has several fields.

Keys around the Space key also change, as shown in Figure 4-1. The keys that appear help you type email addresses and Web pages and are described in the later section "Using special keys for special characters."

Also see the next section for accessing the number-and-symbol keys on the Samsung keypad onscreen keyboard.

- ✔ A blinking cursor on the touchscreen shows where new text appears, which is similar to how text input works on your computer.
- ✔ When you make a mistake, press the Del key to back up and erase.
- ✔ See the later section "Text Editing" for more details on editing your text.
- ✔ Above all, it helps to *type slowly* until you get used to the keyboard.
- ✔ When you type a password, the character you type appears briefly, but for security reasons it's then replaced by a black dot.

- ✔ In addition to pressing the Hide Keyboard button on the Samsung keypad, you can also dismiss the onscreen keyboard by pressing the Back soft button.
- ✔ If you see all capital letters on the alphabetic keyboard, the Shift key has been pressed.
- ✔ Press the Shift key twice to enter All Caps mode.

- Press the Shift key again to turn off all caps mode.

- You can press the Keyboard Settings (Gear) key to make adjustments to the onscreen keyboard.

- Press and hold the Keyboard Settings key to display a pop-up menu from which you can choose to switch to the Swype keyboard.

- Some applications show the keyboard when the Tab is in landscape orientation. If so, the keyboard shows the same keys, but offers more room for your stubby fingers to type.

- Not every application features a horizontal keyboard, however, so you might be stuck using the narrower version of the keyboard.

- When you tire of typing, you can always touch the Microphone button on the keyboard and enter Dictation mode. See the section "Galaxy Tab Dictation," later in this chapter.

Accessing other symbols

You're not limited to typing only the symbols you see on the alphabetic keyboard, shown in Figure 4-1. The onscreen keyboard has many more symbols available, which you can see by touching the 123 key, shown in the margin. Touching this key displays one of three additional keyboard layouts, as shown in Figure 4-11.

Touch the 1/3, 2/3, or 3/3 key to switch between various symbol keyboards, as illustrated in Figure 4-11.

To return to the standard, "alpha" keyboard (refer to Figure 4-1), touch the ABC key.

You can get to some of the keys from the main alphabetic keyboard. The secret is to long-press (press and hold) a key. When you do, you see a pop-up palette of additional characters, similar to the ones shown for the A key in Figure 4-12.

Choose a character from the pop-up palette, or touch the X button to close the pop-up palette.

Not every character has a special pop-up palette. The top row, however, has the numbers in those character's pop-up palettes so that you can quickly access numbers without switching to the symbol keyboard.

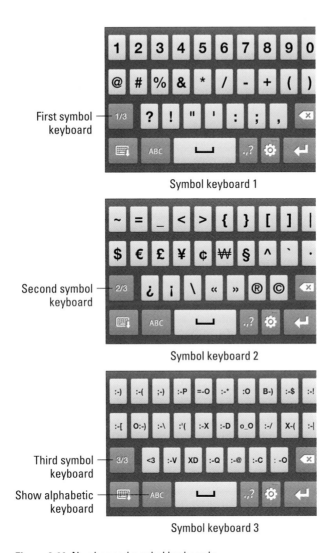

First symbol keyboard

Symbol keyboard 1

Second symbol keyboard

Symbol keyboard 2

Third symbol keyboard

Show alphabetic keyboard

Symbol keyboard 3

Figure 4-11: Number and symbol keyboards.

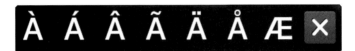

Figure 4-12: Special symbol pop-up palette thing.

Using special keys for special characters

To aid you in typing characters without switching keyboards, the Samsung keypad doubles up on certain keys. For example, in Figure 4-1, you see the . , ? key, which is used to type a period, a comma, or a question mark:

Press the key once to type a period. Press the key again to change the period to a comma. Press the key again to change the comma to a question mark.

When you're typing an email address, the . , ? key changes to the . - ; key but works the same. Ditto for the . : ; key, which appears when you're typing a Web page address.

Two additional keys pop up when typing an email or Web page address. The . com key inserts the text . com with one key press. The www. key inserts the letters *www* followed by a period.

Unlike the other special keys, the www. and . com keys don't insert one letter at a time.

Adding spell check and typing correction

Anyone can type, but it's the rare individual who can spell. In fact, if it weren't for my word processor's spell-checker (and my adept editor), my spelling would be ~~uhtrohshush~~ atrocious. So, with great relief and joy, I present to you the method you use to add typing correction to the Samsung keypad. Follow these steps:

1. **Press the Gear key to summon the Samsung Keypad Settings screen.**

2. **Ensure that a check mark appears by the option XT9.**

   To place a check mark by that option, touch the gray check mark box.

3. **Ensure that a check mark appears by the option Automatic Full Stop.**

   Setting this option directs the Galaxy Tab to add a period anytime you press the Space key twice.

4. **Ensure that a check mark appears by the option Auto-Capitalization.**

   When this option is set, the Tab automatically capitalizes any character you type after typing a period and a space.

5. **Press the Back soft button to return to whatever you were doing earlier.**

When the XT9 option is on, you see a list of text suggestions appear as you use the onscreen keyboard, as shown in Figure 4-13. Choose a word from the list by touching it with your finger, or in some cases the most logical word automatically appears.

Text you're typing   Suggestions   Show more suggestions

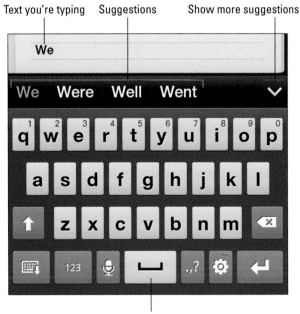

Accept highlighted suggestion

Figure 4-13: Automatic word selection.

To undo an automatic word selection, press the Del key on the keyboard.

To automatically choose the highlighted word, press the Space key.

- ✔ If you find the XT9 setting annoying (and many do), repeat the steps in this section to disable it.

- ✔ I have no idea why it's XT9 and not something easier to remember, like Word-Suggestion-o-Rama.

- ✔ Well, actually, XT9 comes from T9, a predictive-text technology designed for cell phones. *T9* stands for typing *text* on *nine* keys, which is what you would find on a phone. The XT9 is an extension of that predictive-typing technology.

Text Editing

Though email is a bastion of bad text composition, and most people forgive sloppiness in text messaging, it's true that you can do a fair amount of text editing on your Galaxy Tab. Beyond spiffing up your typos, text editing also means nifty tricks, such as copying and pasting text from a Web page. This section uncovers the secrets.

A great app on which to test your text-editing skill is the Memo app. It's found on the Applications screen, along with all the other apps on your Galaxy Tab.

Moving the cursor

The first part of editing text is to move the cursor to the right spot. The *cursor* is that blinking, vertical line where text appears. On most computing devices, moving the cursor is done by using a pointing device. The Galaxy Tab has no pointing device, but you do: your finger.

To move the cursor, simply touch the spot on the text where you want to move the cursor. To help your precision, a cursor tab appears below the text, as shown in the margin. You can move that tab with your finger to move the cursor around in the text.

The cursor tab is also the key to select text, which is covered in the next section. (That section explains the cartoon bubble with a *T* in it that appears when you stop dragging the cursor tab around.)

After you move the cursor, you can continue to type, use the Del key to back up and erase, or paste in text copied from elsewhere. See the later section "Cutting, copying, and pasting" for more information.

Selecting text

Selecting text on the Galaxy Tab works just like selecting text in a word processor: You mark the start of a block, and then you select text to the end of the block. That chunk of text then appears highlighted on the screen.

Just to confuse you, you have several ways to select text.

The first way to select text is to drag over it with your finger. Heed these directions:

1. **Move the cursor to the start of the block of text.**

2. **Touch the Text Selection icon that appears below the cursor tab, shown in the margin.**

   After you touch the icon, the cursor tab gets darker. It's your clue that Text Selection mode is now active.

3. **Drag the cursor tab around the text to select a block.**

   As you drag, the text becomes highlighted and is ready for further manipulation and taunting.

To replace the selected text, type something on the keyboard. Or, you can press the Del key to delete the block. Otherwise, see the later section "Cutting, copying, and pasting" to find out how to cut, copy, search, or share the text.

The second way to select text is to use a special menu. With the onscreen keyboard visible, press and hold your finger on any editable text. You see the Edit Text menu appear, as shown in Figure 4-14. Here are your options for selecting text:

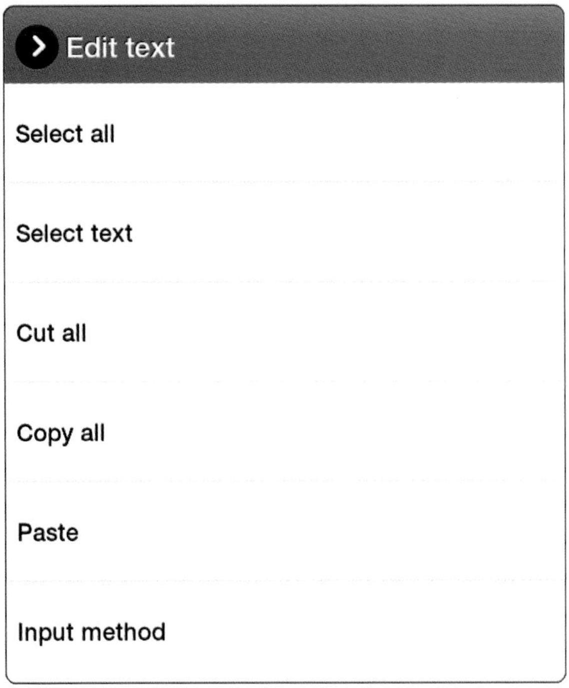

> **Edit text**

Select all

Select text

Cut all

Copy all

Paste

Input method

Figure 4-14: The Edit Text menu.

    Select All: Selects all the text

    Select Text: Enters a special, and especially useless, text-selecting mode — an option better suited for selecting text on a Web page

    Cut All: Cuts all the text, placing it into the clipboard for pasting

    Copy All: Copies all the text, placing it into the clipboard for pasting

My advice is to avoid the Select Text command for anything other than selecting text on a Web page, which is covered in the next section.

✔ You can quickly select a word by double-tapping it with your finger, though this method isn't reliable.

✔ A Clipboard icon next to the Text Selection icon indicates that text has already been copied or cut and can be pasted at that point, replacing the selected text. Later in this chapter, see Figure 4-18 and the section "Cutting, copying, and pasting."

✔ To cancel text selection, or to undo any selected block, press the Back soft button.

Selecting text on a Web page

It's possible to select text from a Web page, even though the text there isn't "editable" text. Because the text isn't editable, or even edible, you need to follow these steps:

1. Long-press the Web page near the text you want to copy.

You can only copy text from a Web page. Obviously, you cannot cut text. See Chapter 8 for information on saving pictures from a Web page.

2. Move the cursor tabs to mark the beginning and end of the block.

A special magnifier appears, as shown in Figure 4-15, to help you pinpoint the block's start or end point on the Web page.

When you select a larger chunk of text on a Web page, the selection block becomes a rectangle, as shown in Figure 4-16. Use the handles on the rectangle's edges to resize the selection.

3. Choose Copy from the pop-up menu that appears.

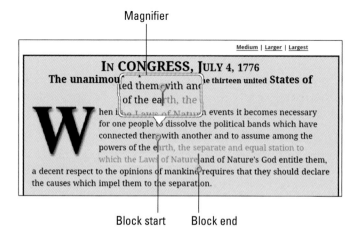

Figure 4-15: Selecting text on a Web page.

Drag to resize block.

He has refused his Assent to Laws, the most wholesome and necessary for
the public good.

He has forbidden his Governors to pass Laws of immediate and pressing
importance, unless suspended in their operation till his Assent should be
obtained; and when so suspended, he has utterly neglected to attend to them.

He has refused to pass other Laws for the accommodation of large districts of
people, unless those people would relinquish the right of Representation in
the Legislature, a right inestimable to them and formidable to tyrants only.

He has called together legislative bodies at places unusual, uncomfortable,
and distant from the depository of their Public Records, for the sole purpose
of fatiguing them into compliance with his measures.

Figure 4-16: Selecting a block of text on a Web page.

The text is copied into the Galaxy Tab clipboard. From there, it can be pasted
into any app that accepts text input. See the next section.

- ✔ Seeing the onscreen keyboard is a good indication that you can edit and
  select text.

- ✔ Copying text from a Web page allows you to paste that text into an email
  message or Facebook status update or into any field where you can
  paste text on the Galaxy Tab.

- ✔ The two other commands on the text-selection pop-up menu are Search
  and Share. Choose Search to look for text within the selected block. Choose
  the Share command to share the block as text or as an image via email,
  instant message, Facebook, or any other sharing app installed on your Tab.

- ✔ Refer to Chapter 8 for more information on surfing the Web with your
  Galaxy Tab.

Cutting, copying, and pasting

Selected text is primed for cutting or copying, which works just like it does
in your favorite word processor. After you select the text, a pop-up slate of
icons appears, as shown in Figure 4-17. To copy the text, choose the Copy
icon. To cut the text, choose the Cut icon.

Just like on your computer, cut or copied text on the Galaxy Tab is stored in
a clipboard. To paste any previously cut or copied text, move the cursor to
the spot where you want the text pasted. It can be anywhere text is input on
the Tab, such as in an email message, a Twitter tweet, or any text field. Then
touch the Paste Text icon that appears, as shown in Figure 4-18.

Copy Cut Paste Search Share

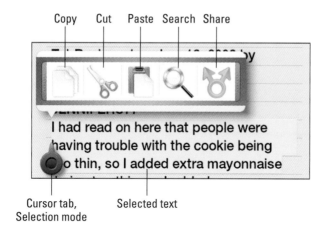

Cursor tab,
Selection mode

Selected text

Figure 4-17: Copying or cutting selected text.

Select text Paste text

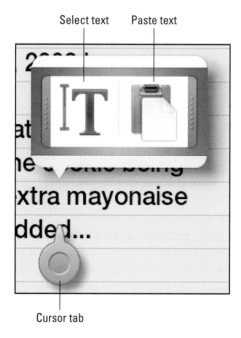

Cursor tab

Figure 4-18: Pasting text.

REMEMBER

~ The Paste Text icon (refer to Figure 4-18) shows up only when there's text to paste.

~ You can paste text only into locations where text is allowed. Odds are good that if you can type, or whenever you see the onscreen keyboard, you can paste text.

Galaxy Tab Dictation

The Galaxy Tab has the amazing ability to interpret your dictation as text. It works almost as well as computer dictation in science fiction movies, though I can't seem to find the command to launch photon torpedoes.

To ensure that voice input is activated on your Tab, follow these steps:

1. **At the Home screen, press the Menu soft button.**

2. **Choose Settings.**

3. **Choose Language and Keyboard.**

4. **Choose Samsung Keypad.**

5. **Ensure that a check mark appears by the option Voice Input.**

6. **Press the Home soft button when you're done.**

The key to voice input is to locate the Microphone icon, similar to the one shown in the margin. To begin voice input, touch the icon. A voice-input screen appears, as shown in Figure 4-19.

Figure 4-19: The voice-input thing.

When you see the text *Speak Now,* speak directly into the Tab.

As you speak, the Microphone icon (refer to Figure 4-19) flashes. The flashing doesn't mean that the Galaxy Tab is embarrassed by what you're saying. No, the flashing merely indicates that the Tab is listening, detecting the volume of your voice.

After you stop talking, the Tab digests what you said. You see your voice input appear as a wavelike pattern on the screen. Eventually, the text you spoke — or a close approximation — appears on the screen. It's magical, and sometimes comical.

✏ The first time you try voice input, you might see a description displayed. Touch the OK button to continue.

✏ A Microphone key lives on the onscreen keyboard for when you tire of typing and want to take a stab at some dictation.

✏ The Microphone icon appears only when voice input is allowed. Not every application features voice input as an option.

✏ The better your diction, the better your results. Also, it helps to speak only a sentence or less.

✏ You can edit your voice input just as you edit any text. See the section "Text Editing," earlier in this chapter.

✏ Speak the punctuation in your text. For example, you would say, "I'm sorry comma Christine" to have the Galaxy Tab produce the text I'm sorry, Christine (or similar wording).

✏ Common punctuation you can dictate includes the comma, period, exclamation point, question mark, and colon.

✏ Pause your speech before and after speaking punctuation.

✏ Dictation may not work where no Internet connection exists.

✏ The Galaxy Tab features a voice censor, which replaces any naughty words you might utter with a series of pound (#) symbols. The Galaxy Tab knows a lot of blue terms, including the infamous "Seven Words You Can Never Say on Television," but apparently the terms *crap* and *damn* are fine. Don't ask me how much time I spent researching this topic.

Part II
The Communications Tab

The 5th Wave   By Rich Tennant

"That's exactly why I only tweet in my basement."

In this part . . .

As time goes by, coming up with excuses for not keeping in touch is becoming more difficult. In the digital age, with the Internet connecting everyone around the world in a matter of microseconds, you have plenty of ways to get hold of people: You can send text messages and email, consult on social networking sites, and even video-chat. These methods are all handy ways to stay connected, and I highly recommend trying them before you do something silly, like write a letter or visit someone in person.

The topic in this part of the book is communications. One technological pillar that supports the Galaxy Tab is communications. No matter where you go, as long as you take the Tab with you, you can keep in touch with your friends. You can even take the Tab right up to their front doors and text them instead of knocking. Talk about modern conveniences!

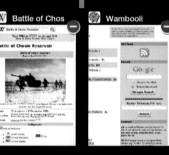

5

All Your Friends in the Galaxy

In This Chapter

▶ Exploring the Contacts app
▶ Searching and sorting your contacts
▶ Sending a group text message or email
▶ Adding new contacts
▶ Editing and changing contacts
▶ Deleting contacts

C an you recite, off the top of your head, the names and phone numbers of everyone you know? How about their email addresses? The names of their favorite childhood pets? Nope — you probably don't even know their bank account PINs or where they keep guns in their houses. That's because this type of information is most likely stored on your computer, where it's far easier to access than from your sluggish, old-fashioned brain.

As a communications device, your Galaxy Tab has a need to harbor information about all the people you know — specifically, those with whom you want to communicate electronically. From sending email and text messaging to social networking, you want to have access to your list of friends, pals, and cohorts. This chapter explains how do that on your Galaxy Tab.

Meet Your Friends

You may already have some friends in your Galaxy Tab. That's because your Google account was synchronized with the Tab when you first set things up. Because all your Gmail and other types of contacts on the Internet were duplicated on the Tab, you already have a host of friends available. The place where you can access those contacts is the Contacts app.

✓ If you haven't yet set up a Google account, refer to Chapter 2.

✓ Adding more contacts is covered later in this chapter, in the section, "Invite Friends to Your Galaxy."

✓ Most apps on the Galaxy Tab use contact information from the Contacts app. Those apps include Email, Gmail, Latitude, and Messaging as well as any app that lets you share information, such as photographs or videos.

✓ Information from your social networking apps is also coordinated with the Contacts app. See Chapter 9 for more information on using the Galaxy Tab as your social networking hub.

Using the Contacts app

To peruse the Galaxy Tab address book, start the Contacts app. The way the Tab ships out of the box, it has a Contacts app shortcut on the second Home screen (panel 2, just to the left of the main Home screen). You can also find the Contacts app on the Applications screen.

The Contacts app shows a list of all contacts in your Galaxy Tab, organized alphabetically by last name, similar to the ones shown in Figure 5-1.

Scroll the list by swiping with your finger. Or, you can touch a letter on the left side of the screen to quickly hop to that part of the list, as shown in Figure 5-1.

To do anything with a contact, you first have to choose it: Touch a contact name and you see detailed information in the right side of the screen, as shown in Figure 5-1. The list of activities you can do with the contact appears on the Info tab. Here are some options:

Send text message: Choose a Text option to send the contact a text message. For example, in Figure 5-1 you would choose Text Home to text Mr. Obama's home number. See Chapter 6 for information on text messaging on the Galaxy Tab.

Send email: Touch an Email option to compose an email message to the contact. When the contact has more than one email address, you can choose to which one you want to send the message. Chapter 7 covers using email on your Tab.

View address: When the contact has a home or business address, you can choose that option to view the address on a map or get directions. Refer to Chapter 12 for all the fun stuff you can do with Maps on your Galaxy Tab.

View social networking status: When a contact is one of your social networking buddies, that person's current status appears as shown in Figure 5-1. The status might also appear at the bottom of the info list, you may see a View Profile item to choose, or you may see a Social Network Feeds button, which lets you see all of the contact's social networking status updates. See Chapter 9 for more information on social networking with the Galaxy Tab.

Figure 5-1: Your Galaxy Tab address book.

You can't do things with certain tidbits of information that show up for a contact. For example, the Galaxy Tab in the United States doesn't make phone calls. Neither does the Tab sing *Happy Birthday* when you touch a contact's birthday information.

✔ Not every phone number can receive text messages. President Obama's home number, shown in Figure 5-1, is the White House main line, which doesn't accept text messages.

✔ After you choose a contact's email address, you see a pop-up menu asking which email program to use: Gmail or another email account.

✔ Not every contact has a picture, and the picture can come from a number of sources (Gmail or Facebook, for example). See the section "Adding a picture to a contact" for more information.

✔ In Figure 5-1, the item referenced as *contact sources* shows the different places from which the contact information is culled. Contacts can be gathered from your Google account, from Facebook, from Twitter, or imported directly into the Tab. The section "Invite Friends to Your Galaxy," later in this chapter, describes how to add contacts from multiple sources.

Sorting your contacts

Your contacts are displayed in the Contacts app in a certain order: alphabetically by last name but listed first name first. You can change that order, if you like. Here's how:

1. **Start the Contacts app.**

2. **Press the Menu soft button.**

3. **Choose Display Options.**

   The Display Options screen appears, which shows you the settings for viewing your contacts.

4. **Choose the View By command to specify how contacts are sorted: first name or last name.**

   The Contacts app is configured to show contacts by last name.

5. **Choose Display Contacts By to specify how the contacts appear in the list: first name first or last name first.**

   The Contacts app shows the contacts listed by first name first.

6. **Touch the Done button when you've made your selections.**

There's no right or wrong way to display your contacts — only whichever method you're used to. I prefer them sorted by last name and listed first name first.

Searching contacts

You can have a massive number of contacts. Though the Contacts app doesn't provide a running total, I'm certain that I have more than 500 contacts on my Tab. That number combines my Facebook, Gmail, Twitter, and other accounts. I have a lot of contacts, and I have the potential for even more contacts.

 Rather than endlessly scroll the Contacts list and run the risk of rubbing your fingers to nubs, you can employ the Galaxy Tab's powerful Search command. You can do so by either touching the Search soft button or choosing the Search text box, shown in Figure 5-1. Use the onscreen keyboard to start typing all or part of a contact's name. The list of contacts quickly narrows to show only the contacts that contain the text you type.

- ✔ You can also voice-search for a contact. Touch the Microphone icon on the onscreen keyboard and then speak the contact's name when you see the Speak Now prompt. The sounds you utter appear in the Search text box, which you can then use to search the list.

- ✔ Don't let the Samsung keypad's autocorrections or suggestions throw you: Continue to type your search text. The Search command uses the text you type, not the suggestions that appear.

- ✔ See Chapter 4 for additional information on using the onscreen keyboard and turning off the XT9 autocorrection and word suggestion feature.

- ✔ Also see Chapter 4 to read up on using dictation with your Galaxy Tab.

- ✔ To clear a search, touch the X button, found at the far right side of the Search box.

- ✔ No, there's no correlation between the number of contacts you have and how popular you are in real life.

Using a contact shortcut

A helpful way to keep popular contacts handy is to place them directly on the Home screen as shortcuts. In Figure 5-2, you see several contacts' shortcut icons on the Home screen. Touching an icon displays that contact's social networking status as well as a series of quick actions, as illustrated in the figure.

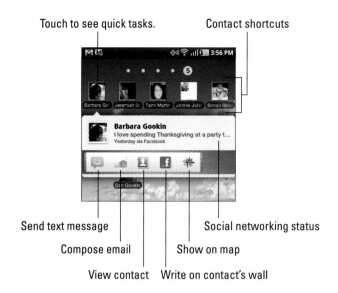

Touch to see quick tasks.   Contact shortcuts

Send text message   Social networking status
Compose email   Show on map
View contact   Write on contact's wall

Figure 5-2: A contact's shortcut icon on the Home screen.

To place a contact icon on the Home screen, obey these steps:

1. **Long-press the Home screen.**

    The Home screen must have enough room for the contact's shortcut icon; if the Home screen is full, the shortcut icon doesn't stick.

2. **Choose Shortcuts from the Add to Home Screen menu.**

3. **Choose Contact.**

4. **Scroll your list of contacts and choose a contact for the shortcut icon.**

    You can also use the Search box to quickly locate a contact.

The contact's icon is placed on the Home screen, ready for action, as illustrated in Figure 5-2. The variety of quick actions available for a contact depends on how detailed the contact's information is. Also, not all contacts have updates for their social networking statuses.

> There may be additional ways to place contacts on the Home screen, such as custom widgets available from your Galaxy Tab's cellular service provider.

> To dismiss the contact's list of quick actions, press the Back soft button or simply touch another location on the Home screen.

✔ You can place any type of contact on the Home screen, even nonhuman contacts, such as businesses, parks, parole offices, and other places you frequent.

✔ The navigation option Show on Map (in Figure 5-2) is unique to the Verizon Galaxy Tab. Other unique options are available depending on the apps you have installed on your Tab.

✔ To add more quick actions for a contact, edit the contact's information. For example, adding a contact's street address means that navigation and map options appear for that contact's quick actions.

✔ Chapter 21 discusses additional shortcut icons you can place on the Home screen, moving them around and deleting them, as well as information such as how you can expand the Home screen to hold more icons.

Working with contact groups

You can take advantage of contact groups to send a gang email or text message. The secret is to use the Groups tab in the Contacts list (refer to Figure 5-1).

After touching the Groups tab, you see all the groups you've created, with either your Gmail, Facebook, or Twitter groups or groups you've made on the Galaxy Tab or elsewhere.

To send a group an email or text message, follow these steps:

1. **Choose the Groups tab in the Contacts app.**

2. **Choose a group from the list.**

   The names of the contacts in that group appear on the right side of the screen.

3. **Touch the Send button.**

4. **Choose Send Message to send the group a text message, or choose Send Email to compose a gang email.**

   You're presented with a list of the names in the group and asked to choose which phone numbers or email addresses to use for the message.

5. **Place a check mark by each contact to whom you want to text or email.**

   The reason you have to complete this chore is that some contacts feature multiple phone numbers and email addresses.

6. **Touch the Send button.**

7. **Use the Complete Action Using menu to choose how to send the message.**

   The options presented depend on the type of contact you've chosen (email address or phone number) and which apps are installed on your Tab. For example, if you choose a phone number, you see options for sending a text message or using a phone app to make a call.

8. **Complete the operation using the app you've chosen.**

   For example, send a text message or compose a Gmail message.

See Chapter 6 for information on sending a text message; Chapter 7 for sending email; and Chapter 10 for using the Galaxy Tab to make phone calls or initiate a video chat.

> ✔ See the section "Building a group of contacts," later in this chapter, for information on creating contact groups.
>
> ✔ The contact groups you create on the Galaxy Tab are listed in the Device section of the Groups tab.
>
> ✔ The best way to create Gmail contact groups is by using Gmail on the Internet. Go to http://gmail.google.com.

Invite Friends to Your Galaxy

You can add even more friends to your Contacts list: Import them from your computer's email program or address book, add them from your social networking sites, receive them via email or text messages, or create new ones from scratch.

Importing contacts from your computer

Your computer's email program is doubtless a useful repository of contacts — a collection of names and addresses that you've built up over the years. You can export those contacts from your email program and then import them into the Galaxy Tab's Contacts app. It's not easy, but it's possible.

The key to the exporting-and-importing business is to bribe the proper customs officials. For electronic records on the Galaxy Tab, the key is to keep the records in the *vCard* (.vcf) file format. In most sophisticated email programs, exporting in the vCard file format is a common feature.

After the vCard files are created on your computer, connect the Galaxy Tab to the computer and transfer them. Transferring files from your computer to the Galaxy Tab is covered in Chapter 19.

Finally, with the vCard files on the Galaxy Tab, you start the Contacts app and follow these steps:

1. **Press the Menu soft button.**

2. **Choose the Import/Export command.**

3. **Choose Import from SD Card.**

4. **Choose the Phone option from the Save Contact To menu.**

   Yes, the option should be titled Device because the Galaxy Tab isn't a phone.

The contacts are imported and appear in the Contacts app as soon as the import operation has been completed.

The importing process may create some duplicates. That's okay: You can join two entries for the same person in the Contacts app. See the section "Joining identical contacts," later in this chapter.

✔ The key to exporting vCard files from your computer's email program is to look for an Export command. It's typically found on the File menu.

✔ In the Windows Live Mail program, choose Go⇨Contacts and then choose File⇨Export⇨Business Card (.VCF) to export the contacts.

✔ In Windows Mail, choose File⇨Export⇨Windows Contacts and then choose vCards (Folder of .VCF Files) from the Export Windows Contacts dialog box. Click the Export button.

✔ On the Mac, open the Address Book program and choose File⇨Export⇨ Export vCard.

✔ You can delete the vCard files you exported from your computer's email program after you're done copying them over to the Galaxy Tab.

✔ The vCard file format uses the `.vcf` filename extension.

✔ You don't need to copy the vCard files to any specific folder on the Galaxy Tab's MicroSD card. Placing them in the root folder is fine. If this bullet point makes sense to you, I give you permission to delete the vCard files after you've imported them into the Contacts app.

Adding contacts from Facebook and Twitter

The Galaxy Tab is keenly aware of your social networking relationships and how vital they are to keeping your online persona popular. For example, all your Facebook and Twitter friends can quickly be linked into the Tab's Contacts list.

Follow these steps in the Contacts app:

1. **Press the Menu soft button.**

2. **Choose the command Get Friends.**

   You see the Get Friends screen, which lists associated accounts on the Galaxy Tab. If you don't see any accounts, refer to Chapter 9 for information on setting up social networking on your Tab.

3. **Choose an account, such as Facebook.**

   You see a list of all your Facebook friends, or perhaps only new friends you've made recently.

4. **Touch the green check mark by the top item, Select All.**

5. **Touch the Get button.**

   The contact or contacts you've selected are added to the Contacts list.

6. **Repeat Steps 3 through 5 for additional accounts listed on the Get Friends screen.**

The accounts you see listed on the Get Friends screen are set up using the Accounts and Sync screen, covered in Chapter 9. You can use that screen to add Facebook, MySpace, Twitter , and other social networking accounts, as well as other accounts you may have on the Tab.

✔ Generally speaking, anytime you install an app that maintains a Contacts list, you're asked whether you want to synchronize that app's contacts with other contacts on your Galaxy Tab. My advice is to choose whatever option synchronizes all the contact information.

✔ See Chapter 10 for information on integrating your Skype contacts with the Contacts app.

✔ Synchronizing contacts across multiple apps or accounts often creates duplicates in your Contacts list. See the section "Joining identical contacts," later in this chapter, for instructions on how to fix that problem.

Creating a new contact from scratch

Sometimes it's necessary to create a contact when you actually meet another human being in the real world. In that case, you have more information to input, and it starts like this:

1. **Open the Contacts app.**

2. **Touch the Add Contact button.**

3. **From the Save Contact To menu, choose Google.**

   When you choose Device, the contact is saved only on your Galaxy Tab. By choosing Google, you're assured that the contact is backed up to the

Internet and available on other Android devices as well as on any computer you use to access your Google account.

4. **Fill in the information on the Add Contact screen as best you can.**

   Fill in the text fields with the information you know, as illustrated in Figure 5-3.

   To add items, touch the green Plus button.

   Touch the red Minus button to remove a field, though you don't need to remove empty fields.

5. **Touch the Done button to complete editing and add the new contact.**

The new contact is automatically synched with your Google account on the Internet — as long as you chose Google in Step 3. That's one beauty of the Android operating system used by the Galaxy Tab: You have no need to duplicate your efforts; contacts you create on the Tab are instantly synchronized with your Google account on the Internet.

Touch to add photo.

Contact location (where it is saved)

Expand to add details

Add another email address

Remove item

Touch to expand.

Scroll down to add more info.

Save and close

Choose phone contact type.

Figure 5-3: Creating a new contact.

Getting a contact from the Maps app

When you use the Maps app to locate a restaurant, haberdasher, or liquor store (or all three in one place), you can quickly create a contact for that location. Here's how:

1. **After searching for your location, touch the cartoon bubble that appears on the map.**

   You see more details for the location, as shown in Figure 5-4.

Details about the
map location   More button

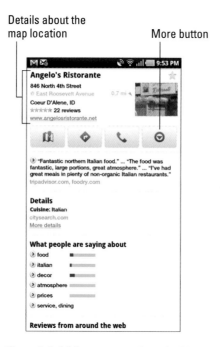

Figure 5-4: Adding a contact from the Maps app.

2. **Touch the More button, shown in Figure 5-4.**

3. **Choose Add As a Contact.**

4. **Choose Google.**

   I recommend saving the contact to your Google account because it's automatically synchronized and backed up on the Internet.

   The next screen shows the contact information just as when you create a new contact, though the Galaxy Tab has already filled in most of the information. That's the beauty of adding a contact by using the Maps app.

5. **Optionally, add more information, if you know it.**

6. **Touch the Done button.**

   The new contact is created.

See Chapter 12 for detailed information on how to search for a location using the Maps application.

Manage Your Friends

Nothing is truly perfect the first time, especially when you create things on a Galaxy Tab while typing with your thumbs at 34,000 feet during turbulence. You can do a whole slate of things with your Galaxy Tab contacts, from making minor changes and additions to creating groups to removing contacts no longer deserving of your attention.

Making basic changes

To make minor touch-ups on any contact, start by locating and displaying the contact's information: Choose the contact's name from the Contacts app. On the right side of the screen, touch the Edit button. Make any changes as you see fit, and then touch the Done button to save things when you're finished editing.

When a contact comes from several sources, you see those sources appear atop the Edit Contacts screen, as shown in Figure 5-5. Each tab represents the source, such as Google, Device (the Galaxy Tab), Skype, and Facebook, as shown in the figure. Choose a tab to make changes for that specific source, though you cannot edit information pulled from a social networking site, such as Facebook, or Skype.

✔ See Figure 5-1 for the location of the Edit button.

✔ The screen for editing the contact is the same one you used to create the contact, as shown in Figure 5-3.

✔ Seeing the message "Unable to edit SNS contacts on device" means that you're unable to edit social networking contact information using the Contacts app. That's because the contact's Facebook, Skype, Twitter and other types of information comes from those locations. It cannot be modified on the Galaxy Tab. (SNS stands for Social Networking Service.)

Contact info for the selected source

Contact sources

Figure 5-5: Editing a joined contact.

Adding a picture to a contact

The easiest way to add a picture to a contact is to already have the picture stored on the Tab. You can transfer the picture from a computer (covered in Chapter 19), or you can snap a shot with the Tab anytime you see the contact or a person or an object that resembles the contact.

After the contact's photo, or any other suitable image, is stored on your Galaxy Tab, follow these steps to update the contact's information:

1. **Locate and display the contact's information.**

2. **Touch the Edit button.**

3. **Touch the Picture icon.**

    Refer to Figure 5-3.

4. **Choose the Album option.**

    Of course, if the contact is right there with you, choose the Take Photo option and take a picture.

5. **Browse the Gallery to look for a suitable image.**

    See Chapter 14 for more information on using the Gallery.

6. **Touch the image you want to use for the contact.**

7. **Select the size and portion of the image you want to use for the contact.**

   Use Figure 5-6 as your guide. You can choose which portion of the image to use by moving the cropping box, and you can resize the cropping box to select more or less of the image.

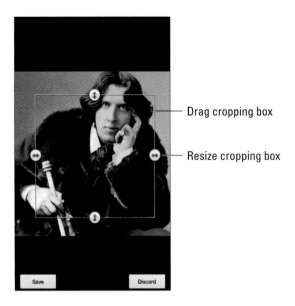

Drag cropping box

Resize cropping box

Figure 5-6: Cropping a contact's image.

8. **Touch Save to assign the image to the contact.**

9. **Touch Done to complete editing the contact.**

The image is now assigned, and it appears whenever the contact is referenced on your Galaxy Tab.

- ✔ The cropping box (see Figure 5-6) is square. You cannot resize one edge without resizing all edges proportionally.

- ✔ You can add pictures to contacts on your Google account using any computer. Just visit your Gmail Contacts list to edit a contact. You can then add to that contact any picture stored on your computer. The picture is eventually synched with the same contact on your Galaxy Tab.

- ✔ Accounts you synchronize from Facebook, Twitter, and other social networking apps also bring along their associated contact pictures.

- ✔ To remove or change a contact's picture, follow Steps 1 through 3 and choose Remove Icon from the menu that pops up.

Making a favorite

A *favorite* contact is someone you stay in touch with most often. It doesn't have to be someone you like — just someone you (perhaps unfortunately) contact often, like your mechanic or plumber.

The list of favorite contacts is kept on the Contact apps' Favorites tab (refer to Figure 5-1). Adding a contact to the list is cinchy: Display the contact's information and touch the Favorite button (the star) in the contact's upper right corner, as shown in Figure 5-1. When the star is gold, the contact is one of your favorites.

To remove a favorite, touch the contact's star again and it loses its color. Removing a favorite doesn't delete the contact, but it removes it from the Favorites list. Also, contacts have no idea whether they're a favorite, so don't believe that you're hurting anyone's feelings by not making them a favorite.

Joining identical contacts

Because the Galaxy Tab can pull contacts from multiple sources (Facebook, Gmail, Twitter), you may discover duplicate contact entries in the Contacts app. Rather than fuss over which entry to use, you can join the contacts. Here's how:

1. **Wildly scroll the Contacts list until you locate a duplicate.**

   Well, maybe not *wildly* scroll, but locate a duplicated entry. Because the Contacts list is sorted, the duplicates appear close together (though that may not always be the case).

2. **Select one of the contacts.**

3. **Press the Menu soft button.**

4. **Choose More and then choose Join Contact.**

   The Join Contact screen appears, as shown in Figure 5-7. If the contact already is joined to several sources, they appear on the right side of the screen, as illustrated in the figure.

5. **Choose an account to join from the left side of the screen.**

   The accounts are merged. Well, they appear together on your Galaxy Tab.

6. **Press the Back soft button when you're done joining accounts.**

The Galaxy Tab limits you to joining only five accounts. That number may seem like a lot, but between your social networking sites, Gmail, and the Tab itself, it can increase rather rapidly.

- When you have more than five joined accounts, you just have to live with having duplicate entries in your Contacts list.

- One joined account is the *primary* account, or the main account for that contact. To set another account as the primary account, touch the Set As Primary button, illustrated in Figure 5-7.

- To unjoin an account, touch the red Minus button, shown in Figure 5-7.

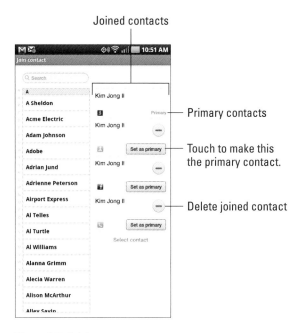

Figure 5-7: Joining a contact.

Building a group of contacts

The Galaxy Tab automatically synchronizes any contact groups you may have on Gmail or from other sources. You can use the groups to send a bunch of people email or a text message. It's handy.

You can create new groups at any time. Follow these steps:

1. **Start the Contacts app.**

2. **Touch the Groups tab.**

   It's found at the top of the screen (refer to Figure 5-1).

3. **Touch the Add Group button.**

4. **Type a name for the group.**

   Keep the group name simple and descriptive. For example, I have a group named Boys, which contains contact information for my sons.

5. **Touch the Edit Member(s) button.**

6. **On the Edit Group Members screen, choose the contacts to add to the group.**

   Scroll the list and touch every contact you want to place in the group. As you touch a contact, it's added to the group.

   If you've accidentally added a contact to the group, touch the red Minus button to remove that person. (The person is only removed from the group, not deleted from your Contacts list.)

7. **Press the Back soft button when you're done adding group members.**

The group is ready to use at once. See the section "Working with contact groups," earlier in this chapter.

To remove a group, choose the Groups tab in the Contacts app and long-press the group you want to remove. Choose the Delete Group command from the menu that appears, and then touch the Delete button to confirm.

You can delete only groups created on the Galaxy Tab. You cannot delete groups that are imported from your Gmail or social networking accounts. To manage those groups, use the original service, such as Gmail on the Internet.

Removing a contact

Every so often, consider reviewing your contacts. Purge those folks whom you no longer recognize or you've forgotten. It's simple:

1. **Locate the contact in your Contacts list and display the contact's information.**

2. **Touch the Delete button.**

   It's found in the lower right corner of the screen, as shown in Figure 5-1.

3. **Touch OK to remove the contact from your Galaxy Tab.**

Because the Contacts list is synchronized with your Gmail contacts for your Google account, the contact is also removed there.

For some linked accounts, such as Facebook, deleting the account from your Tab doesn't remove the human from your Facebook account. The warning that appears (before Step 3 in the preceding list) explains as much.

Removing a contact doesn't kill the person in real life.

6

The Joy of Texting

In This Chapter

▶ Composing a text message

▶ Getting a text message

▶ Changing the text message ringtone

▶ Texting pictures, videos, and media

▶ Managing your text messages

*T*exting is more than a craze. For some people, it's an obsession. I've seen people texting while they're driving, which is outright frightening. Worse, I see people texting while riding bicycles. I see mothers pushing baby carriages while texting and drinking cups of on-the-go coffee. It's nuts, though I must admit that texting does come in quite handy for sending short notes or for those times when a phone call isn't necessary or wanted. Yet some people text more than they talk.

Whether you're a casual texting user or rabid thumb warrior, the Galaxy Tab can easily sate your texting desires. You use the Messaging app to send and receive text messages to other devices.

Message for You!

Texting headquarters on the Galaxy Tab is an app named Messaging. It's where you discover the art of *texting*, or sending a text message. Truly, Messaging is the app that will sate your voracious text-messaging appetite.

> Move your head!

> What? Oh, you mean move it like this?
> 1:20 PM

> Yes. Now I can s

✔ Some Android applications can affect messaging. You're alerted to whether the program affects messaging before it's installed. See Chapter 17.

✔ As far as I know, there's no surcharge for text messaging on the Galaxy Tab. I believe that text messaging is either free or included as part of your monthly data plan. If it's the latter, rest assured that text messaging doesn't eat up a lot of data: Texting is basically unlimited on the Tab.

✔ You can use other apps for text messaging on the Galaxy Tab, though they're more like chatting applications as opposed to traditional, cell phone texting applications. Skype offers a chat feature, as does Google Talk. None of them is a true replacement for text messaging, however.

✔ You can access Google Talk by opening the Talk app on your Galaxy Tab.

✔ The nerdy term for texting is *SMS*, which stands for Short Message Service.

Creating a new text message

You can compose a message to one of your contacts, to the phone number of a mobile device, or to an email address. It works like this:

1. **Open the Messaging app.**

   It can be found on the second Home screen (panel 2) or, like all apps on your Galaxy Tab, on the Applications screen.

   When you first open the Messaging app, you see a list of current conversations (if any), organized by contact name or phone number. See Figure 6-1.

   If you don't see the list, as shown in Figure 6-1, press the Back soft button.

2. **Touch the Compose button.**

3. **Input a mobile number, an email address, or a contact name in the To field.**

   If the text you type matches one or more existing contacts, you see those contacts displayed. Choose one to send a message to that person; otherwise, continue typing the phone number or email address.

4. **Touch the Enter Message Here text box.**

5. **Type your text message.**

   You have only 160 characters to make your point.

6. **Touch the Send button to send the message.**

Unknown contact   Compose

New text message notification │ New text waiting

Touch to view conversation.

Figure 6-1: Text messaging conversations.

The message is sent instantly. You can wait for a reply or do something else with the Tab, such as snooze it or choose to talk with a real person, face to face. Or, you can always get back to work.

✔ You can also use the Contact button on the New Message screen to browse your Contacts list and find a message recipient: Simply touch the check mark next to a phone number or an email address to include that person in the message. Touch the Add button to stick that contact into the To field.

✔ Yes, you can send a single text message to multiple people. See the side-bar "Whether to send a text message or an email?" for my thoughts on sending a text message versus sending an email.

✔ A text message sent from the Galaxy Tab is received via email using a special return address. On the Verizon network, the address is the device's mobile number @vtext.com. You can reply to the message via email, in which case the reply is received on the Galaxy Tab as a text message.

Whether to send a text message or an email?

The concept of sending a text message is similar to sending an email message. Both methods of communication have advantages and disadvantages.

Text messages are short and to the point. They're informal, more like quick chats. Indeed, the speed of reply is often what makes text messaging useful. But, like email, sending a text message doesn't guarantee a reply.

An email message can be longer than a text message. You can receive email on any computer or device that accesses the Internet. Email message attachments are handled better, and more consistently, than text message (MMS) media. Though email isn't considered formal communication, not like a paper letter or a phone call, it ranks a bit higher in importance than text messaging.

Sending a text message to a contact

You can send a text message to any of your contacts, if they have a cell phone that can pick up text messages (not every cell phone can do so) or an email address. Here's how it works:

1. **Open the Contacts app.**

   It's found on the Applications screen, or maybe a shortcut icon is on the Home screen somewhere.

2. **Choose a contact to whom you want to send a text message.**

3. **Touch the Text Mobile item in the contact's Info tab.**

   The phone number may not say *Text Mobile*. It all depends on how you first input information for that contact. It might say *Text Home, Text Work,* or *Text Something-or-Other*. Just ensure that it's a cell phone or mobile device number.

4. **Touch the Message button.**

5. **If prompted by the Complete Action Using menu, choose Messaging, the texting app.**

   A message composition window appears, which also tracks your text conversation, similar to the one shown in Figure 6-2.

6. **Type the message text.**

   Be brief. A text message has a 160-character limit. See the later sidebar "Common text message abbreviations," for some common and useful text message shortcuts and acronyms.

7. Touch the Send button.

The message is sent instantly. When the person replies, you see their message displayed (refer to Figure 6-2).

8. Read the reply.

9. Repeat Steps 6 through 8 as needed — or eternally, whichever comes first.

Contact you're texting   Delete this thread

What the contact typed   What you type

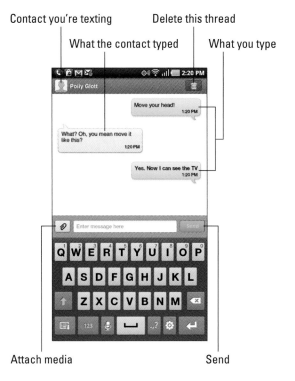

Attach media   Send

Figure 6-2: Typing a text message.

There's no need to continually look at the Tab, waiting for a text message. Whenever your contact chooses to reply, you see that person's text presented as part of an ongoing conversation. See the later section "Receiving a text message."

✔ You can send text messages only to cell phones or other mobile devices that can receive them. Aunt Rowena cannot receive text messages on her landline that she's had since the 1960s.

- The messaging app on the Galaxy Tab can also send a text message to an email address. See the next section.

- Typing on the Swype keyboard is much faster than using the standard onscreen keyboard. See Chapter 4.

- You can also dictate text messages by clicking the Microphone button on the onscreen keyboard. See Chapter 4 for more information on voice input.

- Add a subject to your message by touching the Menu soft button and choosing Add Subject.

- Phone numbers and email addresses sent in text messages become links. You can touch a link to call its number or visit its Web page.

- On Android devices, any smiley faces you put in a text message appear as special Android icons. Press the Menu soft button and choose Insert Smiley to see the gamut.

- Press the Back soft button to dismiss the onscreen keyboard, which can be useful when the keyboard obscures all or part of a message.

- Continue a conversation at any time: Open the Text Messaging application, peruse the list of existing conversations, and touch one to review what has been said or to pick up the conversation.

- Do not text and drive. Do not text and drive. Do not text and drive.

Making a direct contact shortcut for text messaging

For the contacts you text most often, consider creating a texting Home screen shortcut. Obey these directions:

1. **Long-press the Home screen.**

2. **Choose Shortcuts from the Add to Home Screen menu.**

3. **To create a text messaging shortcut, choose Direct Message.**

4. **Choose the contact you want to use for text messaging.**

   The Contacts list displays only those contacts with phone numbers.

You can send a text message only to a cell phone, and not all cell phones are capable of receiving text messages.

The Direct Message contact shortcut appears on the Home screen. The icon features the contact's picture (if the contact has one), and the letter *M* appears, which is your clue that the shortcut is a text message shortcut.

Common text message abbreviations

Texting isn't about proper English. Indeed, many abbreviations and shortcuts used in texting are slowly becoming part of the English language, such as LOL and BRB.

The weird news is that these acronyms weren't invented by teenagers. Sure, the kids use them, but the acronyms find their roots in the Internet chat rooms of yesteryear. Regardless of their source, you might find them handy for typing messages quickly. Or, maybe you can use this reference for deciphering an acronym's meaning (you can type acronyms in either upper- or lowercase):

2	To, also	K	Okay	TC	Take care
411	Information	L8R	Later	THX	Thanks
BRB	Be right back	LMAO	Laughing my [rear] off	TIA	Thanks in advance
BTW	By the way			TMI	Too much information
CYA	See you	LMK	Let me know	TTFN	Ta-ta for now (goodbye)
FWIW	For what it's worth	LOL	Laugh out loud		
FYI	For your information	NC	No comment	TTYL	Talk to you later
GB	Goodbye	NP	No problem	TY	Thank you
GJ	Good job	OMG	Oh my goodness!	U2	You, too
GR8	Great	PIR	People in room (watching)	UR	Your, you are
GTG	Got to go			VM	Voice mail
HOAS	Hold on a second	POS	Person over shoulder (watching)	W8	Wait
IC	I see			XOXO	Hugs and kisses
IDK	I don't know	QT	Cutie	Y	Why?
IMO	In my opinion	ROFL	Rolling on the floor, laughing	YW	You're welcome
JK	Just kidding	SOS	Someone over shoulder (watching)	ZZZ	Sleeping

After touching the direct contact shortcut, you may see the pop-up Complete Action Using menu. Choose Messaging to send the contact a text message using the Messaging app. Other options may appear on the menu, depending on which apps you have installed on your Galaxy Tab.

Receiving a text message

Whenever a new text message comes in, you see a message appear at the top of the touchscreen. The message goes away quickly, and then you see the New Text Message notification, shown in the margin.

To view the message, pull down the notifications, as described in Chapter 3. Touch the messaging notification and that conversation window immediately opens.

Setting the new text message ringtone

Receiving a new text message is accompanied by a pleasant, or not so pleasant, sound. It's the new message *ringtone,* and you can change it at your whim. Follow these steps:

1. **Open the Messaging app.**

2. **Ensure that you're at the main message screen.**

   The main message screen is shown in Figure 6-1. If you don't see this screen, press the Back soft button to back out of a conversation.

3. **Press the Menu soft button.**

4. **Choose the Settings command.**

5. **Choose Select Ringtone.**

6. **If you see a Complete Action Using prompt, choose Android System.**

   Or, you can choose another option to select a ringtone by using another app, such as Zedge. (See Chapter 25 for information about Zedge.)

7. **Browse the list and choose the sound you want.**

   The sound isn't set until you complete Step 8, so feel free to play around with the various sounds.

   If you prefer to have no sound play, choose the option Silent, found near the top of the Alarm Tone list.

8. **Touch the OK button to set the new sound or touch Cancel to keep the current sound unchanged.**

9. **Press the Back soft button to return to the Messaging app.**

The sound plays the next time the Galaxy Tab receives a text message.

You can also determine whether the Tab vibrates when a new text message is received. Place a check mark by the Vibrate item, after Step 7 in the preceding list.

Multimedia Messages

When a text message contains a bit of audio or video or a picture, it ceases becoming a mere text message and transforms into — brace yourself — a *multimedia* message. This type of message even has its own acronym, MMS, which supposedly stands for Multimedia Messaging Service.

- ✔ You can send pictures, video, and audio using multimedia messaging.

- ✔ There's no need to run a separate program or do anything fancy to send media in a text message; the same Text Messaging app is used on the Galaxy Tab for sending both text and media messages. Just follow the advice in this section.

- ✔ Not every mobile device has the ability to receive MMS messages. Rather than get the media, the recipient is directed to a Web page where the media can be viewed on the Internet.

Composing a multimedia message

One of the easiest ways to send a multimedia message is to start with the source, such as a picture or video stored on your Galaxy Tab. You can then choose to use MMS to share that media item, by heeding these directions:

1. **Use the Gallery app to locate the image or video you want to share.**

   You have to be viewing the image or video, so if it appears in a folder or an album, open the album and then touch the image to view it.

   See Chapter 14 for more information on how the Gallery works.

2. **Press the Menu soft button.**

3. **Choose Share.**

4. **Choose Messaging from the pop-up menu.**

   When the image or video is too large to send as a text message, you see a warning message. Dismiss the warning and try again with a smaller image or video. Otherwise, you see the MMS Composition window, shown in Figure 6-3.

5. **Type a contact name or phone number into the To text field.**

   Type only the first part of a contact name and then choose the proper contact from the list that appears.

6. **Type a message in the Enter Message Here text box.**

7. **Touch the Send button to send the multimedia message.**

Unlike sending a text message, sending a multimedia message takes some time.

- ✓ After the message is sent, you see a copy of the image or video in the message history list.

- ✓ Though you can use multimedia messaging to send media to an email address, keep in mind that the media size is limited. The limit is designed for MMS, not for email, so if you want to send large media items, compose an email message instead.

- ✓ As with sending a text message to an email address, the multimedia message has an interesting return email address. You might want to identify yourself to recipients of this type of message so that no one assumes it's unwanted email or spam.

Enter contact's name or phone number.

Remove attachment

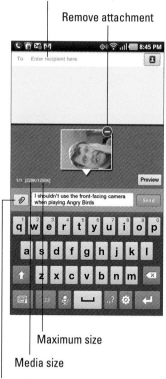

Maximum size

Media size

Attach button

Figure 6-3: Composing a multimedia message.

Attaching media to a message

You don't need to go hunting for already created multimedia to send in a message; you can attach media directly to any message or ongoing conversation. It works like this:

1. **Compose a text message as you normally do.**

   Fill in the To field, or simply continue an existing conversation.

2. **Touch the Attach button.**

   Refer to Figure 6-3 for the location of the Attach button.

   After touching the Attach button, you see a pop-up menu listing various media items you can attach to a text message. Here's a summary:

   > *Picture:* Choose an image stored in the Gallery.

   > *Video:* Choose a video you've taken with the Tab and stored in the Gallery.

   > *Audio:* Browse the folders on the Galaxy Tab to find an audio file to attach.

   > *Capture Picture:* Take a picture right now and send it in a text message.

   > *Capture Video:* Record a video and then send it as media in a text message.

   > *Record Audio:* Record an audio clip, such as your voice, and then send it.

   > *Slide:* Create a collection of photos to send together.

   More options may appear on the menu, depending on which apps you have installed on your Galaxy Tab.

3. **Type a message to go with the media attachment.**

4. **Touch the Send button to send your media text message.**

In just a few, short, cellular moments, the receiving party will enjoy your multimedia text message.

- ✓ Not every mobile device is capable of receiving multimedia messages.

- ✓ Be aware of the size limit on the amount of media you can send; try to keep your video and audio attachments brief.

- ✓ Options exist in the Camera app for taking smaller-size pictures and videos. See Chapter 13 for more information.

✏ When you choose the Audio option, you see a list of folders on the Galaxy Tab. They work just like folders on your computer: Your job is to browse to a location to find audio to send. You can look in the `Music` folder to find songs used by the Music app. Also look in the `media/ audio` or `download` folders for other audio files that may be stored on your Tab.

✏ Multimedia messages can be sent over the cellular data connection, not over a Wi-Fi connection. Be aware of that, especially if you have a limited data plan or else you may incur excess charges.

Receiving a multimedia message

Multimedia attachments come into your Galaxy Tab just like any other text message does, but you see a thumbnail preview of whatever media was sent. To preview the attachment, touch the green Play button, shown in the margin. You see a special window where the attachment "plays."

Yes, even still images play.

To save the attachment on the Tab, press the Menu soft button while viewing the attachment (watching it play). Choose Save Attachment and then touch the Save button. Pictures and videos are saved to the Gallery. Audio is saved in the `download` folder.

Some types of attachments, such as audio, cannot be saved.

To return to the message after playing its media attachment, press the Back soft button.

Message Management

Even though I'm a stickler for deleting email after I read it, I don't bother deleting my text message threads. That might be because I get far more email than text messages. Anyway, were I to delete a text message conversation, I would follow these exact steps:

1. **Go to the main screen in the Messaging app.**

   It's the screen that lists all your conversations, as shown in Figure 6-1.

2. **Long-press the message thread you want to delete.**

3. **Choose Delete Thread from the pop-up menu.**

4. **Touch the Delete button to confirm.**

   The conversation is gone.

If I wanted to delete multiple conversations, I'd follow these steps:

1. **Touch the Menu soft button.**
2. **Choose Delete Threads.**
3. **Touch the box next to each conversation you want to zap.**

   Obviously, if you want to keep one, don't touch its box.

   A green check mark appears by conversations slated for execution.
4. **Touch the Delete button.**
5. **Touch the Delete button to confirm.**

The selected messages are gone.

You've Got Email

*T*hese days, it seems odd when you ask people for their email address and they don't have one. You have a better chance of standing behind an orangutan in an ATM line than you do of finding someone without an email address, though I admit that I haven't used every ATM in the world.

One of the Galaxy Tab's communications feats is its ability to handle your email. The Tab receives your email messages, letting you read them anywhere. You can also compose new missives, forward messages, attach media files, and do basically the entire email enchilada. Forget being tied to a computer — using your Galaxy Tab, you can do email anywhere.

Inbox	
(5)	12/1/201◆
ePope@vatican.va	
...o much going on	
custserv@oldnavy.com	
Order Status for Order #14B8	
d.corleone@themob.org	
Re: An offer you can't refuse	
God@heaven.gov	
¨wd: LOL	
...ort@comcast.net	
...admit that we could do better	
	...oad more messages

Email Roundup

Two apps on the Galaxy Tab handle email: one app for Gmail, which is your Google email, and an app named Email, which handles all other types of email. It includes Web-based email, such as Yahoo! Mail, Windows Live Mail, and others, plus whatever ISP email you have or email from work.

✔ You can run the Gmail and Email apps by touching the Applications button on the Home screen and then locating the apps on the Applications screen.

✔ Adding the Gmail or Email app icon to the Home screen is easy: See Chapter 21.

✔ A Gmail account was created for you when you signed up for a Google account. See Chapter 2 for more information about setting up a Google account.

✔ The Email program can be configured to handle multiple email accounts. That way, all your different email account messages arrive in one universal inbox. Setting up your email is covered later in this chapter.

✔ Though you can use your Tab's Web browser to visit the Gmail Web site, you should use the Gmail app to pick up your Gmail.

✔ Likewise, you should use the Email app to pick up your Yahoo! Mail, AOL Mail, Hotmail, and other Web-based email systems.

✔ If you forget your Gmail password, visit this Web address:

        www.google.com/accounts/ForgotPasswd

✔ Every so often, Google updates the Gmail app, adding new features. If anything changes after this book goes to press, refer to my Web page for updates and additional information:

        www.wambooli.com/help/galaxytab

Mail of the Electronic Kind

As a Google device, your Galaxy Tab works seamlessly with Gmail. In fact, if Gmail is already set up to be your main email address, you'll enjoy having access to your messages all the time by using your Tab.

Regular email, handled by the Email program, must be set up before it can be used. See the later section "Email Configuration" for instructions. After completing that painless-yet-cumbersome process, you can receive email on your Tab just as you do on your computer.

Getting a new message

You're alerted to the arrival of a new email message in your Galaxy Tab by a notification icon as well as by a ringtone or sound. The icon differs between a new Gmail message and an Email message.

For a new Gmail message, you see the New Gmail notification, shown in the margin, appear at the top of the touchscreen.

For a new email message, you see the New Email notification.

To deal with the new-message notification, pull down the notifications and choose the appropriate one. You're taken right to your inbox to read the new message.

✔ See the later section "Setting email options" to set up how the Galaxy Tab reacts when you get a new email message.

✔ Refer to Chapter 3 for information on accessing notifications.

Checking the inbox

To peruse the mail you have, start your email program — Gmail for your Google mail or Email for other mail you have configured to work with the Galaxy Tab — and open your electronic inbox.

To check your Gmail inbox, start the Gmail app. It can be found on the Applications screen. The Gmail inbox is shown in Figure 7-1.

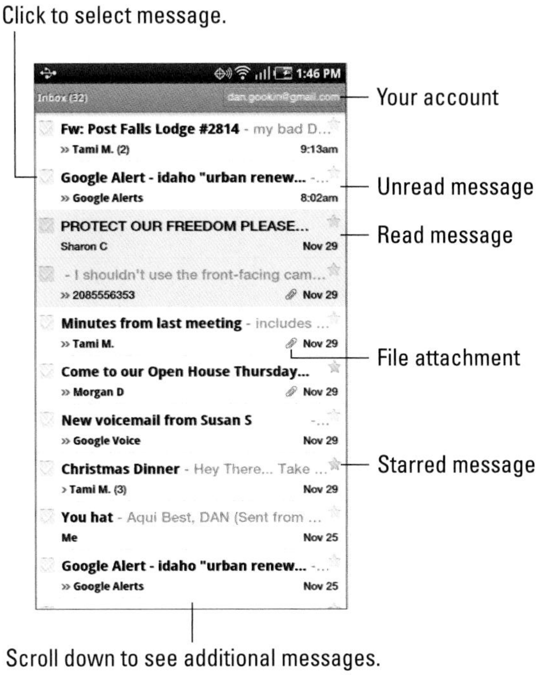

Click to select message.

Your account

Unread message

Read message

File attachment

Starred message

Scroll down to see additional messages.

Figure 7-1: The Gmail inbox.

To get to the inbox screen when you're reading a message, touch the Menu soft button and choose the command Go to Inbox.

To check your Email inbox, open the Email app. A shortcut to the Email app is at the bottom of every Home screen as a preset on the Galaxy Tab. Or, you can open the Email app from the Applications screen.

In the Email app, you find multiple inboxes — one for each email account you've configured on the Tab. Figure 7-2 shows a single account's inbox.

Unread message

Mail account   Mailbox   Compose

Get new mail

Figure 7-2: An email account inbox.

To view your universal inbox, which shows all incoming email for all your email accounts, touch the mail account button (shown in Figure 7-2) and choose All Inboxes. Likewise, to view messages from a specific account, choose the account name from the same menu, shown in the figure.

The mailbox button is used to peruse the various mailboxes associated with each account. As with your email program on your computer, you have an inbox and an outbox and sent, trash, and other boxes, which helps keep your email organized.

✓ You won't find your Gmail inbox in the list of accounts for the Email program.

✓ Gmail is organized using *labels*, not folders. To see your Gmail labels from the inbox, touch the Menu soft button and choose Go to Labels.

✓ Email messages on your Galaxy Tab aren't deleted from the mail server. That way, you can read the same email messages later, using a computer. Most computer email programs, however, are configured to delete messages from the mail server. When they do, those messages no longer show up on the Tab.

Reading an email message

As mail comes in, you can read it by choosing the new-email notification, described earlier in this chapter. You can also choose new email by viewing the inbox. The message appears on the screen, as shown in Figures 7-3 and Figure 7-4 for Gmail and Email, respectively.

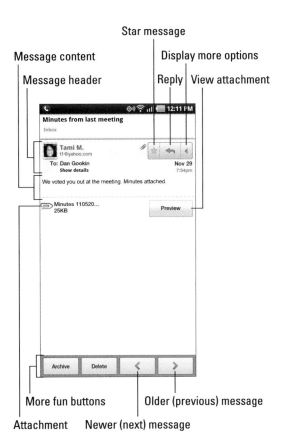

Figure 7-3: Reading a Gmail message.

Older (previous) message   Delete message

Newer (next) message

Message subject

Move message
to folder

Reply/Reply All/Forward

Compose new message

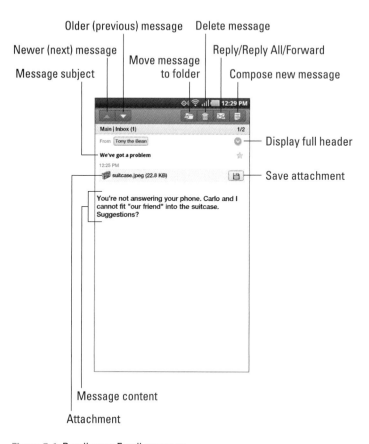

Display full header

Save attachment

Message content

Attachment

Figure 7-4: Reading an Email message.

Reading and working with a message operate much the same as in any email program you've used. Refer to the figures for locating common email actions, as described in this list:

- To reply to a message, touch the Reply button in the Gmail program; in the Email program, choose the Reply command from the Reply button menu.

- The Reply All command is hidden in Gmail: Touch the Display More Options button to see it. In the Email program, choose Reply All from the Reply button menu.

- To forward a Gmail message, touch the Display More Options button and choose the Forward command. In the Email program, the Forward command is found on the Reply button menu.

- Refer to the later section "Write the message" for information on (surprisingly) writing a new electronic message, which also applies when you forward or reply to an email.

- To delete a message in Gmail, touch the Delete button. In the Email program, you also touch the Delete message button to remove a message, though I see no reason to delete messages in the Email program, because they're deleted automatically when your computer's email program picks them up later.

- Use the Older and Newer buttons to continue to read your email messages.

- When you're done with a message, you can press the Back soft button to return to the inbox.

Here are some general email notes:

- I find it easier to manage Gmail using a computer.

- The non-Gmail email you read on your Galaxy Tab isn't deleted from the email server. That means you can pick up the same email all over again using your computer.

- When you touch the Star icon in a Gmail message, you're flagging the message. Those starred messages can be viewed or searched separately, making them easier to locate later.

- Use the Reply All command only when everyone else *must* get a copy of your reply. Because most people find endless Reply All email threads annoying, use the Reply All option judiciously.

Searching your messages

You can use the Search soft button to search the email on your Galaxy Tab. This feature works best with Gmail; you can search only the message headers in the Email app.

To search for any tidbit of text in your Gmail, heed these directions:

1. **Open the Gmail inbox.**

2. **Touch the Search soft button.**

3. **Type the text to find.**

   You can also dictate the text by first pressing the Microphone button on the keyboard and then speaking what you're trying to find.

4. **Touch the Search button to begin the search.**

   Peruse the results.

The search results are limited to text in those program's messages. To perform a wider search throughout the entire Galaxy Tab, touch the Search soft button when viewing the Home screen.

When searching the Email program, display the universal inbox: From the mail account button (refer to Figure 7-2), choose All Inboxes. Press the Search soft button to search the message sender and Subject fields. Yes, that's the extent of using the Search command for regular email on the Galaxy Tab.

Write That Message

The best way to get email is to send email. Speaking for a great majority of the Internet, I would favor that you send original email, a photo of yourself, or a personal story as opposed to merely forwarding something cute, political hyperbole, or a ribald joke. That's just me. Otherwise, for composing your Galaxy Tab email, refer to this section.

Composing a new Gmail message

Crafting a Gmail epistle on the Galaxy Tab works similarly to creating email on your computer. So if you're frustrated with that process on your computer, you'll be equally frustrated on the Galaxy Tab.

Figure 7-5 shows the basic Gmail composition setup. Follow these steps to craft your missive:

1. **Start the Gmail app.**

2. **Ensure that you're viewing the inbox.**

   If not, press the Back soft button.

 3. **Press the Menu soft button.**

4. **Choose Compose.**

   A new message screen appears, looking similar to Figure 7-5 but with none of the fields filled in.

5. **Type the first few letters of a contact name, and then choose a matching contact from the list that's displayed.**

   You can also send to any valid email address not found in your Contacts list, by typing that address.

 To summon the Cc field, press the Menu soft button and choose the command Add Cc/Bcc.

6. **Type a subject.**

7. **Type or dictate the message.**

8. **Touch the Send button to whisk your missive to the Internet for immediate delivery.**

Copies of the messages you send are saved in your Gmail account, which is accessed from your Galaxy Tab or from any computer connected to the Internet.

Message content

Message subject   Save as draft

To (recipient)   Send

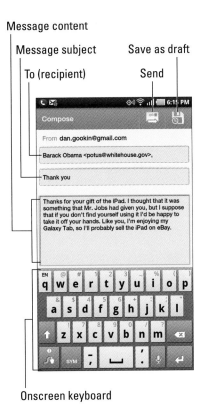

Onscreen keyboard

Figure 7-5: Writing a new Gmail message.

Composing a non-Gmail message

Sending an email message for an email account other than Gmail is handled by the Email app. It works like this:

1. **Open the Email app.**

2. **Choose a specific email account from the Accounts button.**

   You cannot compose a new message when viewing the universal inbox. Instead, choose a specific account.

   Even though you choose a specific account, the email is sent from whichever account you've specified as your main email account. See the section "Setting up a new email account," later in this chapter, for details on setting the main email account.

3. **Touch the Compose button found in the upper right part of the screen.**

4. **Craft the message.**

   Figure 7-6 illustrates the New Mail window. Fill in the blanks just as you would when composing an email message on your computer.

5. **Touch the Send button to send the message.**

Message subject

Touch to expand Cc/Bcc fields.

Message recipients   Choose contacts

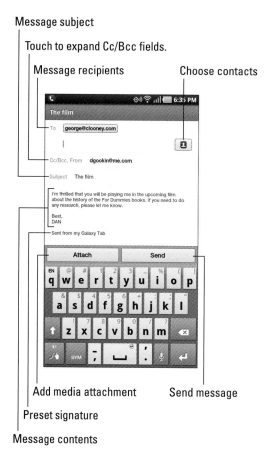

Add media attachment   Send message

Preset signature

Message contents

Figure 7-6: Composing an email message.

Copies of the messages you send in the Email program are stored in the specific account's Sent mailbox. To see that mailbox, choose Sent from the Mailbox button (refer to Figure 7-2).

✔ Mail is sent right away, unless no digital network is available. In that case, mail is stored in the outbox until a signal is acquired.

✔ To display the Cc and Bcc fields, touch the Cc/Bcc, From text, as shown in Figure 7-6.

✔ See the later section "Creating a signature" for changing the signature automatically attached to your outgoing messages.

✔ To cancel the message, press the Menu soft button and choose Discard.

✔ To save the message for later, press the Menu soft button and choose Save As Draft.

Starting a new message from a contact

A quick and easy way to compose a new message is to find a contact and then create a message using that contact's information. Quickly follow these steps:

1. **Open the Contacts app.**

2. **Locate the contact to whom you want to send an electronic message.**

   Review Chapter 5 for ways to hunt down contacts in a long list.

3. **Choose an Email option from the contact's Info tab.**

   For example, choose Email Work, Email Home, or Email Other.

4. **Choose the Compose command to use Gmail to send the message or choose Email to send an email message using your main email account.**

   At this point, creating the message works as described in the preceding sections; refer to them for additional information.

Message Attachments

You can send and receive email attachments on your Galaxy Tab just as you can send and receive them on your computer. Even so, email attachments work better in the computer kingdom than they do in Tablet Land. Therefore, don't expect to do the same things with email attachments on your Tab as you can do on a computer.

For receiving attachments, the Tab lets you view the attachment, to see (or hear) its contents. Not every attachment is viewable, however. It all depends on the type of file attached to the message.

Find your email attachments

Any email attachments you save are stored on the MicroSD card, the Galaxy Tab's removable storage device. Specifically, the attachments are placed in the `download` folder. To display the contents of that folder, start the My Files app and choose the `download` folder. The folder's contents are displayed on the touchscreen, just as your computer's folder contents are displayed. Same deal.

Touch a file's icon in the `download` folder to view that file. Image and video files are played in the Gallery app; audio files are played using the Music app; the ThinkFree Office app is used to view Microsoft Office documents as well as Acrobat Reader (PDF) files.

After viewing a file, press the Back soft button to return to the `download` folder in the My Files app.

You can transfer the information stored on the MicroSD card to your computer, which includes transferring saved email attachments from the `download` folder. See Chapter 19 for information on synchronizing files between the Galaxy Tab and your computer.

Email messages with attachments are flagged in the inbox with paper clip icons, which seems to be the standard I-have-an-attachment icon from most email programs. When you open one of those messages, you may see the attachment name appear along with either a Preview or Save button.

 Touch the Preview button to view the attachment. What happens after you touch the Preview button depends on the type of attachment. Sometimes you see a list of apps from which you can choose one to open the attachment. Many Microsoft Office documents are opened by the QuickOffice app.

Touch the Save button to save the attachment to the MicroSD card, in the `download` folder. If the attachment can be viewed, you see (or hear) it after it's been saved.

Some attachments can be neither previewed nor saved. In those cases, use a computer to fetch the message and attempt to open the attachment. Or, you can reply to the message and inform the sender that you cannot open the attachment on your mobile device.

✐ Sometimes, pictures included in an email message aren't displayed. You find a Show Pictures button in the message, which you can choose to display the pictures.

✐ You can add an attachment to an email message you create: In the Gmail program, press the Menu soft button and choose the Attach command. In the Email program, use the Attach button, as shown in Figure 7-6.

  ✔ You can browse the Gallery and choose a photo or video to email: Long-press the photo and choose the Share command from the bottom of the screen. Choose Email or Gmail from the pop-up menu to begin a new message with that photo or video attached.

  ✔ See Chapter 14 for more information on the Gallery.

Email Configuration

It's possible to customize your email experience on the Galaxy Tab. Though some changes and modifications may make things easier, other options are just so boring that there's no point in covering them in this section. So I don't.

Setting up a new email account

The Gmail app is limited to using only Google's email system. The Email app, on the other hand, can be set up to work with multiple email accounts, from free Web-based email accounts to the Email account you have with your ISP or at work. Obey these steps to set things up:

1. **Open the Email app.**

   You should see the Set Up Email screen, listing the various types of email accounts you can add (though your selection is by no means limited to those icons). If so, skip to Step 6; otherwise, you probably already have some accounts configured. Continue with Step 2:

2. **Ensure that you're viewing an inbox.**

   It can be All Inboxes or any specific account's inbox. Just make sure that you're not reading an email message.

3. **Press the Menu soft button.**

4. **Choose Account Manager.**

   You see a list of all current email accounts configured for use on your Galaxy Tab.

5. **Touch the Add Account button.**

6. **Choose an icon to add an email account from that service or provider.**

   For example, choose AOL or Yahoo! if you have an email account at AOL or Yahoo!.

   Choose Hotmail if you have an account on Hotmail, MSN, or Windows Live.

   If you have an ISP account, such as a Comcast or Road Runner account, choose Others. For work, you probably have to choose the Microsoft Exchange icon.

Over the next few steps, you need to know some information about your email account.

7. If the option appears, choose the proper domain from the Select Service menu.

For example, choose `hotmail.com`, `msn.com`, or `live.com`.

8. Type the email address you use for the account.

You need to type a full email address.

9. Type the password for that account.

You must type your password one character at a time when using the Swype keyboard.

After you've added the first account, you see an option to make the new account (the one you're adding) the main account. If that's what you want to do:

10. Place a check mark by the option Send Email from This Account By Default.

The main account is the one the Tab uses to send all your email. Only one account can be the main account.

11a. If you're configuring a Web-based email account, such as Hotmail or AOL, touch the Next button; skip to Step 19.

11b. If you're configuring an Exchange Server account, fill in the information on the Exchange Server Settings screen.

Use the information provided by your organization to fill in all the proper fields; skip to Step 19.

11c. For configuring an ISP email account, choose Manual Setup.

Manual setup is required for non-Web-based email because you need to supply specific information to configure it. That's the tedious part.

12. Because you're configuring your ISP email account, touch the POP3 Account button.

13. Fill in the POP3 information provided by your email service.

For example, for a POP3 server, you input the proper POP3 server name provided by your ISP. The Galaxy Tab guesses at the name, though that name (in the POP3 Server field) might be incorrect.

Ensure that the Delete Email from Server option is set to Never. By setting this option, you ensure that any email you pick up on the Galaxy Tab is also available to your computer.

14. **Touch the Next button.**

15. **Fill in the SMTP server information provided by your ISP.**

    Most of the information on the screen should be accurate, but check the SMTP Server field and ensure that it shows the server name as provided by your ISP.

16. **Touch the Next button.**

    If the outgoing server settings fail, try deselecting the Require Password item, and try again.

17. **Choose an email check frequency.**

    Especially if the option Never is preset, choose something more frequent.

18. **Touch the Next button.**

19. **Give the account a name.**

    I use the name of the service for the account name, except for my main email account with my ISP. I gave that account the name *Main*.

20. **Optionally, change the name that's set in the Your Name field.**

    It's the name that appears for outgoing mail.

21. **Touch the Done button.**

    Your email account is set up.

You can set up all your email accounts on your Galaxy Tab — even multiple accounts for different services. So if you have more than one Microsoft Live account, for example, add them all.

Not every Web-based email account can be accessed by the Galaxy Tab. When doubt exists, you see an appropriate warning message. In most cases, the warning message also explains how to properly configure the Web-based email account to work with your Galaxy Tab.

Creating a signature

I highly recommend that you create a custom email signature for sending messages from the Galaxy Tab. Here's my signature:

```
DAN

This was sent from my Galaxy Tab.
Please forgive the typos.
```

To create a signature for Gmail, obey these directions:

1. **Start Gmail.**

2. **Press the Menu soft button.**

3. **Choose More and then Settings.**

   If you see no settings, choose Back to Inbox and repeat Steps 2 and 3.

4. **Choose Signature.**

5. **Type or dictate your signature.**

   The signature can be on two lines, even though it looks like just one line is available.

6. **Touch OK.**

7. **Press the Back soft button to return to your Gmail inbox.**

You can obey these same steps to change your signature; the existing signature shows up after Step 4.

To set a signature for the Email program, heed these steps:

1. **Press the Menu soft button.**

   If nothing happens, go to an inbox and try again.

2. **Choose Account Manager.**

3. **Long-press an account.**

   The Account Settings screen appears.

4. **Choose Signature.**

5. **Add or edit your email account signature.**

   You may see a preset signature, one that may plug your wireless provider. Whatever. Feel free to type whatever you like as a signature.

6. **Touch the OK button.**

7. **Press the Back soft button to return to the account manager.**

8. **Press the Back soft button again to return to the Email inbox.**

The signature you set appears in all outgoing messages for the account you long-pressed in Step 3. To set the signature for another account, repeat these steps for that specific account.

You can copy and paste your signature from one account to another. See Chapter 4 for information on how copy and paste works on the Galaxy Tab.

Setting email options

A smattering of interesting email settings are worth looking into. To reach the Settings screen in Gmail or Email, follow Steps 1 through 3 in the preceding set of steps for Gmail and Email, respectively.

Here are some items worthy of note:

- Set a default email account in the Email program by choosing Default Email Account. Only one account can be the default.

- To specify how frequently the Email program checks for new messages, choose Email Check Frequency. I like to set my check frequency to 5 minutes.

- Gmail is checked all the time for new mail, so there's no option to set its update frequency.

- Choose Email Notifications to have the Tab alert you to new messages.

- Choose a specific ringtone for the account by touching Select Ringtone.

- Specify whether the Tab vibrates upon the receipt of new email by choosing Vibrate.

- The ringtone and vibration options are available only when Email Notifications is selected.

- Options in the Email program must be set for each of your email accounts.

Tablet Web Browsing

In This Chapter

▶ Browsing the Web on your Tab

▶ Adding a bookmark

▶ Working with multiple Web page windows

▶ Sharing and saving Web pages

▶ Downloading images and files

▶ Setting a new home page

▶ Configuring the Browser app

*H*ave you ever browsed the Web on a cell phone? It's like trying to view all of China through a porthole. Yeah, it's possible, but not much fun. Like China, the Web was designed to be viewed using a computer, complete with a large monitor and full-size keyboard. That doinky screen on a cell phone doesn't do the Web justice.

The Galaxy Tab has a nice, roomy screen. Viewing the Web on the Tab is like seeing China in person, which is the best way to see China or, really, anything else on the Internet. Truly, using the Web on your Galaxy Tab is an enjoyable experience. When it isn't, refer to this chapter for advice and suggestions.

ᴚ **Chosin Reservoir**

Battle of Chosin Reservoir
Part of the Korean War

▸ If possible, activate the Galaxy Tab's Wi-Fi connection before you venture out on the Web. Though you can use the Tab's cellular data connection, the Wi-Fi connection is often faster and incurs no data usage charges.

▸ Many places you visit on the Web can instead be accessed directly and more effectively by using specific apps. Facebook, Gmail, Twitter, and YouTube, and potentially other popular Web destinations, have apps that are either preinstalled on the Tab or can be downloaded for free from the Android Market. Use them instead of the Browser app.

✏️ The Browser isn't the only app for surfing the Web. Another popular app is Dolphin Browser, which is available at the Android Market. See Chapter 17.

Mobile Web Browsing

Rare is the person these days who has had no experience with the World Wide Web. More common is someone who has used the Web on a computer but has yet to taste the Internet waters on a mobile device. If that's you, consider this section your quick mobile Web orientation.

Viewing the Web

Your Galaxy Tab's Web-browsing app is named Browser. It dwells as a primary shortcut, found just to the left of the Applications button on every Home screen. Figure 8-1 illustrates the Browser app's interface.

Address box   Bookmarks, Most Visited, History

Forward   Windows

                                        Web page
Back   Refresh/Stop   contents

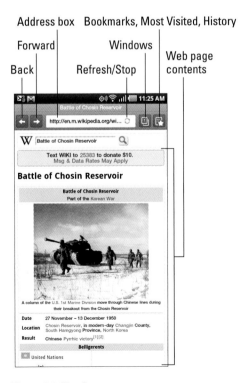

Figure 8-1: The Browser.

Here are some handy Galaxy Tab Web browsing tips:

✔ Pan the Web page by dragging your finger across the touchscreen. You can pan up, down, left, or right.

✔ Double-tap the screen to zoom in or zoom out.

✔ Pinch the screen to zoom out, or spread two fingers to zoom in.

✔ You can orient the Tab horizontally to read a Web page in Landscape mode. Then you can spread or double-tap the touchscreen to make teensy text more readable.

Visiting a Web page

To visit a Web page, type its address into the Address box (refer to Figure 8-1). You can also type a search word, if you don't know the exact address of a Web page. Touch the Go button on the Samsung keypad onscreen keyboard or the Go button by the Address box (see the margin) to search the Web or visit a specific Web page.

If you don't see the Address box, swipe your finger so that you can see the top of the window, where the Address box lurks.

You "click" links on a page by touching them with your finger. If you have trouble stabbing the right link, zoom in on the page and try again.

✔ To reload a Web page, touch the Refresh symbol on the right end of the Address bar.

✔ To stop a Web page from loading, touch the X that appears to the right of the Address bar. The X replaces the Refresh button and appears only when a Web page is loading.

Browsing back and forth

To return to a Web page, you can touch the Browser's Back button, illustrated in Figure 8-1, or press the Back soft button.

Touch the Browser's Forward button to go forward or to return to a page you were visiting before you touched the Back button.

To review the long-term history of your Web browsing adventures, touch the Bookmarks button in the upper right corner of the Browser window, as shown in Figure 8-2. Choose History to view your Web browsing history.

To view a page you visited weeks or months ago, you can choose a Web page from the History list.

Bookmarks tab

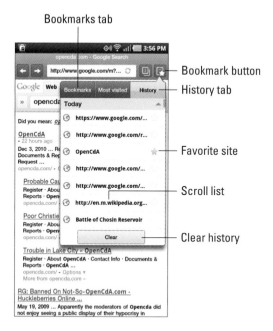

Bookmark button

History tab

Favorite site

Scroll list

Clear history

Figure 8-2: The Browser's history list.

To clear the History list, touch the Clear button, shown in Figure 8-2.

Using bookmarks

Bookmarks are those electronic breadcrumbs you can drop as you wander the Web. Need to revisit a Web site? Just look up its bookmark. This advice assumes, of course, that you bother to create (I prefer *drop*) a bookmark when you first visit the site. Here's how it works:

1. **Visit the Web page you want to bookmark.**

2. **Touch the Bookmark button, found at the top of the Browser window.**

    Refer to Figure 8-2 to see the location of the Bookmark button.

3. **If necessary, touch the Bookmarks tab to see the list of bookmarks.**

4. **Touch the Add Bookmark button.**

    You see the Add Bookmark window, shown in Figure 8-3.

5. **If necessary, edit the bookmark name.**

    The bookmark is given the Web page name, which might be kind of long. I usually edit the name to a shorter one that can fit beneath the thumbnail square.

6. **Touch OK.**

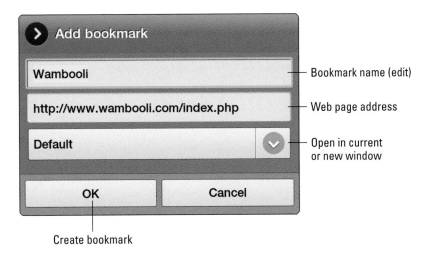

Figure 8-3: Adding a bookmark.

After the bookmark is set, it appears in the list of bookmarks. You can swipe the list downward to see the bookmarks and all their fun thumbnails.

 Another way to add a bookmark is to summon the Most Visited tab, shown in Figure 8-2. Touch the Star button by one of the Web pages you visit most often to bookmark that site.

　✔ To visit a bookmark, choose it from the Bookmarks list.

　✔ Remove a bookmark by long-pressing its entry in the Bookmarks list. Choose the command Delete Bookmark. The bookmark is gone.

　✔ Bookmarked Web sites can also be placed on the Home screen: Long-press the bookmark thumbnail and choose the command Add Shortcut to Home.

 　✔ The MyBookmarks app, obtained from the Android Market, can import your Internet Explorer, Firefox, and Chrome bookmarks from your Windows computer into the Galaxy Tab. See Chapter 17 for more information on the Android Market.

　✔ Refer to Chapter 4 for information on editing text on the Galaxy Tab.

Managing multiple Web page windows

The Browser app sports more than one window, which is a feature you find on computer Web browsers. It's possible to open Web pages in new windows and manage those multiple Web page windows on the Galaxy Tab. You have several ways to do it:

✓ *To open a link in another window,* long-press that link. Choose the command Open in New Window from the menu that appears.

✓ *To open a bookmark in a new window,* long-press the bookmark and choose the command Open in New Window.

✓ *To open a blank browser window,* touch the Windows button and then press the Plus button, shown in Figure 8-4.

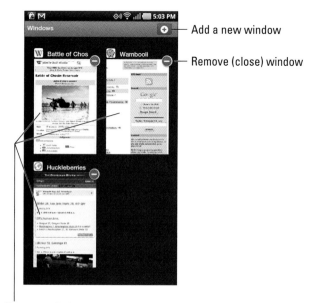

Add a new window

Remove (close) window

Choose a window

Figure 8-4: Working with browser windows.

You switch between windows by choosing one from the Windows screen, as shown in Figure 8-4. Open that screen by touching the Windows button at the top of the Browser app's screen (refer to Figure 8-1).

Close a window by touching the Minus button next to the window's thumbnail.

✓ The teensy number shown on the Windows button indicates how many windows the browser has open.

✓ New windows open using the home page that's set for the Browser application. See the section "Setting a home page," later in this chapter, for information.

Searching the Web

The handiest way to find things on the Web is to use the Google widget, often found floating on the fourth panel of the Home screen (just to the right of the main Home screen) and shown in Figure 8-5. Use the Google widget to type something to search for, or touch the Microphone button to dictate what you want to find on the Internet.

Figure 8-5: The Google widget.

To search for something anytime you're viewing a Web page in the Browser app, press the Search soft button. Type the search term into the box. You can choose from a list of suggestions.

To find text on the Web page you're looking at, as opposed to searching the entire Internet, follow these steps:

1. **Visit the Web page where you want to find a specific tidbit o' text.**

2. **Press the Menu soft button.**

3. **Choose Find on Page.**

4. **Type the text you're searching for.**

5. **Use the left- or right-arrow button to locate that text on the page — backward or forward, respectively.**

   The found text appears highlighted in green.

6. **Touch the X button when you're done searching.**

See Chapter 21 for more information on widgets, such as the Google widget.

The Google Search app, found on the Applications screen, works like a full-screen version of the Google widget. Use the app to search the Web.

Sharing a page

There it is! That Web page that you just *have* to talk about to everyone you know. The gauche way to share the page is to copy and paste it. Because you're reading this book, though, you know the better way to share a Web page. Heed these steps:

1. **Long-press the link or bookmark you want to share.**

2. **Choose the command Share Link.**

   A pop-up menu of places to share appears, looking similar to Figure 8-6. The variety and number of items on the Share Via menu depend on the applications installed on your Tab. For example, you might see Twitter or Facebook appear, if you've set up those social networking sites as covered in Chapter 9.

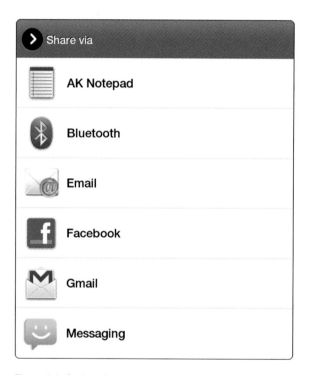

Figure 8-6: Options for sharing a Web page.

3. **Choose a method to share the link.**

   For example, choose Email to send the link by mail, or Text Messaging to share via a text message.

4. **Do whatever happens next.**

   Whatever happens next depends on how you're sharing the link: Compose the email or text message, for example. Refer to various chapters in this book for specific directions.

The best way to share a Web page is to share a link to the Web page. Ditto for YouTube videos and other media: Links are text. They take no time to send, consume only a tiny sip of data, and are more welcome by experienced Internet users than the old copy-and-paste job.

The easiest way to find the link to the page you're looking at is to use the Back command and visit the previous page; long-press the link.

When you can't find the link to the page, copy the text from the Address bar. That text is basically the link to the page. To copy, long-press the Address bar and choose either the Copy or Copy All command from the Edit Text pop-up menu. You can then paste the link into an email or text message.

Saving a Web page

I like to save some Web pages for later reading. It's not an obvious thing to do, but I save the Web pages of long diatribes or interesting text so that I can read them later, such as when I'm cooped up in an airplane for a cross-country trip, sitting around bored at the car repair shop, or visiting other locations where time slows and boredom grows.

To save a Web page to the Galaxy Tab's MicroSD card, follow these steps:

1. **Long-press the link to the page you want to save.**

   You can only save a Web page that's being linked to; you cannot save a Web page you're viewing.

2. **Choose the command Save Link.**

   The page is downloaded.

The Web page is saved in the `download` folder on the MicroSD card. The page can be viewed by opening the My Files app and then opening the `download` folder.

- ✔ Web pages you save are given the name `downloadfile.htm`. Additional pages you save have the names `downloadfile-1.htm`, `downloadfile-2.htm`, and so on.

- ✔ Refer to Chapter 20 for information on using your Galaxy Tab on an airplane.

The Art of Downloading

There's nothing to downloading, other than understanding that most people use the term without knowing exactly what it means. Officially, a *download* is a transfer of information over a network from another source to your gizmo. For your Galaxy Tab, that network is the Internet, and the other source is a Web page.

- When the Galaxy Tab is downloading information, you see the Downloading notification.

- There's no need to download program files to the Galaxy Tab. If you want new software, you can obtain it from the Android Market, covered in Chapter 17.

- Most people use the term *download* to refer to copying or transferring a file or other information. That's technically inaccurate, but the description passes for social discussion.

- The opposite of downloading is *uploading*. That's the process of sending information from your gizmo to another location on a network.

Grabbing an image from a Web page

The simplest thing to download is an image from a Web page. It's cinchy: Long-press the image. You see a pop-up menu appear, from which you choose the command Save Image.

To view images you download from the Web, you use the Gallery app. Downloaded images are saved in a folder, or "pile," that's titled Download.

- Refer to Chapter 14 for information on the Gallery.

- Technically, the image is stored on the Tab's MicroSD card. It can be found in the `download` folder. You can read about storage on the MicroSD card in Chapter 19.

Downloading a file

The Web is full of links that don't open in a Web browser window. For example, some links automatically download, such as links to PDF files or Microsoft Word documents or other types of files that can't be displayed by a Web browser. To save this type of document on the Galaxy Tab, long-press the link and choose the command Save Link from the menu that appears.

- You can view the saved file by referring to the Download Manager. See the next section.

- Some links may automatically download; clicking the link downloads the file instead of opening it in a new window.

- The ThinkFree Office app is used on the Galaxy Tab to display PDF and Microsoft Office files.

Reviewing your downloads

The Browser app keeps a list of all the stuff you download from the Web. To review your download history, follow these steps:

1. **Press the Menu soft button.**

2. **Choose the command Download Manager.**

   The Download Manager list appears, similar to the one shown in Figure 8-7. You can peruse the list, remove items from the list, or touch the Go to My Files button to examine the files.

Downloaded stuff   Remove from list (doesn't delete the download)

Open the My Files app   Scroll to see more downloads

Figure 8-7: The Download Manager.

3. **To exit the Download Manager, press the Back soft button.**

When you touch the Go to My Files button, you're switched to the My Files app, where you can then choose the download folder to witness your downloads face-to-face. You can then touch a downloaded file's icon to open and view the file.

- ✔ The Download Manager also lists any Web pages you've downloaded.

- ✔ Touching the Clear button doesn't delete the downloaded file — it only removes the file's name from the Download Manager's list.

- ✔ There are some things you can download that you cannot view. When that happens, you see an appropriately rude error message.

- ✔ You can quickly review any download by choosing the Download notification.

Web Controls and Settings

More options and settings and controls exist for the Browser program than just about any other program I've used on the Galaxy Tab. It's complex. Rather than bore you with every dang doodle detail, I thought I'd present just a few of the options worthy of your attention.

Setting a home page

The *home page* is the first page you see when you start the Browser application, and it's the first page that's loaded when you fire up a blank window. To set your home page, heed these directions:

1. **Browse to the page you want to set as the home page.**

2. **Press the Menu soft button.**

3. **Choose Settings.**

   A massive list of options and settings appears.

4. **Choose Set Home Page.**

5. **Touch the Use Current Page button.**

6. **Touch OK.**

   The home page is set.

I changed the home page on my Tab because it was preset to my cellular provider's page, and that page took forever to load. Remember: You don't have to use your cellular provider's home page.

If you want your home page to be blank (not set to any particular Web page), type **about:blank** in the text box instead of touching the Use Current Page button (refer to Step 5). That's the word *about,* a colon, and then the word *blank,* with no period at the end and no spaces in the middle. I prefer a blank home page because it's the fastest Web page to load. It's also the Web page with the most accurate information.

Changing the way the Web looks

You can do a few things to improve the way the Web looks on your Galaxy Tab. First and foremost, don't forget that you can orient the device horizontally to see a wide view on any Web page.

From the Settings screen, you can also adjust the zoom setting used to display a Web page. Heed these steps when using the Browser app:

1. **Press the Menu soft button.**
2. **Choose Settings.**
3. **Choose Default Zoom.**
4. **Select Close from the menu.**
5. **Press the Back soft button to return to the Web page screen.**

The Close setting might not be "big" enough, so remember that you can spread your fingers to zoom in on any Web page.

Setting privacy and security options

With regard to security, my advice is always to be smart and think before doing anything questionable on the Web. Use common sense. One of the most effective ways that the Bad Guys win is by using *human engineering* to try to trick you into doing something you normally wouldn't do, such as click a link to see a cute animation or a racy picture of a celebrity or politician. As long as you use your noggin, you should be safe.

As far as the Galaxy Tab's browser settings go, most of the security options are already enabled for you, including the blocking of pop-up windows (which normally spew ads).

If Web page cookies concern you, you can clear them from the Settings window. Follow Steps 1 and 2 in the preceding section and choose the option Clear All Cookie Data.

You can also choose the command Clear Form Data and remove the check mark from Remember Forum Data. These two settings prevent any characters you've input into a text field from being summoned automatically by someone who may steal your Tab.

You might be concerned about various warnings regarding location data. What they mean is that the Galaxy Tab can take advantage of your location on planet earth (using the GPS or satellite position system) to help locate businesses and people near you. I see no security problem in leaving that feature on, though you can disable location services from the Browser's Settings screen: Remove the check mark by Enable Location. You can also choose the item Clear Location Access to wipe out any information saved in the Tab and used by certain Web pages.

See the earlier section "Browsing back and forth" for steps on clearing your Web browsing history.

9

The Digital Social Life

In This Chapter

▷ Accessing social updates for your contacts

▷ Getting Facebook on the Galaxy Tab

▷ Sharing your life on Facebook

▷ Sending pictures to Facebook

▷ Tweeting on Twitter

▷ Exploring other social networking opportunities

*O*nce upon a clock tick, I wrote that the number-one reason for people to use the Internet was email. That's no longer true. I'm thinking today that the number-one reason to use the Internet is social networking. It's the ability to connect with friends, communicate, and share your life with thoughts, pictures, videos, and games. It's "that Facebook thing," as one of my older relatives calls it.

Armed with your Galaxy Tab, you can keep your digital social life up-to-date wherever you go. You can communicate with your online friends, let them know where you are, upload pictures and videos you take on the Tab, or just share your personal, private, intimate thoughts with all of humanity.

Your Social Networking Contacts

The Galaxy Tab briefly tastes the social networking waters by integrating your social networking friends with the Contacts list. It's not full-on social networking — not the same as using specific apps as covered elsewhere in this chapter — but it's a start.

The best way to configure social networking on the Tab is to already have established social networking accounts. If you haven't already, create yourself an account on Facebook or Twitter or whatever other social networking sites you plan to use. Create those accounts using your computer first, and then integrate them with your Galaxy Tab as described in this section.

Integrating your social networking contacts

You may have already configured your Galaxy Tab to play nice with your Facebook or Twitter or other social networking hubs. If not, follow these steps:

1. **Open the Settings app.**

   Or, from the Home screen, you can press the Menu soft button and choose the Settings command.

2. **Choose Accounts and Sync.**

   You're presented with a list of accounts you've associated with the Galaxy Tab. If you've just set things up, the only account you see is your Google (Gmail) account.

3. **Touch the Add Account button.**

   The Add an Account screen lists a bunch of accounts you can add to your Tab, including popular social networking sites.

4. **Choose the social networking account you want to add.**

   Three are listed: Facebook, Twitter, and MySpace.

   The Add an Account screen also shows other accounts that may be available on your Galaxy Tab. The list, which appears on the bottom of the screen in the More Accounts area, depends on which apps are installed on the Tab.

5. **Type your username or email address for the account you want to add.**

6. **Type the account's password.**

   You can place a check mark next to the Show Password item if you need help typing the password.

7. **Touch the Log In button.**

   The Galaxy Tab attempts to connect with your account.

8. **Choose how often to synchronize the Tab with your account, and then touch the Next button.**

   I like the 3 Hours option.

9. **Choose how to synchronize your social networking contacts.**

   I recommend keeping check marks by all the options, which fully integrates your social networking information with the Galaxy Tab.

10. **Touch the Done button.**

You can either repeat these steps to add other social networking sites or press the Home soft button to return to the Home screen.

The final step required to integrate your social networking friends with your contacts on the Galaxy Tab is to use the Get Friends command. Refer to the section in Chapter 5 about adding contacts from Facebook and Twitter for the details.

Viewing contact social networking info

Any of your contacts who were synchronized with your social networking sites, or who have multiple (joined) accounts on the Galaxy Tab, show their social networking statuses in the Contacts app. There are two places to look.

First, you may find a button beneath the contact's picture, as shown in Figure 9-1. The button may read Social Network Feeds, as it does in the figure, or it may contain the first part of the contact's most recent status update. Either way, touch the button to see a pop-up window where you can scroll through the contact's latest updates.

Figure 9-1: Social networking updates for a contact.

The second way to check a contact's social networking status is to scroll all the way to the bottom of the Info tab, where you might find more status updates. By touching that entry, you see more details.

✔ Of course, the best way to view social networking info is to use a social networking app, as covered in the next section.

✔ When a contact has no recent updates, or the Galaxy Tab is unable to access the social networking site's status, you see the No Activities icon displayed in the contact's Social Networking Feeds pop-up window.

In Your Facebook

Of all the social networking sites, Facebook is the king. It's the online place to go to catch up with friends, send messages, express your thoughts, share pictures and video, play games, and waste more time than you ever thought you had.

✔ Though you can access Facebook on the Web by using the Browser app, I highly recommend that you use the Facebook app described in this section.

✔ Updates to your contacts' Facebook status can be accessed from the Contacts app, as discussed earlier in this chapter.

✔ Facebook is one of the most popular sites on the Internet at the time this book goes to press. On some days, it sees more Internet traffic than Google.

Setting up your Facebook account

The best way to use Facebook is to have a Facebook account, and the best way to do that is to sign up at www.facebook.com using your computer. Register for a new account by setting up your username and password.

Don't forget your Facebook username and password!

Eventually, the Facebook robots send you a confirmation email. You reply to that message, and the online social networking community braces itself for your long-awaited arrival.

After you're all set up, you're ready to access Facebook on your Galaxy Tab. You can add your Facebook friends to your Tab's Contacts list, as described earlier in this chapter. But to get the most from Facebook, you need the official Facebook app, covered in the next section.

Getting the Facebook app

The Galaxy Tab doesn't come with a Facebook app, but you can get the official Facebook app for free from the Android Market. That app is your red carpet to Facebook's social networking kingdom.

 To get the Facebook app, you can scan the barcode shown in the margin. Or, you can go to the Android Market and search for the Facebook for Android app. See Chapter 17.

 The Facebook app is installed on your Galaxy Tab when you see the Successful Install notification, shown in the margin. You can choose this notification to start the Facebook app, or just refer to the next section.

Running Facebook on your Galaxy Tab

You access Facebook by running the Facebook app. If you can't find the Facebook app, you need to install it; refer to the preceding section.

The first time you behold the Facebook app, you'll probably be asked to log in. Do so: Type the email address you used to sign up for Facebook and then type your Facebook password. Touch the Login button.

If you're asked to sync your contacts, do so. I recommend choosing the option Sync All, which brings in all your Facebook friends to the Contacts list. Touch the Next button, and then touch Finish to begin using Facebook.

Eventually, you see the Facebook news or status updates feed. To go to the main Facebook page, shown in Figure 9-2, press the Back soft button.

 When you're done using Facebook, press the Home soft button to return to the Home screen.

The Facebook app continues to run, until you either sign out or turn off the Galaxy Tab. To sign out of Facebook, press the Menu soft button and choose the Logout command.

   ✔ Refer to Chapter 21 for information on placing a Facebook app shortcut on the Home screen.

   ✔ Also see Chapter 21 for information on adding a widget to the Home screen. Facebook comes with a Facebook widget that displays recent status updates and allows you to share your thoughts directly from the Home screen.

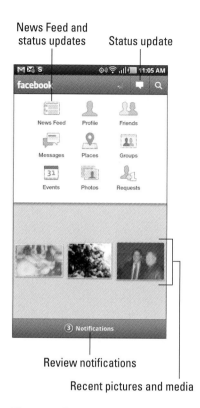

News Feed and
status updates   Status update

Review notifications

Recent pictures and media

Figure 9-2: Facebook on the Galaxy Tab.

⯈ To see more details on an item in the News Feed, choose that item. It appears on another screen, along with any comments and more details.

⯈ Whenever something new happens on Facebook, you see the Facebook notification appear, similar to the one shown in the margin. (Different icons are used for different Facebook activities.) Pull down the notifications and choose the Facebook item to see what's up.

⯈ Notifications also appear at the bottom of the main Facebook page, as shown in Figure 9-2.

Setting your status

The primary thing you live for on Facebook, besides having more friends than anyone else, is to update your status. It's the best way to share your thoughts with the universe, far cheaper than skywriting and far less offensive than a robocall.

To set your status on the Galaxy Tab, follow these steps in the Facebook app:

1. **Touch the Comment button.**

   It's shown in the margin but also appears atop the main Facebook screen, shown in Figure 9-2.

2. **Touch the What's On Your Mind text box.**

3. **Type your comment.**

   You can also dictate the comment if you touch the keyboard's Microphone button.

4. **Touch the Share button.**

You can also set your status by using the Facebook widget on the Home page, if it's been installed: Touch the What's on Your Mind text box, type your important news tidbit, and touch the Share button.

Uploading a picture to Facebook

One of the many things your Galaxy Tab can do is take pictures. Combine that feature with the Facebook app and you have an all-in-one gizmo designed for sharing the various intimate and private moments of your life with the ogling throngs of the Internet.

The key to sharing a picture on Facebook is to locate the wee Camera icon, which is found to the left of the What's On Your Mind text box on the Facebook app's News Feed page. Here's how to work that button and upload an image or a video to Facebook:

1. **Touch the Camera icon on the News Feed screen.**

   There's also a Camera button on the My Albums page, which you get to by touching the Photos icon on the main Facebook app screen (see Figure 9-2).

2. **Choose an option from the Upload Photo menu.**

   You have two options for uploading a picture:

   Choose from Gallery: If you choose this option, browse the Gallery to look for the picture you want to upload. (See Chapter 14 for more information on how the Gallery app works.)

   Capture a Photo: Use the Galaxy Tab's camera to snap a picture of whatever is around you. Touch the Camera button to snap the picture; touch Save to continue or Discard to start over and take a new picture. (See Chapter 13 for more information on how to use the Camera app.)

After selecting or taking a picture, you see the Upload Photo screen, shown in Figure 9-3.

 3. **Optionally, choose an album by touching the Album button, shown in Figure 9-3.**

Unless you choose otherwise, the Facebook app uploads your picture to the Mobile album.

 4. **Optionally, type a caption.**

Touch the Add a Caption Here text box and the onscreen keyboard appears. Type or dictate a caption for your image. The caption is also uploaded to Facebook.

 5. **Touch the Upload button.**

The image is posted as soon as it's transferred over the Internet and digested by Facebook.

Send image and caption to Facebook

Online album

Choose online album

Image

Caption text

Figure 9-3: Uploading an image to Facebook.

The image can be found as part of your status update/news feed, but it's also saved to whichever album you specified (refer to Step 2).

✔ You can use the Facebook app to view the image in Facebook, or you can use Facebook on any computer connected to the Internet.

✔ Even though you can use the Camera app to shoot video, that feature is disabled when you go to take a picture for Facebook.

✔ Facebook also appears on the various Share menus you find on the Galaxy Tab. Choose Facebook from the Share menu to send to Facebook a copy of whatever it is you're looking at. Other chapters in this book give you more information about the various Share menus and where they appear.

Configuring Facebook

The commands that control Facebook are stored on the Settings screen, which you access by touching the Menu soft button while viewing the main Facebook screen (refer to Figure 9-2) and choosing the Settings command.

Most settings are self explanatory: You simply choose which Facebook events you want the Galaxy Tab to monitor. Two items you might want to set are the refresh interval and the way the Tab alerts you to new Facebook activities.

Choose Refresh Interval to specify how often the Tab checks for new Facebook activities. You might find the one-hour value to be too long for your active Facebook social life, so choose something quicker. Or, to disable Facebook notifications, choose Never.

The following two options determine how the Galaxy Tab reacts to Facebook updates:

Vibrate: Vibrates the Tab

Notification Ringtone: Plays a specific ringtone

For the notification ringtone, choose the Silent option when you want the Tab not to make noise upon encountering a Facebook update.

Tweet Suite

Twitter is a social networking site, similar to Facebook but far more brief. On Twitter, you write short spurts of text that express your thoughts or observations or share links. Or, you can just use Twitter to follow the thoughts and twitterings, or *tweets*, of other people.

✔ A message posted on Twitter is a *tweet*.

✔ A tweet can be no more than 140 characters long. That number includes spaces and punctuation.

✔ You can post messages on Twitter or follow others who post messages.

✔ They say that of all the people who have accounts on Twitter, only a small portion of them actively use the service.

✔ I'm not a big fan of Twitter. Even more so than Facebook, Twitter seems to exist to sate some people's craving for attention. It provides the bricks that pave the road to pseudo-fame, so a lot of what I read on Twitter seems to me to be self-centered junk. Then again, I've seen some good news feeds on Twitter, so I don't dislike it completely.

Setting up Twitter

The best way to use Twitter on the Galaxy Tab is to already have a Twitter account. Start by going to http://twitter.com on a computer and follow the directions there for creating a new account.

You can do two things on the Galaxy Tab after you get a Twitter account.

The first thing to do is to add in your Twitter friends and followers with your Galaxy Tab contacts. Follow the steps outlined earlier in this chapter, in the section "Integrating your social networking contacts."

The second thing you need to do is get a Twitter app. It provides a better interface for using Twitter than visiting the Twitter Web page on the Browser.

 The Twitter app can be obtained from the Android Market. Use the barcode in the margin to get a quick link to the app. Refer to Chapter 17 for additional information on installing the Twitter app on your Galaxy Tab.

When you start the Twitter app for the first time, you're asked to type your Twitter ID or email address, plus your Twitter password. After that, you can use Twitter without having to log in again — until you turn off the Tab or exit the Twitter app.

Figure 9-4 shows the Twitter app's Home screen.

To exit the Twitter app, press the Menu soft button at the Twitter Home screen and choose Sign Out.

✔ The Twitter app I recommend, named Twitter, was developed by the Twitter people themselves. Twitter is free and available at the Android Market.

✔ You can use other Twitter apps as well, including the popular Twidroyd.

✔ Configure the Twitter app by pressing the Menu soft button at the Twitter Home screen (refer to Figure 9-4) and choosing the Settings command.

✔ Refer to Chapter 17 for information on the Android Market.

Read tweets   Create tweet

Figure 9-4: The Twitter app.

Tweeting

The Twitter app (refer to Figure 9-4) provides an excellent interface to the many wonderful and interesting things that Twitter does. Of course, the two most basic tasks are reading and writing tweets.

To read tweets, choose the Tweets item. Recent tweets are displayed in a list, with the most recent information at the top. Scroll the list by swiping it with your finger.

To tweet, touch the Create Tweet icon. Use the Create Tweet screen to send text, upload an image from the Gallery, or take a new picture.

✔ You have only 140 characters for creating your tweet. That includes spaces.

✔ The character counter in the Twitter app lets you know how close you're getting to the 140-character limit.

✔ Twitter itself doesn't display pictures, other than your account picture. When you send a picture to Twitter, you use an image hosting service and then share the link, or URL, to the image. All that complexity is handled by the Twitter app.

✔ The Twitter app may appear on various Share menus in other apps on your Galaxy Tab. You use those Share menus to send to Twitter a copy of whatever you're looking at.

Even More Social Networking

The Web goes through crazes. You may have experienced the online shopping site craze, the auction site craze, or blogging, and now we're in the midst of the social networking craze. It seems like a new social networking site pops up every week. Beyond Facebook and Twitter, other social networking sites include, but are not limited to,

✔ Google Buzz

✔ Google Latitude

✔ LinkedIn

✔ Meebo

✔ MySpace

I recommend first setting up the social networking account on your computer, similar to the way I describe it earlier in this chapter for Facebook and Twitter. After that, obtain an app for the social networking site using the Android Market. Set up and configure that app on your Galaxy Tab to connect with your existing account.

✔ These sites may have special Android apps you can install on your Galaxy Tab, such as the MySpace Mobile app for MySpace.

✔ As with Facebook and Twitter, you may find your social networking apps appearing on various Share menus on the Galaxy Tab. That way, you can easily share your pictures and other types of media with your online social networking pals.

10

Yes, the Tab Does Phone Calls and Video Chat

In This Chapter

▶ Understanding phone calls on the Galaxy Tab

▶ Working with the Skype app

▶ Getting Skype contacts

▶ Chatting on Skype

▶ Using Skype to make phone calls

▶ Making a video call with Tango

▶ Reviewing various phone apps

Gloria Swanson

Incoming call

The most original way to communicate with someone is to be there in person. That's how communications started, until the post office was developed by the Persians in 550 BC. It was followed by the Philistines' invention of junk mail in 549 BC. And, of course, SPAM was invented by the fine folks at Hormel in 1937.

Thanks to technology, it seems that the trend has been for mankind to drift away from face-to-face communications. After 2,400 years of sending letters, along came the telephone, and then email, and then cell phones, and then texting. Now, finally, after decades of promises, you can have good-ol' face-to-face communications again, thanks to the Galaxy Tab with its front-facing camera and the proper video chat app.

⊬ This chapter features apps that let you make phone calls, video-chat, and otherwise connect with other humans.

⊬ More apps are available for communications on the Galaxy Tab than can be listed in this chapter. Plus, these apps may be updated from time to time. For the latest information on communications apps for the Galaxy Tab, please visit this book's support page on my Web site:

        www.wambooli.com/help/galaxytab

The Galaxy Tab Is Not a Phone

It's sad, but the Galaxy Tab *could* be a cell phone. It's not. It has the guts. In fact, if you activated your Tab to work with a cellular service, you made an actual phone call. If you were observant, you probably saw a telephone icon appear on the Tab's status bar. Yes, the Galaxy Tab can make phone calls, but it doesn't. Not unless you're sneaky.

Well, maybe not sneaky, but my point is that plenty of apps are available that let you communicate with other individuals using your voice. These apps don't turn the Galaxy Tab into a cell phone, but they allow you to use the Tab and the Internet to connect with another person for vocal and even visual communications.

The person with whom you're communicating can be using a computer, a cell phone, a mobile device, or even a traditional telephone. A single app can't handle all those communications methods, but plenty of apps are available that cover all the bases.

⊬ The version of the Galaxy Tab sold overseas has phone service available.

⊬ Some advertisements you see for the Galaxy Tab feature software that allows for phone or video chat. This software is apparently available only overseas.

⊬ Someday, with the permission of the government, cellular carriers may make phone service available on the Galaxy Tab in the United States. I don't believe it would require a hardware update to your Tab, but it definitely would require a cellular subscription and the painful monthly bill that accompanies the subscription.

Connect to the World with Skype

Perhaps the most versatile app for converting the phoneless Galaxy Tab into a phone is Skype. It's one of the most popular Internet communications programs, allowing you to text, voice, or video chat with others on the Internet as well as use the Internet to make phone calls.

✔ At the time this book went to press, you could use Skype on the Galaxy Tab to call other Skype users and place phone calls, but the current version of Skype doesn't support video calls on the Tab.

✔ See the later section "Video Phone Calls with Tango" for information on making video calls.

Obtaining a Skype account

Get started with Skype by creating an account. I recommend visiting www. skype.com on a computer, where you can enjoy the full screen and keyboard, though you can use the Browser on the Galaxy Tab if you've completely shunned computers.

At the Skype Web site, click the Join Skype button or, if the page has been updated since this book went to press, find and click a similar-sounding button. Sign up according to the directions offered on the Web site.

After you have a Skype account, the next step is to obtain a copy of the Skype app for your Galaxy Tab, as covered in the next section.

✔ As with other Web services, you create a Skype name to identify your user account. It's the name you use to identify yourself to others who use Skype.

✔ If you want to use Skype to place phone calls, you need to stuff some cash into your account. Log in to the Skype Web site and follow the directions for getting Skype Credit.

✔ There's no charge for using Skype to chat with other Skype users. As long as you know the other party's Skype name, connecting and chatting is simple. See the later section "Chatting with another Skype user."

Getting Skype for the Galaxy Tab

Your Galaxy Tab doesn't come with Skype software preinstalled. To get Skype, saunter on over to the Android Market and download the app. If you have a bar code scanning app, you can also scan the icon in the margin, as described in this book's Introduction.

After installing Skype on your Tab, follow these steps to get started:

1. **Start the Skype app.**

2. **Touch the Continue button after reading the initial propaganda screen.**

   Well, you don't have to read the screen; I never do.

3. **Sign in using the account name and password you set when you first signed up.**

4. **Touch the Sign In button.**

   You can't make emergency calls using Skype.

5. **Touch the Accept button.**

   You're given the option to have a brief tour of the Skype app.

6. **Optionally, touch the Leave Tour button.**

7. **Choose Don't Sync.**

   The next section explains how to create new Skype contacts, so you can save that step for later.

8. **Touch the Continue button.**

The main Skype screen is shown in Figure 10-1. The Contacts tab lists people and phone numbers you've connected with on Skype. The later section "Building your Skype Contacts list" describes how to get more contacts than just Skype Test Call.

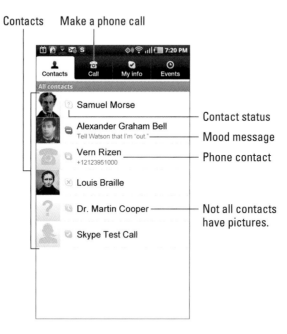

Figure 10-1: Skype's contact screen.

The Skype app stays active the entire time your Tab is on. If you desire to sign out of Skype, follow these steps:

1. **Touch the My Info tab in the Skype app.**

   Refer to Figure 10-1.

2. **Press the Menu soft button.**

3. **Choose Sign Out.**

4. **Touch the Sign Out button.**

You're prompted to sign back in to Skype the next time you run the app.

   ✔ The Sign In screen has a Sign In Automatically option. If you select this option, Skype logs you in every time you start the Skype app.

   ✔ To reset the Sign In Automatically option, touch the My Info tab and press the Menu soft button. Choose Settings. Remove the check mark by Sign In Automatically.

   ✔ To quickly access Skype, pull down the Skype notification, shown in the margin.

   ✔ The Skype app lacks the ability to video-chat, though that situation may change.

   ✔ You can make phone calls on Skype only when you've added Skype Credit to your account.

Managing your Skype status

On the Info tab in the Skype app, you can set your Skype status, which is your presentation to the rest of the Skype universe. The Info tab is illustrated in Figure 10-2.

To set your mood message, touch the Mood Message item beneath your name, as shown in Figure 10-2. Type a new mood message into the Edit Mood message dialog box.

Set your Skype status by touching a Status item. You see a menu of status options, as shown in Figure 10-3. If you don't want to be bothered while using Skype, set your status appropriately.

When you're online, the status of your Skype friends appears on the Contacts tab in the Skype app, as shown in Figure 10-1.

Your account image

Your mood message

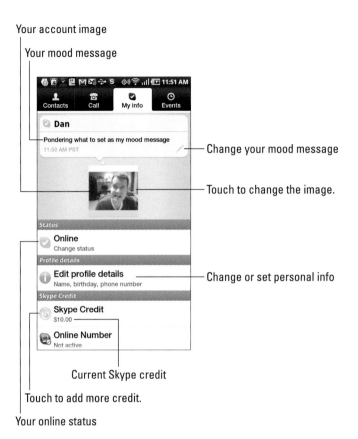

Change your mood message

Touch to change the image.

Change or set personal info

Current Skype credit

Touch to add more credit.

Your online status

Figure 10-2: Your Skype status.

One status item that doesn't appear in Figure 10-3 is the question mark, shown as the status for Samuel Morse in Figure 10-1. The question mark means that the user's status is unknown or that the user hasn't yet accepted your invitation to become a Skype contact.

✔ If you set your status (see Figure 10-3) as Offline, you can't use certain Skype features, such as adding more Skype Credit, nor do you see the status of your Skype contacts.

✔ Setting your status to Sign Out is the same as signing out of Skype.

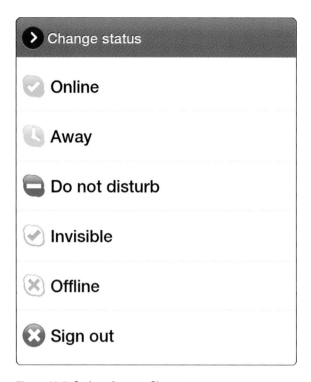

Figure 10-3: Options for your Skype status.

Building your Skype Contacts list

Voice and text chat on Skype over the Internet are free. If you can use a Wi-Fi connection, you can chat without incurring a loss of your cellular plan's data quota. Before you can talk, however, you need to connect with another Skype user.

Yes, the other person must have a Skype account. Further, the person must agree to your request to become a Skype contact.

To find your friends on Skype, follow these steps:

1. **Touch the Contacts tab in the Skype app.**

2. **Press the Menu soft button.**

3. Choose Add.

The Add Contact menu appears.

4. Choose Check Address Book.

You most likely already have a gaggle of contacts in your Tab. The Skype app can search your Contacts list and discover which ones are already on Skype.

5. Touch the Continue button.

This operation can take some time. (I'm serious — more than an hour). Be patient.

You can snooze the Tab while Skype is scouring your Contacts list.

Eventually, you see a list of Skype contacts that the Skype app has found in your Contacts list.

6. Remove the check marks by the contacts you do not want to add.

The Skype app lists all contacts it could find who have Skype accounts. If you continue (see Step 7), a new contact request is sent to each of those contacts. If you don't want to send a request to someone in the list, remove the check mark by that contact's name.

Be sure to check the list! Skype searches for matching text, not for individuals, so random and unusual Skype contacts will doubtlessly show up in the list, especially ones that list multiple Skype names; look for `Customer Care` and `noreply`, and be sure to remove them.

7. Touch the Add Selected button.

You see a final list of contacts. The contacts must approve your request to be added. Until then, they have a blank Skype icon, as illustrated in Figure 10-1.

8. Touch the Continue button.

The contacts are added to the Contacts tab, but they sport a question mark status until they agree to accept your Skype invitation.

If searching the Galaxy Tab's Contacts list doesn't do the job, you search for a specific contact: Follow Steps 1 through 3 in this section, and then continue here:

1. Choose the Search for a Contact option.

2. Type the contact's name into the Search Skype Directory text box.

3. Touch the Search soft button to start the search.

4. Scroll the list of results to find the exact person you're looking for.

If your friend has a common name, the list will be quite extensive. You can use city information to help narrow the list, but not every Skype user specifies a current city. The Skype username may also help you identify specific people.

5. Touch an entry to add it to your Contacts list.

You see a full-page description for the contact, where you can choose to call them, chat on Skype, or add them to your Contacts list.

6. Touch the Add button.

7. Optionally, type a Hello message to the contact.

8. Touch the Send button.

9. Touch Continue.

No matter how you add people to your list, you see the question mark icon as a person's status until they agree to accept your request.

- You can always email people you know and ask them whether they're on Skype.

- If you get a friend's Skype username, you can manually add them to your Skype Contacts list: From the Add Contact menu, choose Add a New Contact and type the Skype username.

- Some people may not use Skype often, so it takes a while for them to respond to your friend request.

- If you're hot to use Skype, send a pending contact a text message or an email. See Chapters 6 and 7, respectively.

- If you accidentally add unusual or odd Skype contacts, my advice is to delete them. To remove a contact, long-press that contact's name in the list and choose the command Remove Contact from the pop-up menu.

- You can block a contact by long-pressing their entry and choosing the command Block Contact from the pop-up menu.

- If the Skype app crashes during a contact searching operation, it's probably because you've collected some bogus Skype contacts. It happens. A good way to get out of this situation is to use the Skype program on a computer to clean up and remove unwanted contacts. You may also need to uninstall and then reinstall the Skype app. See Chapter 17 for information on uninstalling apps.

Chatting with another Skype user

You can text-chat with any Skype user, which works similarly to texting, though with no maximum-character limitations. The only restriction is that you can chat only with other Skype users.

To chat, choose a contact from the Contacts list (refer To Figure 10-1). You see a screen with more detailed information about the contact. Touch the Chat button at the bottom of the screen. Figure 10-4 illustrates the Chat screen.

Stuff they write

Show Contacts tab   Show Events tab

Type here   Send

Smiley face palette   Stuff you write

Figure 10-4: Chatting on Skype.

Type your text in the box, as illustrated in Figure 10-4. Touch the Send button to publish your comment. You can also use the Smiley button to insert a cute graphic into your text. The conversation unfolds as shown in Figure 10-4.

✔ The Skype Chat notification, shown in the margin, appears whenever someone starts a chat with you. It's handy to see, especially when you may have switched away from the Skype app to do something else on the Galaxy Tab. Simply pull down the notifications and choose the Skype Chat item to get into the conversation.

✔ You can add more people to the conversation, if you like: Touch the Menu soft button and choose the command Add Participants. Select the contacts you want to join with your chat session, and then touch the Add Selected button. It's a gang chat!

✔ To stop chatting, press the Back soft button. The conversation is kept in the Skype app, even when the other person has disconnected.

✔ Old chats stored in the Skype app are accessed from the Events tab (refer to Figure 10-4).

✔ To remove an old chat event, touch the Events tab and long-press the chat event. Choose the command Remove Event from the pop-up menu.

✔ For the chat to work, the other user must be online and available.

Speaking on Skype (voice chat)

Perhaps the number-one reason for getting Skype is to transmogrify your Galaxy Tab into a phone. The trick works: As long as your pal has a Skype account, you can chat it up all you want, pretending all the while that the Tab is a phone. Follow these steps:

1. **Touch the Contacts tab in the Skype app.**

2. **Choose a contact.**

   The contact needs to be available: Look for a green check mark icon by their name.

3. **Touch the green Call button on the contact's information page.**

   In a few Internet seconds, the other person picks up and you're speaking with each other. You see the In-Call screen, lovingly illustrated in Figure 10-5.

4. **Talk.**

   Blah-blah-blah. There's no time limit, though Internet connection problems may inadvertently hang you up.

To disconnect the call, touch the End Call button, shown in Figure 10-5.

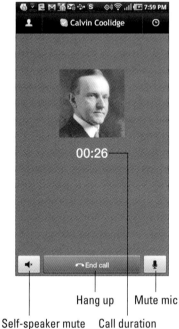

Hang up | Mute mic

Self-speaker mute   Call duration

Figure 10-5: A Skype voice chat.

If someone calls you on Skype, you see a pop-up window, similar to the one shown in Figure 10-6. Touch the Answer button to accept the call and start talking. Touch Decline to dismiss the call, especially when it's someone who annoys you.

The Incoming Call screen (see Figure 10-6) appears even when the Galaxy Tab is sleeping. The incoming call wakes up the Tab.

- ✔ Voice chat on Skype over the Internet is free. If you use a Wi-Fi connection, you can chat without incurring a loss of your cellular plan's data minutes.

- ✔ You can chat with any user in your Skype contacts list, by using a mobile device, a computer, or any other gizmo on which Skype is installed.

- ✔ To mute the microphone, press the Mute Mic button, illustrated earlier, in Figure 10-5.

- ✔ The self-speaker Mute button (see Figure 10-5) helps reduce audio feedback. It's on (muted) by default. Even so:

- ✔ If you plan to use Skype a lot, get a good headset.

✔ When a headset is plugged in, the self-speaker Mute button switches between headphones and the Tab's built-in speakers.

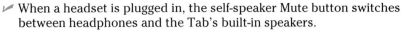

✔ Missed Skype calls are flagged by a special notification icon, as shown in the margin. Pull down the notifications to see who called. You can also review the Events tab in the Skype app to see who called and when. (Touch that item in the Skype Events list to return a missed call.)

✔ You can text-chat while you're talking: Press the Menu soft button and choose the Chat command. Then, while you talk, you can type messages to the contact you're talking with. This seems like doubling up on the communications thing, but I've done it a few times.

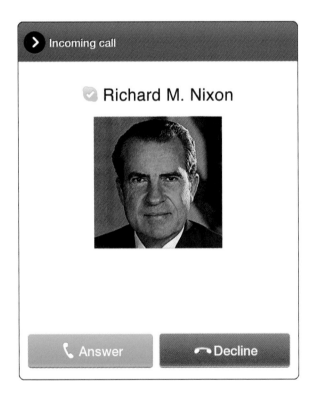

Figure 10-6: An incoming Skype voice call.

Making a Skype phone call

Voice chat is okay on Skype, and it comes a close second to the real thing: making a phone call. Yep, you can use Skype to call any phone number on the planet, but most easily you can call people's phone numbers as listed in the Galaxy Tab's Contacts list. Here's what to do:

1. **Ensure that you have Skype Credit.**

   You cannot make a "real" phone call unless you have Skype Credit on your account. You add Skype Credit by using the Info tab, shown earlier, in Figure 10-2.

2. **In the Skype app, touch the Call tab.**

   The Call tab is illustrated in Figure 10-7.

Phone number goes here.

Choose international prefix   Choose Galaxy Tab contact

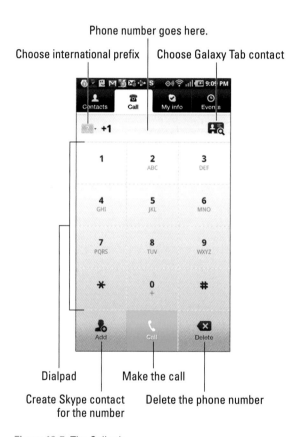

Dialpad   Make the call

Create Skype contact   Delete the phone number
for the number

Figure 10-7: The Call tab.

3. **Input the phone number to dial.**

   Or, use the Contacts button, shown in Figure 10-7, to summon a contact. If you do so, use the text box that (eventually) appears at the top of the screen to search for specific names or numbers. Choosing a contact places their number on the Call tab.

REMEMBER

Always input the full phone number when making a Skype phone call, including the country code, shown as +1 for the United States in Figure 10-7, as well as the area code.

4. Touch the Call button to place the call.

This step works just like using a cell phone. Indeed, at this point, the Galaxy Tab has been transformed by the Skype app into a cell phone (albeit a cell phone that uses Internet telephony to make the call).

5. Talk.

The In-Call screen is shown in Figure 10-8.

Contact info (if available)

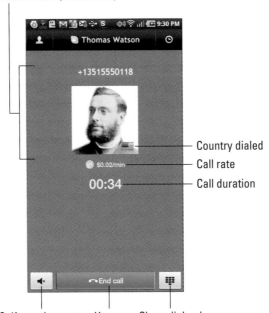

Country dialed

Call rate

Call duration

Self-speaker mute   Hang up   Show dialpad

Figure 10-8: A Skype phone call.

To mute the Tab's microphone, press the Menu soft button and choose the Mute command.

6. To end the call, touch the End Call button.

7. If the number you dialed isn't a current Skype contact, touch the Add Contact button to create a Skype contact for that person.

Skype contacts are separate from Galaxy Tab contacts. By touching the Add Contact button, you create a phone number contact for the number you just dialed.

Lamentably, you cannot receive a phone call using Skype on your Galaxy Tab from a cell phone or landline unless you pay for a Skype online number. In that case, you can use Skype to both send and receive regular phone calls. This book doesn't cover the Online Number option.

✔ Choosing a contact from the Call tab screen (see Figure 10-7) isn't the same as choosing a Skype contact from the Contacts tab. If you choose to add the contact, as described in Step 7, your Galaxy Tab contact's number appears on the Skype Contact tab.

✔ When a Galaxy Tab contact has multiple numbers, you can choose a number from the menu that appears.

✔ When dialing a non-Skype contact, only the phone number appears onscreen. The contact's name and picture show up only for Skype contacts; the picture appears only if the Skype user has assigned an image to their account.

✔ Skype phone calls aren't free. The call rate you're paying appears below the contact's information, as illustrated in Figure 10-8.

✔ You can check the Skype Web site for a current list of call rates, for both domestic and international calls: www.skype.com.

✔ Unless you've paid Skype to have a specific phone number, the phone number shown on the recipient's Caller ID screen is something unexpected, often merely the text Unknown. Because of that, you might want to email or text whoever you're calling and let them know that you're placing a Skype call. That way, they won't skip the call because they don't recognize the Caller ID number.

Video Phone Calls with Tango

I blame that front-facing camera. I mean, what's the point of having a front-facing camera unless you can do video chat? Sure, you can take pictures of yourself (self-portraits), which is covered in Chapter 13. But video chat is the new rage on mobile devices.

The problem is that the Galaxy Tab lacks a preinstalled video chat app. It's up to you to hunt down such an app. Or, you can just read this section, which covers the Tango app. It happens to be the video chat app that I hunted down and wrote about for this book.

✔ Other video chat apps are available from the Android Market. See Chapter 17.

✔ Also see the later section "Phone App Roundup" for some video (and phone) app suggestions.

Setting up Tango on your Tab

 As with other apps you don't have on your Galaxy Tab, you obtain a copy of Tango from the Android Market. You can visit the Market and search for Tango, or use the bar code shown in the margin to quickly download a copy.

After downloading and installing Tango, follow these steps:

1. **Start the Tango app.**

2. **Create your account.**

   The app automatically captures the Tab's phone number. Input your first name and last name and an email address.

   You must add the email address because it's one of the ways Tango lets you connect with other Tango users for video chat.

3. **Touch the Save button to create your Tango account.**

Magically, Tango instantly finds friends of yours who have downloaded and installed the Tango app. Those friends are listed on the Contacts tab, though you're not limited to communicating with only those friends.

✔ Tango is available only on mobile devices. Unlike with Skype, you cannot use Tango to call someone on a computer.

✔ To add more friends, touch the Invite tab. You can send Tango invites via email or SMS.

 ✔ Other users must have Tango installed on their phones or mobile devices, and their gizmos need a front-facing camera for video chat to work.

✔ You can invite someone only if they're an existing contact on your Galaxy Tab. See Chapter 5 for information on creating new contacts.

✔ It's also possible to install Tango on mobile devices that don't have front-facing cameras. In that case, you can talk to, but not see, the other person. The person can, however, see you because your Galaxy Tab features a front-facing camera.

✔ The Tango app has neither an Exit nor Sign Out command. To quit Tango, press the Back soft button until you see the Home screen.

Calling someone with Tango

Ah, it's the moment you've been waiting for: Making the actual video call on Tango is easy — after you've set up friends in your Tango Contacts list. Follow these steps:

1. **Start the Tango app.**

2. **If necessary, touch the Contact tab.**

3. **Choose a contact to call.**

   You can only call Tango contacts.

4. **When the other person answers, touch the Tango button.**

   The In-Call screen is shown in Figure 10-9. At this point, the Galaxy Tab is used like a telephone — though you probably won't put the thing to your ear.

Contact info   Call duration

Turn on video   Mute speaker

Mute microphone   Hang up

Figure 10-9: The Tango In-Call screen.

The big enchilada with Tango, of course, is video chat:

5. Touch the Tango (camera) button to initiate video chat.

Ta-da. Finally, video chat. They promised such a thing in the 1960s. Glad to see it's finally here. Figure 10-10 illustrates the in-call video screen.

Switch between front and rear cameras

The person calling

You   Mute   Hang up   Turn your
                          camera on or off

Figure 10-10: Video chat on the Galaxy Tab.

The other user must turn on her camera so that you can see both of you. If you desire privacy, you can turn off your camera, as illustrated in Figure 10-10.

6. To end the call, touch the End button.

Tango isn't the only app that provides video chat. See the later section "Phone App Roundup" for more app suggestions.

- ✔ The contact's picture is pulled from the Galaxy Tab's Contacts list.

- ✔ If a contact lacks a picture, you see a generic Android icon.

- ✔ To keep the person you're talking to from throwing up, consider keeping the Tab in a docking stand or another stable location. Moving the Tab around while you speak can make some people dizzy. Oh, and even when you keep the Tab steady, do look appropriate.

Receiving a Tango call

With Tango installed on your Galaxy Tab, the gizmo becomes as close to a phone as it can be. An incoming Tango call appears on the screen, as shown in Figure 10-11. The setup should be familiar to you, if you've used a cell phone with the Android operating system. It works the same way.

To answer the call, slide the green Phone button to the right, as illustrated in the figure.

To ignore the call, slide the red Ignore button to the left.

Caller's contact info

Slide right to answer the call.

Slide left to ignore the call.

Figure 10-11: Tango is calling.

If you choose to answer, the call proceeds as described in the preceding section.

- ✒ When you dismiss the call, the other party sees a message explaining that you didn't answer. It doesn't mean that you ignored them; they see the same message whether you ignore the call or simply aren't available to answer.

- ✒ If you call someone and he doesn't answer, you see the message "So-and-so did not answer. Try again later." Touch the OK button.

- ✒ Incoming calls can be received even when Tango isn't running or when the Galaxy Tab is in Snooze mode.

Phone App Roundup

With the proliferation of cell phones and mobile devices with front-facing cameras, you're going to see a lot of phone and video chat apps coming to the Android Market. Skype is the king, though that doesn't mean some other app (such as Tango) won't come up and steal Skype's crown.

Table 10-1 lists a sampling of other video or phone apps available for the Galaxy Tab. I don't have room in this book to write about all of them in detail. Check them out at the Android Market.

Table 10-1	Various and Sundry Phone and Video Chat Apps
App Bar Code	**App Name**
	Fring
	ClearSea
	SIPDroid
	Yahoo Messenger

- ✒ Refer to Chapter 17 for more information on the Android Market.

- ✒ The video chat feature of the Yahoo! Messenger app was in *beta,* a testing phase, at the time this book went to press.

- ✒ Be careful when shopping for video chat apps in the Android Market. Some apps are porn. As you probably don't know, but I do because I research these things for scientific purposes, "video chat" has an entirely different meaning in the pornography business.

Tab voice mail with Google Voice

Google Voice is a service offered by Google. It does a lot, so it's difficult to explain in just a few paragraphs. Basically, *Google Voice* is a phone service. You can use it to make calls to any phone number, but also to organize your calls by using a Google Voice phone number.

 A Google Voice app is available for the Galaxy Tab from the Android Market. Unlike on other Android devices, the Google Voice app on the Galaxy Tab is restricted: You cannot use Google Voice to send or receive phone calls. You can, however, use Google Voice on the Galaxy Tab to receive voice mail — that is, if you survive the

Google Voice installation process, which doesn't run smoothly on the Tab.

My advice is to install Google Voice only if you already have and use the Google Voice service. The installation program will appear to fail; that's because you can't verify the Tab's "phone number" with Google Voice. Even so, Google Voice is installed and will pick up and play your voice mail.

Hopefully, a future release of Google Voice will work around the limitations of the Galaxy Tab and allow you access to more features.

Part III
The Everything Else Tab

In this part . . .

For years, I yearned for a single gizmo that I could carry with me. It would do all the tasks done by the other things that I carried: phone, address book, camera, MP3 player, video player, picture album, death ray — even the books I would lug on the airplane with me. Oh, to have such a device would be a dream come true.

Time to wake up!

The Galaxy Tab is perhaps the ultimate gadget. It can do just about anything, go just about anywhere, and replace just about everything else you tote along with you during your busy day. This part of the book explores some of those wonderful, unusual, and potentially great things the Galaxy Tab can do.

Your Digital Library

*P*aper was invented thousands of years ago. It was the latest gizmo for carrying the written word, much easier than toting about stone tablets and pyramids. Then some genius combined pieces of paper into a scroll. Then about 2,000 years ago, the bound book made the scroll obsolete. Unlike scrolls, text could be written on both sides of the page in a book. Books were also smaller, easier to store, and much easier to pinch from the library.

The latest improvement on carrying the written word is the eBook. Rather than load yourself down with several bulky tomes, especially those trashy novels that would look embarrassing on any bookshelf, you can tote around your reading material on the Galaxy Tab.

Why Don't You Read It on the Road?

Welcome to the latest craze in publishing: eBooks, or electronic books. It's important to know that eBooks is pronounced "ee-books," not "eb-ooks," which makes no sense but, honestly, given weird technology jargon, who really knows?

An *eBook* is essentially a digital version of the material you would normally see on paper. The words, formatting, figures, pictures — all that stuff is simply stored digitally so that you can read it on some sort of eBook reader. In the case of the Galaxy Tab, you need eBook software, which is included in the form of the Kindle app.

The primary advantage of an eBook reader is that you can keep an entire library of books with you. So rather than pay way too much for the latest potboiler in an airport bookstore, you can shop online before you leave and take an eBook with you. That way, when you're bored reading your email, the Web, playing games, checking your stocks, or chatting it up with a friend, you can read books on your Galaxy Tab.

- ✔ Other eBook apps are available, including the popular Kobo. See the section "Other Reader Apps," later in this chapter.

- ✔ Just about any current popular title you can buy in a bookstore or online is available in the eBook format.

- ✔ You can also use eBook reader software to view periodicals — magazines and newspapers — as long as you pay for the subscription and the eBook-reading software you're using allows for daily updates.

- ✔ eBook titles cost money, though they're generally cheaper than their real-world equivalents.

- ✔ It's easy and free to build up your eBook library with classics and older books. Most of those titles are free, though some compilations have a modest price tag, such as 99 cents.

The Kindle eBook Reader

The good folks at Amazon recognize that after buying yourself a Galaxy Tab, you'll probably never have use for their fancy eBook reader, the Kindle. Those fools who dare take a Kindle on a transcontinental flight can seethe with jealousy as they sit across the aisle from you, knowing how much better the Galaxy Tab is than the Kindle gizmo.

You'll say, "Hey! I see you have a Kindle." Then you snicker.

The Kindle owner will be miffed, and most likely respond, "Well, I see that you don't have an iPad!"

Just chuckle softly to yourself. That's because both you and the silly Kindle owner are probably using the same software to read your eBooks.

Your Galaxy Tab comes with the Kindle app, illustrated in Figure 11-1. You can start the app by touching the Applications button and then choosing the Kindle app, found on the Applications screen. See the next section for special, first-time instructions on running the Kindle app.

Figure 11-1: Kindle on the Galaxy Tab.

The Kindle app is nearly the same as the software that's included on the Kindle. (Well, I'm guessing at that, though the publisher may twist my arm and make me buy the silly Kindle just to back up my words.) Regardless, as preinstalled software on your Tab, Kindle is the ideal way to get used to getting and reading eBooks.

✔ Consider placing a shortcut to the Kindle app on the Home screen. See Chapter 21 for the complete, scintillating instructions.

✔ As this book goes to press, magazine and newspaper subscriptions aren't available using the Kindle app on your Galaxy Tab.

Setting up the Kindle app

As an Amazon thing, the Kindle app works in conjunction with your Amazon account. If you don't yet have an account on Amazon, get one! Visit www.amazon.com and follow the directions to sign up and create an account.

Maybe even buy a nice sweater or some concrete while you're there. Amazon carries everything.

After you get your Amazon account, start the Kindle app and heed these first-time setup directions:

1. **Type your email address.**

   Use the same address you used to create your Amazon account.

2. **Type your Amazon.com password.**

3. **Touch the Register button.**

After registering, you see the main Kindle screen, shown in Figure 11-1, though your digital bookshelf is empty. See the next section for information on getting eBooks to read.

Getting some reading material

I divide into two categories the kind of eBooks you can get for the Kindle: free and not free. Follow these steps to grab an eBook:

1. **Start the Kindle app on your Galaxy Tab.**

2. **Press the Menu soft button.**

3. **Choose Kindle Store.**

   You're transferred from the Kindle app into the browser app. A special page opens for the Kindle store at Amazon.

4. **Search for the book you want, or browse the categories.**

   As a suggestion, choose the category Free Popular Classics to find something free to download.

5. **Touch to select a title.**

   Ensure that the title description says *Auto-delivered wirelessly.* That way, the title is automatically transferred (downloaded) to your Galaxy Tab.

6. **Touch the Buy Now with 1-Click button.**

   Refer to Figure 11-2 for details about using the purchase screen for a free title.

7. **If you're getting a free title, or if you've already signed in to your Amazon account, skip to Step 12.**

Go to Amazon home page

Touch to buy.

Gizmo to send to

Figure 11-2: Buying an eBook.

8. **If prompted, sign in to your Amazon account.**

   Your email address is already filled in, but you need to touch the password field and type your Amazon password.

9. **Touch the Sign In button.**

10. **If prompted to have the browser automatically remember your password, touch the Never button.**

    If you want, you can touch the Remember button to have the Browser app automatically recall your password. I recommend against it, for security reasons.

11. **If prompted, specifically when purchasing a nonfree eBook, choose the credit card you want to use for making the purchase.**

    For example, if you have multiple credit cards on file at Amazon, select the one to which you want to charge your eBook purchase.

12. **Touch the Go to Kindle for Android button.**

    You return to the Kindle app on your Galaxy Tab.

The title you downloaded appears in the list shortly. If not, press the Menu soft button and choose the Sync command.

If you've already purchased eBooks from the Kindle store for another gizmo, you can archive them to your Galaxy Tab: In the Kindle app, press the Menu soft button and choose the Archived Items command. You instantly see your existing Kindle library on the Tab.

See the next section for information on reading eBooks.

✔ You receive an email confirmation message describing your purchase. The email appears even when you "buy" a free eBook.

✔ For a nonfree eBook, you see a button, not shown in Figure 11-2: Touch the Try a Sample button to download a snippet from the title you're interested in. It's the equivalent of browsing at a bookstore (the real kind of bookstore).

✔ Even though the Kindle store doesn't look it, it's a Web page. If you scroll up the page, you see the Browser app's controls. Refer to Chapter 8 for information on using the Browser app.

✔ Not every title is available as an eBook.

Reading on your Galaxy Tab

The whole point of getting an eBook is so that you can read the thing, flipping the digital pages just the same as you would in a real book, although I don't recommend that you lick your finger to turn the page. (See Chapter 22 for information on cleaning the Galaxy Tab screen.)

After choosing a book in the Kindle app, you see it open on the touchscreen. For the first time you've opened a book, you see the first page. Otherwise, you see the last page you were reading.

Figure 11-3 illustrates the basic reading maneuvers: You can touch the left or right sides of the screen to flip a page left or right, respectively. You can also swipe the pages left or right.

Touching a page in the upper right corner adds a bookmark, as shown in Figure 11-3. Touching that same spot again removes the bookmark.

When you touch the center of the page, you see an overlay that shows your location in the overall document. You can use the slider that appears at the bottom of the screen to quickly move to a new part of the document.

For more precise movement in an eBook, press the Menu soft button and choose the Go To command. Use the Go To menu to choose where to go in the document; if you choose the My Notes & Marks item, you can hop to one of your bookmarks.

Touch to turn back a page.　　　Bookmark

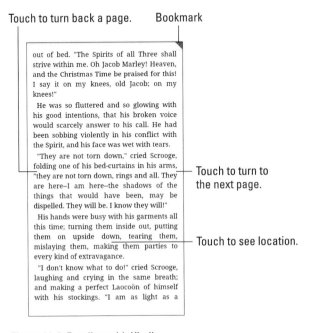

out of bed. "The Spirits of all Three shall strive within me. Oh Jacob Marley! Heaven, and the Christmas Time be praised for this! I say it on my knees, old Jacob; on my knees!"

He was so fluttered and so glowing with his good intentions, that his broken voice would scarcely answer to his call. He had been sobbing violently in his conflict with the Spirit, and his face was wet with tears.

"They are not torn down," cried Scrooge, folding one of his bed-curtains in his arms, "they are not torn down, rings and all. They are here--I am here--the shadows of the things that would have been, may be dispelled. They will be. I know they will!"

His hands were busy with his garments all this time; turning them inside out, putting them on upside down, tearing them, mislaying them, making them parties to every kind of extravagance.

"I don't know what to do!" cried Scrooge, laughing and crying in the same breath; and making a perfect Laocoön of himself with his stockings. "I am as light as a

— Touch to turn to the next page.

— Touch to see location.

Figure 11-3: Reading with Kindle.

To return to the Kindle library (the main page), press the Menu soft button and choose the Home command.

TIP

↙ You can change the size of the text on the page by pressing the Menu soft button and choosing the View Options menu. You choose from five preset text sizes.

↙ As far as I can tell, the Kindle app on the Galaxy Tab lacks a feature to highlight text in an eBook. Normally, you can highlight text by long-pressing the screen. That feature doesn't seem to work, at least not in the version of the Kindle app available as this book goes to press.

↙ The Kindle app also lacks a quick command to keep the screen from reorienting itself. To turn off screen orientation (rotation) on the Galaxy Tab, refer to Chapter 3.

Other Reader Apps

The sure sign of a good idea is imitators. Kindle wasn't the first eBook reader, but it's one of the most popular. In addition to Kindle, you can get other eBook reader apps for your Galaxy Tab. Here's the shortlist:

 Aldiko: The Aldiko reader has a vast public library but also a lot of privately published eBooks. That's because it uses the popular ePub file format. Two versions of Aldiko are available: The free version's barcode is shown in the margin, but you can also find the premium version.

 FBReader: The FBReader app is an open-source eBook reader. It supports many common eBook file formats, and it's available for Windows as well as for Android phones. FB stands for FreeBooks.

 Kobo: The Kobo app is sponsored by the Canadian bookstore chain Indigo (and Chapters). Like Amazon, Chapters also sells the Kobo eBook reading gizmo, which is similar to the Kindle gizmo. Regardless, the Kobo app is the software version of the Kobo gizmo's eBook-reading software.

 Laputa Reader: The popular Laputa Reader consistently receives high rankings by users in the Android Market. It also features that nifty page-flipping effect that's popular on the tablet made by a fruit company.

Generally speaking, these apps work similarly to the Kindle app: You set up an account, and then you download free or paid-for eBooks.

Not every eBook reader has every book available in its library. Some books — specifically, some of the latest bestsellers — may take a while to come out in eBook format. Some eBooks may be available in one format and not another, which is why you might end up having more than one eBook reader on your Galaxy Tab.

 Be careful when searching for eBook-reading software in the Android Market. Some of the results may not be family wholesome — if you catch my drift.

See Chapter 17 for information on the Android Market.

Get from Here to There

In This Chapter

▶ Exploring the galaxy with Maps

▶ Displaying special map options

▶ Searching for people, places, and things

▶ Getting to your destination

▶ Finding a restaurant

▶ Navigating with the Galaxy Tab

▶ Adding a Home screen navigation shortcut

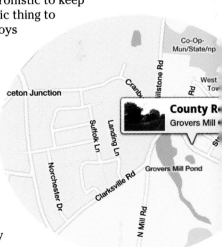

I keep gloves in my car's glove box. It's not often that I wear gloves when I drive; I just think that it's funny and kind of anachronistic to keep gloves in a "glove compartment." Another anachronistic thing to keep in your car's glove compartment is a map. Yes, boys and girls, once upon a time, there were these things called *maps*. People used them to get from here to there. Especially if you'd never been somewhere, you needed a map.

Paper maps are still around, but why bother with them — and all that annoying refolding — when you have a smart gizmo like the Galaxy Tab? Thanks to the Maps app, you can find the spot you're looking for, see what's nearby, get directions, and even hear step-by-step vocal navigation. Though the Galaxy Tab may not fold like an old map, and you probably don't want to put the Tab in your car's glove compartment, it's definitely a worthy improvement.

   ✏ The Galaxy Tab features an app, named Navigation, that handles the chore of getting from here to there, similar to the way a GPS car navigation system works.

   ✏ Another Maps-like app is Places, which helps you search for specific things when you're out and about.

   ✏ Both the Navigation and Places apps can be accessed from with the Maps app.

   ✏ Google frequently updates the Maps app. For information on how the updates apply to the information in this book, please refer to my Web site: www.wambooli.com/help/galaxytab.

The Maps App

Nothing beats having a good map. Combine the Galaxy Tab's ability to read global positioning system (GPS) satellites with a vast database of streets and satellite images and you have one of the best maps available: the Maps app.

Using the Maps app

Start the Maps app by choosing its icon from the Applications screen. If you're starting the app for the first time, or if it's just been updated, you can read the What's New screen; touch the OK button to continue.

The Galaxy Tab uses its GPS abilities to zero in on your current location on planet Earth. You see that location as a blinking blue triangle, as shown in Figure 12-1. If your location isn't exact, the Maps app displays a blue circle around the triangle, which gives you approximate location.

If you don't see your location on the map, touch the Location button (refer to Figure 12-1). Or, you can touch the Location button at any time to return to your current location from whatever other location you're browsing.

Here are some fun things you can do when viewing the map:

Zoom in: To make the map larger (to move it closer), touch the Zoom In button, double-tap the screen, or spread your fingers on the touchscreen.

Zoom out: To make the map smaller (to see more), touch the Zoom Out button or pinch your fingers on the touchscreen.

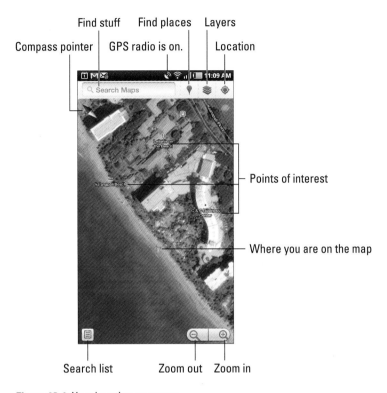

Find stuff   Find places   Layers
Compass pointer   GPS radio is on.   Location

Points of interest

Where you are on the map

Search list   Zoom out   Zoom in

Figure 12-1: Your location on a map.

Pan and scroll: To see what's to the left or right or at the top or bottom of the map, drag your finger on the touchscreen; the map scrolls in the direction you drag your finger.

Rotate: Using two fingers, rotate the map clockwise or counterclockwise. Touch the Compass Pointer (shown in Figure 12-1) to reorient the map with north at the top of the screen.

 Perspective: Tap the Location button to switch to perspective view, where the map is shown at an angle. Touch the Perspective button again to return to a flat-map view.

The closer you zoom in to the map, the more detail you see, such as street names, address block numbers, and businesses and other sites — but no tiny people.

To direct the Maps app to show only streets and points of interest, you peel back the Satellite layer: Touch the Layers button to see the Layers menu, shown in Figure 12-2. Touch the Satellite item to remove the green check mark or just touch the Clear Map button.

Touch to remove layer.

Remove all layers and search items   Layer is visible.

Figure 12-2: The Layers menu.

To return to Satellite view, touch the Layers button and choose Satellite from the list.

To see 3D terrain, touch the Layers button and choose Terrain. You can combine the Terrain view with the Perspective trick to see the layout of the land.

✔ The Galaxy Tab's GPS is the same technology used by car navigation toys as well as by handheld GPS gizmos.

✔ When the Galaxy Tab is using the GPS radio, you see the GPS Is On status icon appear.

✔ The blue triangle (refer to Figure 12-1) shows in which general direction the Tab is pointing.

✔ Perspective view can be entered for only your current location.

✔ The Traffic layer, available from the Layers menu (refer to Figure 12-2) shows current traffic conditions color-coded on the street map. Traffic information may not show up for every location, however.

✔ Also see the later section "Locating an address," for details about the Street View feature.

✔ The Galaxy Tab warns you when various applications access Location features. The warning is nothing serious: The Android operating system is just letting you know that software will access the device's physical location. Some folks may view that action as an invasion of privacy; hence the warnings. I see no issue with letting the Tab know where you are, but I understand that not everyone feels that way. If you'd rather not share location information, simply decline access when prompted.

Adding goodies to the map

There are two ways you can add depth and feeling to a boring map. The first way is to use the Layers menu, as described in the preceding section. Beyond that, Google occasionally tosses some weird, experimental, and potentially useful items into something called Google Labs.

For the Maps app, you can visit the Labs and see what kind of extra, optional features are available. Follow these steps:

1. **Open the Maps app.**

2. **Press the Menu soft button.**

3. **Choose More and then choose Labs.**

    You see a list of options you can add to the Map display.

4. **Choose a Labs item to add to the map.**

    The item is added right away, and you can play with it or see it in action.

The number and type of options available on the Labs menu change with the whims and moods of the mad scientists in the Google labs. Eventually, some Labs options make it to the big-time; the Traffic layer began its life in a test tube in the labs.

My advice is to check the Labs list often to see what's up.

The Android Market app Compass also serves as a virtual compass for your Galaxy Tab. See Chapter 17 for more information on the Android Market.

Pilot Your Way through the Galaxy

Next to your laser blaster, the Maps app is your best friend when it comes to invading another planet. That's because the Maps app can tell you where are and what's around you. Though it doesn't locate enemies or aliens, it can help you find a specific location, such as a safe house in Grover's Mill. Or, it can help you locate something that has no specific address, such as where to find some fresh boron for your landing craft or a decent taco place that's open at 2 a.m.

Locating an address

Your location on the Maps app screen is shown as a blue triangle (refer to Figure 12-1). If you don't see the triangle on the screen, touch the Location button. It helps you find where you are. But, seriously: Where are you? If you wanted to contact a friend to pick you up, you can't just explain that you're a blue triangle on the screen. The friend wouldn't believe you, no matter how much you promised them that you haven't been drinking.

To find out where you are, at your current street address, long-press your location on the Maps app. Or, you can long-press any location to find out that location's specific address. Up pops a bubble, similar to the one shown in Figure 12-3, that gives your approximate address.

Touch bubble to see more information.

Long-press a location to see its address.

Figure 12-3: Finding an address.

If you touch the address bubble (refer to Figure 12-3), you see a screen full of interesting things you can do, as shown in Figure 12-4.

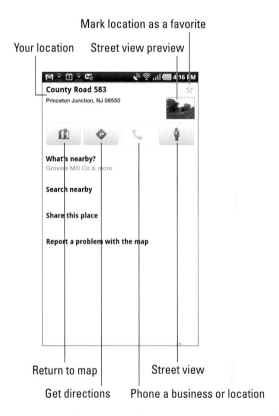

Figure 12-4: Things to do with a location.

The What's Nearby command displays a list of nearby businesses or points of interest. Some of them show up on the screen, and others are available by touching the What's Nearby command.

Choose the Search Nearby item to use the Search command to locate businesses, people, or points of interest near the given location.

The Report a Problem command doesn't connect you with the police; instead, it's used to send information back to Google regarding an improper address or another map malfunction.

What's *really* fun to play with is the Street View command. Choosing this option displays the location from a 360-degree perspective. In Street view, you can browse a locale, pan and tilt, or zoom in on details to familiarize yourself with an area, for example — whether you're familiarizing yourself with a location or planning a burglary.

 Press the Back button to return to regular Map view from Street view.

Finding locations on the map

The Maps app can work like a powerful Web search engine. Unlike when you're finding things on the Internet, however, you use the Maps app to locate things in the real world.

 The secret to search for a location is the press the Search soft button. Or, you can simply touch the Search Maps text field atop the Maps app window. The following sections describe how to search for various things.

Look for a specific addresses

To locate an address, type it into the Search Maps text box; for example:

```
10236 Charing Cross Rd., Los Angeles, CA 90024
```

Touch the Search button to the right of the Search Maps text box and that location is then shown on the map. The next step is getting directions, which you can read about in the later section "Getting directions."

- ✔ You don't need to type the entire address. Often times, all you need is the street number and street name and then either the city name or zip code.
- ✔ You can use dictation by touching the Microphone button and then speaking the address.
- ✔ If you omit the city name or zip code, the Galaxy Tab looks for the closest matching address near your current location.

Look for a type of business, restaurant, or point of interest

You may not know an address, but you know when you crave bulgogi or kimchi. Maybe you need a hotel or gas station. To find a business entity or a point of interest, type its name in the Search box; for example:

```
Movie theater
```

This command flags movie theaters near your current location. Or, you can be specific and look for locations elsewhere by specifying the city name, district, or zip code, such as

```
Korean 92123
```

After typing this command and touching the Search button, you see a smattering of Korean restaurants found in my old neighborhood in San Diego, as shown in Figure 12-5.

Search text   Top search result

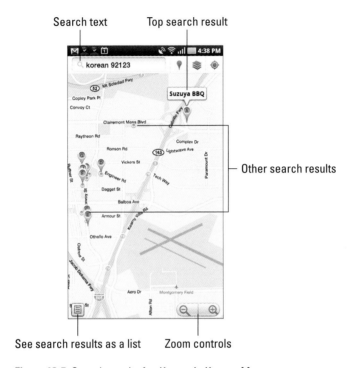

Other search results

See search results as a list   Zoom controls

Figure 12-5: Search results for *Korean* in Kearny Mesa.

To see more information about a result, touch its cartoon bubble, such as the one with Suzuya BBQ, shown in Figure 12-5. The screen that appears offers details, plus perhaps even a Web site address and phone number. You can press the Get Directions button (refer to Figure 12-4) to get driving directions; see the later section "Getting directions."

  ✔ Each letter or dot on the screen represents a search result (refer to Figure 12-5).

  ✔ Use the Zoom controls or spread your fingers to zoom in to the map.

  ✔ You can create a contact for the location, keeping it as a part of your Contacts list: After touching the location balloon, touch the Menu button (shown in the margin). Choose the command Add As a Contact. The contact is created using data known about the business, including its location and phone number and even a Web page address — if that information is available.

✔ The location's information page shows a Phone button, though if you touch that button, you're reminded that the Galaxy Tab cannot make phone calls. That's kind of disappointing because you can make phone calls if you have the proper app installed, just not by touching that Phone button. See Chapter 10 for information on how to get around the Galaxy Tab's lack-of-phone abilities.

✔ Touching the Search List button on the Maps screen displays all search results in list format. Refer to Figure 12-1 for the location of the Search List button.

Search nearby

Maybe you don't know what you're looking for. Maybe you're like my teenage sons, who stand in front of the open refrigerator, waiting for the sandwich fairy to hand them a snack. The Maps app features a sort of "I don't know what I want but I want something" fairy. It's the Search Nearby command.

Touch the Search Nearby button (refer to Figure 12-1) to see a list of places near you: restaurants, coffee, bars, hotels, attractions, and more. Touch an item to see matching locations in your vicinity.

You can use the Add button to create another search category, such as Payday Loan Store, All-Night Denture Repair, or Bingo Casino.

To remove a category, long-press its icon and choose the Remove command.

Look for a contact's location

You can hone in on where your contacts are located by using the map. This trick works when you've specified an address for the contact — either home or work or another location. If so, your Galaxy Tab can easily help you find that location or even give you directions. Heed these directions:

1. **Display information about a contact.**

2. **Touch the contact's address.**

   The address has text above it that reads *View Home Address* or *View Business Address.*

3. **If you see the Complete Action Using menu, choose Maps.**

   The contact's location appears in the Maps app.

You can touch the address bubble to get directions or read more information about the location. Refer to sections elsewhere in this chapter for the specifics.

✔ When your Galaxy Tab features more than one map search application, you see the Complete Action Using menu (refer to Step 3).

✔ Not every contact has address information available, though there's nothing to stop you from editing your contacts and adding their address information.

✔ See Chapter 5 for more information on using the Contacts app.

Getting directions

One command associated with locations on the map is Get Directions. I suppose it's the opposite of the Get Lost command. Here's how to use it:

1. **Touch a location's cartoon bubble displayed by an address, a contact, or a business or from the result of a map search.**

2. **Touch the Get Directions button.**

   See the next section for information on the Navigation options.

3. **Choose Get Directions.**

   You see the directions listed, as shown in Figure 12-6. The Maps app has already chosen your current location (shown as My Location in the figure) as the starting point and the location you searched for or are viewing on the map as the destination.

You can follow the directions on the screen or touch the Map button (refer to Figure 12-6) to see the path you need to take as illustrated on the map. Zoom in or out to see more or less detail.

✔ To receive vocal directions, touch the Navigation button or just read the next section.

✔ Touch the From or To field to change the point of origin or the destination, though I admit that it's easier to simply start over.

✔ The Transportation Method button (refer to Figure 12-6) displays a menu from which you can choose a different way to travel, such as on foot, by bicycle, or via public transportation.

✔ The Maps app may not give you the perfect directions, but for places you've never been, it's a great tool.

Navigating to your destination

Lists are so 20th century. I don't know why anyone would bother, especially when the Galaxy Tab features a digital copilot in the form of voice navigation.

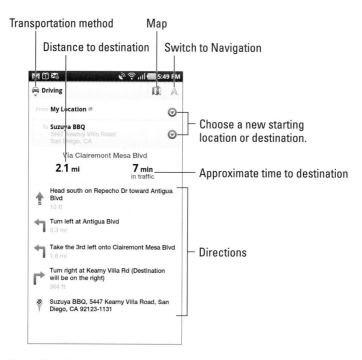

Transportation method   Map

Distance to destination   Switch to Navigation

— Choose a new starting location or destination.

— Approximate time to destination

— Directions

Figure 12-6: Going from here to there.

To use Navigation, choose the Navigation option from any list of directions. Or, touch the Navigation button, as shown in Figure 12-6. You can also enter the Navigation app directly by choosing it from the Applications screen, though then you must input (or speak) your destination, so it's just easier to start in the Maps app.

In Navigation mode, the Galaxy Tab displays an interactive map that shows your current location and turn-by-turn directions for reaching your destination. A digital voice tells you how far to go and when to turn, for example, and gives you other nagging advice — just like a backseat driver, albeit an accurate one.

After choosing Navigation, sit back and have the Galaxy Tab dictate your directions. You can simply listen, or just glance at the Tab for an update of where you're heading.

To stop Navigation, press the Menu soft button and choose the Exit Navigation command.

✔ To remove the navigation route from the screen, exit navigation and return to the Maps app. Touch the Layers button to bring up the Layers menu. Touch the Clear Map button.

✔ When you tire of hearing the Navigation voice, press the Menu soft button and choose the Mute command.

✔ I refer to the navigation voice as *Gertrude*.

✔ You can press the Menu soft button while navigating and choose Route Info to see an overview of your journey.

✔ When viewing the Route Info screen, touch the Gears button to see a handy pop-up menu. From that menu, you can choose options to modify the route so that you avoid highways or avoid toll roads.

✔ The neat thing about Navigation is that whenever you screw up, a new course is immediately calculated.

✔ In Navigation mode, the Galaxy Tab consumes a lot of battery power. I highly recommend that you plug the Tab into your car's power adapter ("cigarette lighter") for the duration of the trip.

Adding a navigation shortcut to the Home screen

When you visit certain places often — such as the parole office — you can save yourself the time you would spend repeatedly inputting navigation information, by creating a navigation shortcut on the Home screen. Here's how:

1. **Long-press a blank part of the Home screen.**

2. **From the pop-up menu, choose Shortcuts.**

3. **Choose Directions & Navigation.**

4. **Type a contact name, address, destination, or business name in the text box.**

   As you type, suggestions appear in a list. You can choose a suggestion to save yourself some typing.

5. **Choose a traveling method.**

   Your options are car, public transportation, bicycle, and on foot (even though the icon of the "on foot" guy doesn't seem to have any feet).

6. **Scroll down a bit to type a shortcut name.**

7. **Choose an icon for the shortcut.**

8. **Touch the Save button.**

   The Navigation shortcut is placed on the Home screen.

To use the shortcut, simply touch it on the Home screen. Instantly, the Maps app starts and enters Navigation mode, steering you from wherever you are to the location referenced by the shortcut.

- ✔ I keep a navigation shortcut to my home on the Home screen. It helps me quickly find my way back to my house when I'm fleeing the authorities.
- ✔ See Chapter 21 for additional information on creating Home screen shortcuts.
- ✔ I keep all navigation shortcuts in one place, on the first Home screen to the right.

Where Are Your Friends?

A feature in the Maps app is Latitude. It's a layer you can apply to a map, but it's also the name of its own app, Latitude.

Latitude is a social networking service that lets you share your physical location with your friends, also assumed to be using Latitude. Being able to more easily know where your friends are makes it possible to meet up with them — or, I suppose, to avoid them. It's all up to you.

To join Latitude, you press the Menu soft button when viewing a map and then choose the Join Latitude command. Or, you can just start the Latitude app.

After opening Latitude, read the information, and then touch the Allow & Share button to continue. If you don't see the Join Latitude command, you've already joined; start Latitude by choosing the Latitude command.

To make Latitude work, you need to add friends to Latitude, and those friends need to use Latitude. After adding Latitude friends, you can share your location with them as well as view their locations on a map. You can also chat with Google Talk, send them email, get directions to their location, and do other interesting things.

To disable Latitude, press the Menu soft button when Latitude is active and choose the Privacy command. Choose the option Sign Out of Latitude or Turn Off Latitude.

It's a Big, Flat Camera

In This Chapter

▷ Taking a picture on the Tab

▷ Reviewing an image

▷ Doing a self-portrait

▷ Creating a panorama

▷ Exploring various camera options

▷ Making a video

1 suppose that the world is getting used to the concept of cameras that no longer look like cameras. For instance, a long time ago, to take a picture, you held the camera right up to your eyeball. You looked into something called a *viewfinder*. Today, you hold the camera away from your face, crook your head back, and squint at a tiny LCD screen. That's the new "normal."

The Galaxy Tab has not one, but two cameras — one on the back and another on the front. Both cameras can be used to take still images or record video. Never mind that it's a unique experience to wield a big, flat camera for recording your memories: With a nice, high-resolution screen, you never have to squint to ensure that you're taking a good picture.

Smile for the Camera

The reason that mankind doesn't have more pictures of UFOs is simple: People don't often carry a camera with them when the rare alien craft shows up. That's no longer the case, thanks to portable all-in-one gizmos like the Galaxy Tab. Now you can have your camera with you wherever you take your Tab — *if* you remember to use the Tab as a camera to capture those pesky aliens.

Snapping a pic

Of the two cameras on the Galaxy Tab, the heavy-duty one is on the Tab's back. It's the 3-megapixel (MP) camera, which also has a flash. The front-facing camera is only 1.3MP and doesn't have a flash, so most of the time you're taking a picture, you hold up the Tab and look at the touchscreen.

To begin your photography adventure on the Tab, start the Camera app, found on the Applications screen. After starting the Camera app, you see the main Camera screen, as illustrated in Figure 13-1.

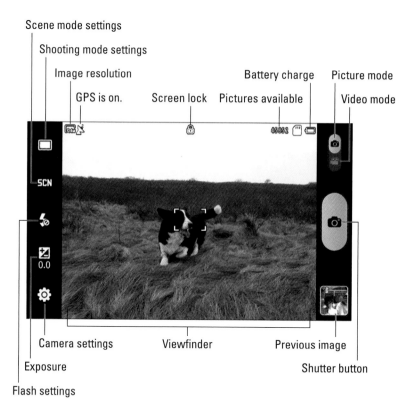

Scene mode settings
Shooting mode settings
Image resolution
GPS is on.
Screen lock
Pictures available
Battery charge
Picture mode
Video mode

Camera settings
Viewfinder
Previous image
Exposure
Shutter button
Flash settings

Figure 13-1: Galaxy Tab in Camera mode.

To take a picture, point the camera at the subject and touch the Shutter button, shown in Figure 13-1.

After you touch the Shutter button, the screen goes blank, you may hear a mechanical shutter sound play, and then you see a review screen, as shown in Figure 13-2.

Send or save the   Add picture to a contact   Delete picture
picture on the Internet   or set as wallpaper

Review previous
picture

Figure 13-2: Reviewing a picture you just shot.

Here are your options:

Back: When the picture looks okay, just press the Back soft button to return to the Camera app and take more pictures.

Share: Touch the Share button to send the image as an attachment to an email or a text message, save it to Facebook, post it in your Picasa album, and so on.

Set As: Touch the Set As button to assign the image as a contact's picture or to set the image as the Galaxy Tab's Home screen wallpaper (background).

Delete: Touch the Delete button to erase the image and return to take another picture. Touch the OK button to confirm.

You can also touch the triangle to review the previous pictures you've taken with the Galaxy Tab. When reviewing pictures, use the triangles that appear on the left and right sides of the screen to page through your images.

If the onscreen menu (shown in Figure 13-2) disappears, just touch the picture to make it visible again.

✒ As on other digital cameras, the shutter doesn't snap instantly when you shoot the picture; the camera takes a moment to focus, the flash may go off, and then you hear the shutter sound effect.

- The Galaxy Tab can be used as a camera in either landscape or portrait orientation, though the controls and gizmos are always presented in landscape format (refer to Figure 13-1).

- If your pictures appear blurry, ensure that the camera lens on the back of the Galaxy Tab isn't dirty.

- The pictures you take with your Galaxy Tab are saved to the MicroSD card. They remain on the MicroSD card until you delete them.

- Reviewing and organizing all the pictures on your Galaxy Tab is the job of the Gallery app. See Chapter 14 for information on the Gallery app.

- Chapter 14 also offers specifics on how to use the Share command (see Figure 13-2).

- There's no zoom function in the Camera app. A zoom function may appear in a future release of the Camera app on the Galaxy Tab.

- Similarly, though the Camera app features automatic focus, you have no way to override or to control the camera's focus. That may change in the future.

- If you press the Tab's Power button while using the Camera app, you lock the screen. The Lock icon appears, as shown in Figure 13-1. Press the Power button again to unlock.

- You can take as many pictures with your Galaxy Tab as you like. The Pictures Available indicator (refer to Figure 13-1) shows how many pictures can be stored on the MicroSD card at the camera's current resolution setting. In Figure 13-1, where the resolution is 0.4MP, there is room for 46,852 pictures.

- The Tab has no easy or obvious way to undelete an image, so be careful! In fact:

- I recommend that you do your deleting and other photo management duties by using the Gallery app, discussed in Chapter 14.

- The Galaxy Tab not only takes a picture but also keeps track of where you were located on planet earth when you took the picture. In Figure 13-1, you see that the GPS indicator is on, which means that location information is being stored. See Chapter 14 for information on reviewing a photograph's location.

- The next time you're face-to-face with a contact, remember to snap that person's photo. Use the picture-review window's Set As button to assign the image as the contact's photo — with the contact's permission, of course.

✔ You can also review the image you just took by touching the Previous Image button (refer to Figure 13-1).

✔ Spread or pinch your fingers on the touchscreen to zoom in or out of a picture you're previewing.

✔ The Galaxy Tab stores pictures in the JPEG image file format. Images are stored in the DCIM/Camera folder on the MicroSD card; they have the JPG filename extension.

Setting the flash

You can use one of three settings for the flash when taking still shots on your Galaxy Tab:

Auto: The flash activates during low-light situations, but not when it's bright out.

On: The flash always activates.

Off: The flash never activates, even in low-light situations.

To change or check the flash setting, touch the Flash settings button on the Camera app screen, as shown in Figure 13-1. The icon that appears reflects the current flash state.

✔ A good time to turn on the flash is when taking pictures of people or objects in front of something bright, such as Aunt Carol holding her prize-winning peach cobbler in front of a burning building.

✔ Only the rear camera features a flash.

Changing the resolution

The Galaxy Tab's rear camera has several resolutions at which you can take an image. To set the resolution, follow these steps before you snap the picture:

1. **Touch the Camera settings button.**

2. **Ensure that the Image tab is selected.**

3. **Choose Resolutions.**

4. **Select a resolution from the list.**

5. **Press the Back soft button to return to the Camera app.**

The current image resolution is noted atop the Camera app's screen, as shown in Figure 13-1.

✔ You cannot change the resolution when taking a self-portrait. See the next section.

   ✔ Resolution settings control the image quality. Technically, the higher the resolution, the more information is in the picture. That concept comes into play when you choose to print an image: Higher resolutions print better. When you plan to take images only for email or posting on the Internet, lower resolutions are fine.

Taking a self-portrait

Who needs to pay all that money for a mirror when you have a Galaxy Tab? Not only is the front-facing camera useful for video chat, but you can also take a picture of yourself, alone or with others, by simply following these steps:

   1. **Start the Camera app.**

   2. **Touch the Shooting Mode Settings button.**

      Refer to Figure 13-1 for its location.

   3. **Choose Self-Shot from the Shooting Mode menu.**

      The front-facing camera is activated. There's no flash, and the resolution cannot be adjusted.

   4. **Smile.**

   5. **Touch the Shutter button to snap your pic.**

As with taking a picture using the rear-facing camera, you get to preview the shot. Refer to Figure 13-2 as well as the information in the earlier section "Snapping a pic."

See Chapter 10 for details on video chat.

Doing a panoramic shot

An interesting shooting mode to play with is the panoramic shot. Using some sort of otherworldly intelligence, the Galaxy Tab can help you line up multiple images that are then pasted together to form a panoramic image. Here's how to accomplish this feat:

   1. **Start the Camera app.**

   2. **Touch the Shooting Mode Settings button.**

   3. **Choose Panorama.**

      An indicator appears at the bottom of the screen. It's your guide to help you take as many as eight sequential shots, which are later assembled into the panorama.

4. **Hold your arms steady.**

   Pivot on your feet as you scan around you to compose the panoramic image.

5. **Touch the Shutter button.**

6. **Pivot slightly to your right (or left, but you must continue in the same direction).**

   As you move the camera, you see a green rectangle. The rectangle frames what will be the next shot in the image.

7. **Keep moving as subsequent shots are taken.**

   Try to keep the green rectangle within the frame of the image you're shooting.

   If you turn too far without hearing the automatic shutter snap, turn back until you can center the green rectangle.

8. **After the last image is snapped, wait while the image is assembled.**

The Camera app sticks each of the different shots together, creating a wide panoramic image. The image is previewed, similar to all other pictures you take with the Tab; refer to the earlier section "Snapping a pic" to see what you can do next.

If you want to take fewer than eight images in your panoramic shot, simply touch the Shutter button to stop.

Making various camera adjustments

Plenty of interesting settings are in the Camera app. Each setting can be accessed from a menu that pops up when you choose one of the buttons on the left ("top") side of the Camera app, as illustrated in Figure 13-1.

Rather than bore you by describing all the settings, here are some of my favorites:

Continuous shots: If you need to take lots of pictures rapidly, such as when photographing sports or family fights, touch the Shooting Mode Settings button and choose Continuous. You can take as many as nine shots, one after the other, by touching and holding the Shutter button. Also consider choosing Sports from the Scene Mode settings menu.

Night photography: In low-light settings, activate the Night screen mode: Touch the Screen Mode Settings button and choose Night.

Shutter noise: To control whether the Camera app makes a noise when you snap a picture, touch the Camera Settings button, choose the Setup tab, and then choose Shutter Sound. Select a sound from the Shutter Sound menu, or choose Off for no sound. Touch the Save button to confirm your choice.

Disable review: You can turn off the picture review by touching the Camera Settings button, choosing the Setup tab, and then choosing Review to remove the green check mark there.

GPS setting: The camera keeps track of the location where you've taken a picture only if you've turned on the GPS option. To enable this option, touch the Camera Settings button, choose the Setup tab, and touch the GPS option to place (or remove) a green check mark there.

Image effects: You can apply only a handful of special effects to images you take with the Galaxy Tab: Negative, Black and White (monochrome), and Sepia Tone. To apply an effect, touch the Camera Settings button, and on the Image tab, choose Effect. Select an effect to apply or choose Normal for no effect, and then touch the Save button.

Live from Your Galaxy Tab, It's Video!

Images are nice, but flat. There may be a thousand words going on in the picture, but none of them makes a sound. There's also little action, which can be artistic, but life is made up of a series of moments. To capture that quality, you can use your Galaxy Tab as a video camera.

Recording a video

The same Camera app that's used to take still images is also used to capture video. The secret is the Video mode switch you drag down that transforms the Camera app from Picture to Video mode, as illustrated in Figure 13-3.

Start shooting the video by pressing the Record button, shown in Figure 13-3. You may hear a sound, and then you see the Recording screen, shown in Figure 13-4.

Touch the Pause button to pause the video recording. To resume recording, touch the Pause button again. (The Pause button turns into the Record button when recording is paused.)

When you're done recording, touch the Stop button.

To review your video, touch the Previous Video button, shown in Figure 13-3.

Recording mode

Video resolution   Maximum recording time   Video mode

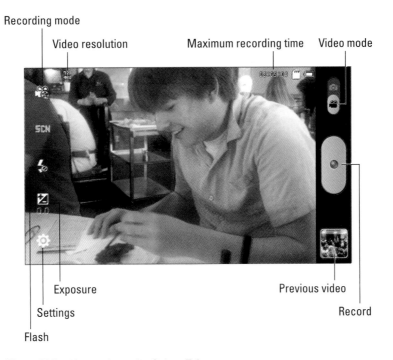

Exposure   Previous video

Settings   Record

Flash

Figure 13-3: Video mode on the Galaxy Tab.

Recording time   Stop recording

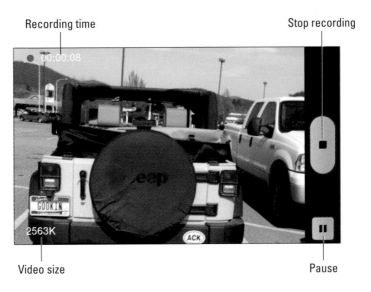

Video size   Pause

Figure 13-4: Recording a video.

✔ Hold the Galaxy Tab steady! The camera still works when you whip around the Tab, but wild gyrations render the video unwatchable.

✔ The length of video you can record is limited by how much storage space is available on the MicroSD card.

✔ To peruse, as well as manage, your videos, use the Gallery app. See Chapter 14.

✔ Pausing a recording doesn't create two recordings — it merely places a break into a single recording.

✔ You cannot record video using the front-facing camera by using the Camera app. That setup may change in the future.

✔ The Recording Mode button displays a menu with two settings. Use the Limit for MMS setting when recording a video you plan to send as a text message (MMS) attachment. See Chapter 6 for information on text messaging with the Galaxy Tab.

✔ There's no need for a "flash" when recording video, though you can touch the Flash button and choose the option On to keep the LED flash lamp turned on for recording indoors. (Yes, keeping the flash lamp on consumes a lot of battery power.)

✔ The Camera app stores your videos on the MicroSD card in the DCIM/Camera folder. The videos are saved in the MP4 video file format and have the MP4 filename extension.

Reviewing the video

To review your video masterpiece, touch the Previous Video button (refer to Figure 13-3). Choose your video from the list (it's the first one shown). Touch the big Play button (the triangle at the bottom center) to review the video.

To delete a video you're reviewing, touch the Delete button.

You can use the Share button to send the video as an email attachment or to publish it to the Internet.

Touch the screen when reviewing a video to summon the onscreen controls.

When your video is done playing, you can press the Back soft button to return to the Camera app.

✔ The best way to review, manage, and delete the videos you've shot is by using the Gallery app. See Chapter 14.

✔ Also see Chapter 14 for information on publishing your video to YouTube.

✔ Though deleting a video frees up storage space on the MicroSD card, recovering a deleted video is pretty much impossible.

14

Galaxy Gallery

Some things just can't stand on their own. For example, a car requires gas. Not only that — the car needs a driver, roads, and somewhere to go. Likewise, a robot requires proper programming to ensure that it doesn't destroy humanity. And you'd be a fool if you bought only one teleporter. Without that second teleporter, where would you beam yourself?

There's no point in the Galaxy Tab having a camera unless it has a place to store pictures. My inner nerd reminds me that the Tab's MicroSD card stores images and videos. Call it "digital film," but all that means nothing unless you have an opportunity to review and enjoy those captured moments at a later time. Accomplishing that task is this chapter's subject.

Where Your Pictures Lurk

Some people hang their pictures on the wall. Some put pictures on a piano, or maybe on a mantle. In the digital realm, pictures are stored electronically, compressed and squeezed into a series of ones and zeroes that mean nothing unless you have an app that lets you view those images. On the Galaxy Tab, that app is the *Gallery*.

Visiting the Gallery

In the distance, you spy Edna. You know she's going to drone on and on about her grandchildren, show you their latest pictures, and explain how spectacular and superhuman they are. Rather than ask her to buzz off, you can thwart her efforts and gain control over the situation by whipping out your Galaxy Tab. She'll be stunned by your high-tech savvy, and you can start the Gallery app to immediately impress her with your images and videos.

Start the Gallery app by choosing its icon from the Applications screen. You may also find a Gallery app shortcut icon on the primary Home screen.

When the Gallery app opens, you see your visual media (pictures and videos) organized into piles, or albums, as shown in Figure 14-1. The number and variety of albums depend on how you synchronize your Tab with your computer, which apps you use for collecting media, or which photo-sharing services you use on the Internet, such as Picasa.

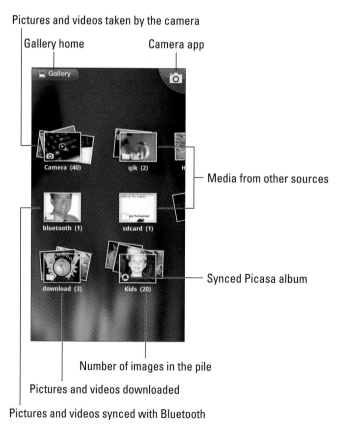

Figure 14-1: The Gallery's main screen.

Touch an album (pile) to open it and view the pictures or videos it contains. The media is displayed in a grid, which you can scroll left or right. Thumbnail previews give you an idea of what the images are.

 Videos stored in a pile appear with the Play button (shown in the margin) on their thumbnails.

Figure 14-2 illustrates how images look when you open an album. You can use the Organize button in the upper right corner of the screen to switch from Grid view to a view that organizes your images by date.

Current pile (folder)   Grid

Gallery Home   Dates

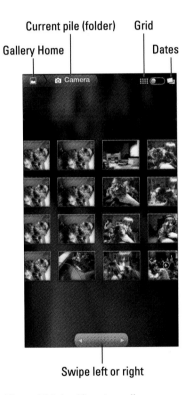

Swipe left or right

Figure 14-2: Looking at an album.

You can view more images in the album by swiping your finger left and right.

To view an image or a video, touch it with your finger. The image appears in full size on the screen, similar to what's shown in Figure 14-3. You can rotate the Tab horizontally (or vertically) to see the image in another orientation.

Later sections describe in more detail what you can do when viewing an image, as shown in Figure 14-3.

Picture number

Album (pile)   Zoom in

Gallery Home   Lovely image   Zoom out

See all images in the album

Do things with the image

Figure 14-3: Examining an image.

Videos play when you choose them. The Video Playing screen is illustrated in Figure 14-4. To see the controls (illustrated in Figure 14-4), touch the screen while the video is playing.

 To return to the main category in the Gallery, press the Back soft button, or you can choose the Gallery Home button from the top of the screen, as shown in Figures 14-2 and 14-3.

✒ Videos in the Gallery play in one orientation only.

✒ Touch a video or an image to redisplay the onscreen menu, as shown in Figures 14-3 and 14-4.

✒ Press the Menu soft button while viewing a video to see more commands, such as the Scene Selection command, which helps you jump around to various spots in long videos.

✔ When playing a video, touch the Set Bookmark button (see Figure 14-4) to drop a yellow triangle on the video's time index. To review the bookmarks you've set, press the Menu soft button and choose the Bookmarks command.

✔ To run a slide show of photos in an album, touch the Slideshow button, shown in Figure 14-3. The Slideshow starts, displaying one image after another.

✔ To keep the Gallery handy, considering placing its shortcut icon on the Home screen. Refer to Chapter 21.

✔ Refer to Chapter 8 for information on downloading photos from the Web.

✔ See Chapter 19 for information on the doubleTwist program, which can be used to synchronize images and videos between the Galaxy Tab and your computer.

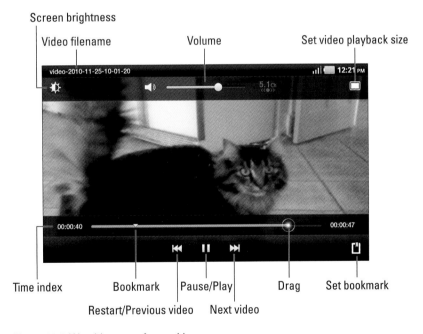

Figure 14-4: Watching one of your videos.

Finding out where you took a picture

In addition to snapping a picture, the Galaxy Tab can save the location where you took the picture. This information is obtained from the Tab's GPS, the same tool used to find your location on a map. In fact, you can use the information saved with a picture to see exactly where the picture was taken.

For example, Figure 14-5 shows the location where I took the image shown in Figure 13-1 (from Chapter 13). The location was saved by using GPS technology and is available as part of the picture's data.

Figure 14-5: A picture's location.

To see where you've taken a picture, follow these steps:

1. **Summon the image in the Gallery.**

2. **Press the Menu soft button.**

3. **Choose the More command.**

4. **Choose Show on Map.**

   The spot where you took the picture appears in the Maps app.

Not every image has location information. In many cases, the Galaxy Tab might be unable to acquire a GPS signal. When that happens, location information is unavailable.

✓ As far as I can tell, videos don't store location information on the Galaxy Tab.

✓ The Tab's GPS can be disabled for images you capture. Refer to Chapter 13 for information on how to turn GPS on or off when taking pictures.

Selecting multiple pictures and videos

The Gallery has a handful of commands you can use to manipulate and manage your pictures and videos. Some commands can affect multiple pictures or videos, but only when you know the secret of how to select multiple pictures or videos. Here's that secret:

1. **Open the album (pile) you want to mess with.**

2. **Press the Menu soft button.**

   Each image in the album is adorned by a tiny check box, as shown in Figure 14-6.

3. **Touch a thumbnail to select it.**

   Or, you can choose the Select All item, shown in Figure 14-6.

4. **Perform an action on the group of images or videos.**

   Later sections describe specifically what you can do.

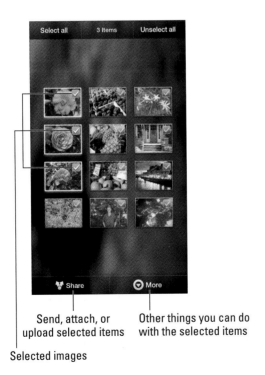

Send, attach, or upload selected items

Other things you can do with the selected items

Selected images

Figure 14-6: Choosing images to mess with.

To unselect items, touch them again. To unselect everything, touch the Unselect All command, shown in Figure 14-6.

The type of commands you can use on a group of items in an album depends on the group. Some commands, such as Delete and Share, can be performed on any old group. Other commands, such as the image rotation commands, work only with pictures, not with videos.

Deleting pictures and videos

It's entirely possible, and often desirable, to remove unwanted, embarrassing, or questionably legal images and videos from the Gallery. To zap a single image or video, follow these steps:

1. **Summon the image or video you want to get rid of.**

2. **Press the Menu soft button.**

3. **Choose Delete.**

4. **Choose Confirm Deletions.**

    Or, touch Cancel to chicken out.

To remove multiple images or videos, follow the directions in the preceding section for selecting multiple items in an album, and then pick up at Step 3 in the preceding list.

- You cannot undelete an image or a video you've deleted. There's no way to recover such an image using available tools on the Galaxy Tab.

- Some images and videos cannot be deleted. Specifically, you cannot remove pictures shared from your Picasa Web albums. You need to visit the Picasa Web site to delete those images: http://picasa.google.com.

Assigning an image to a contact

You can set any image for a contact. It doesn't necessarily have to be an image you've taken with the Galaxy Tab; any image you find in the Gallery will do. Follow these steps:

1. **View an image in the Gallery.**

2. **Press the Menu soft button.**

3. **Choose More and then Set As.**

    If the Set As command doesn't appear, you cannot set that image for a contact; not every album allows its images to be set for contacts.

4. Choose Contact Icon.

5. Scroll the Tab's Contacts list and choose a particular contact.

You can use the Search command to easily locate a contact when you have an abundance of them.

6. Crop the image.

Refer to the later section "Cropping an image" for detailed instructions on working the crop-thing.

7. Touch the Save button.

Or, touch the Discard button to chicken out or change your mind.

The contact's image is set and you're returned to view the image in the Gallery.

Images you set for your Google contacts are instantly synchronized with your Google account on the Internet.

Setting an image as wallpaper

You can choose as the Galaxy Tab's Home screen background or wallpaper any picture that's viewable in the Gallery. Basically, you follow the same steps as outlined in the preceding section, but in Step 4 choose Wallpaper instead of Contact Icon. Then skip to Step 6.

Some images can be set as wallpaper that cannot be assigned to a contact. For those images, you see the command Set As Wallpaper in Step 3. Choose that command and then proceed with Step 6 to crop the image.

Press the Home button to see the new wallpaper.

You can also change wallpaper by long-pressing the Home screen and choosing the Wallpapers command. See Chapter 21.

Cropping an image

One of the few image-editing commands available in the Gallery is Crop. You can use Crop to slice out portions of an image, such as when removing ex-spouses and convicts from a family portrait. To crop an image, obey these directions:

1. Summon the image you want to crop.

2. Press the Menu soft button.

3. **Choose More and then Crop.**

If the Crop command is unavailable, you have to choose another image. (Not every album lets you modify images.)

4. **Work the crop-thing.**

You can drag the orange rectangle around to choose which part of the image to crop. Drag an edge of the rectangle to resize the left and right or top and bottom sides. Or, drag a corner of the rectangle to change the rectangle's size proportionally. Use Figure 14-7 as your guide.

5. **Touch the Save button when you're done cropping.**

Only the portion of the image within the orange rectangle is saved; the rest is discarded.

There's no way to undo a crop action after you've touched the Save button.

Working the orange rectangle to crop an image can be frustrating. When the image zooms in too small, you may have difficulty zooming back out. At that point, you can touch the Discard button and start over again.

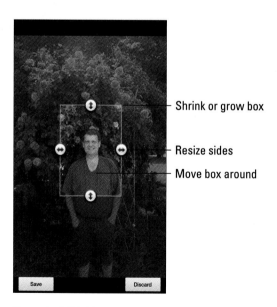

Shrink or grow box

Resize sides

Move box around

Figure 14-7: Working the crop-thing.

Rotating pictures

Which way is up? Well, the answer depends on your situation. For taking pictures with the Galaxy Tab, sometimes images just don't appear "up," no matter how you turn the Tab. To fix that situation, heed these steps:

1. **Choose an image to rotate.**

2. **Press the Menu soft button.**

3. **Choose the More command.**

4. **Choose Rotate Left to rotate the image counterclockwise; choose Rotate Right to rotate the image clockwise.**

 You can rotate a whole slew of images at one time: Select all the images as described in the earlier section "Selecting multiple pictures and videos." Choose More and then Rotate Left or Rotate Right. All the images are rotated at one time.

✔ You cannot rotate videos.

✔ You cannot rotate certain images, such as images shared from your Picasa Web albums.

Printing your pictures

A trick you wouldn't expect to find on a portable gizmo is the ability to print your lovely photos. The Galaxy Tab is more than up to the task, *if* you have a Bluetooth printer and you've survived the ordeal of connecting *(pairing)* the printer to your Tab. If so, printing takes place thusly:

1. **Ensure that the Tab's Bluetooth wireless radio is on.**

   Refer to Chapter 19 for information about Bluetooth.

2. **Ensure that the Bluetooth printer is on, that its Bluetooth radio is on, and that the printer is stocked with ink and paper, ready to print.**

3. **Open the Gallery app and browse to find the image you want to enshrine on paper.**

4. **Press the Menu soft button and choose More and then Print.**

5. **If prompted, choose the Bluetooth printer.**

6. **Make any settings on the Print screen.**

   For example, you can set the number of copies to print or change the orientation.

7. **Touch the Print button to print the picture.**

   In a few moments, you can hold the picture in your hands.

Bluetooth printing isn't perfect. For example, your Galaxy Tab may not recognize the Bluetooth printer. It happens. As an alternative, you can attach an image to an email message, send it to yourself, and then print it on your computer. See the next section.

Set Your Pics and Vids Free

Keeping your precious moments and memories in the Galaxy Tab is an elegant solution to the problem of lugging around photo albums. But when you want to show your pictures to the widest possible audience, you need a much larger stage. That stage is the Internet, and you have many ways to send and save your pictures and videos online, as covered in this section.

Refer to Chapter 19 for information on synchronizing and sharing information between the Galaxy Tab and your computer.

Sharing with the Share menu

Occasionally, you stumble across the Share command when working with photos and videos in the Gallery. This command is used to distribute images and videos from your Galaxy Tab to your pals in the digital realms.

The menu that appears when you choose the Share command contains various options for sharing media, similar to the one shown in Figure 14-8. You may see more or fewer items on the Share menu, depending on which software you have installed on your Tab, which Internet services you belong to, and which type of media is being shared.

Figure 14-8: Sharing options for media.

When viewing a video, pause the video and press the Menu soft button. Choose the command Share Via to see the Share menu.

The following sections describe some of the items you can choose from the menu and how the media is shared.

AllShare

The AllShare program wirelessly connects external monitors and other playback gizmos to your Galaxy Tab. As long as everything works properly, the result is that you can view your pictures or watch your videos on your computer or another gizmo.

See Chapter 19 for more information about the AllShare program and DLNA media sharing.

Bluetooth

Bluetooth is perhaps the most difficult way to share files, mostly because many Bluetooth-enabled gizmos don't have the file-sharing smarts to make the operation work. In fact, I can promise you that it's far easier simply to connect a USB cable to the Galaxy Tab and share your media using a direct connection, which is covered in Chapter 19.

I've been able to transfer images from a Macintosh computer to the Galaxy Tab using Bluetooth, but not the other way around. I've also been able to transfer files to the Galaxy Tab from my Droid phone, which works better than file transfer does on the Mac. Chapter 18 covers setting up the Bluetooth connection, and details about making a file transfer to the Tab are covered in Chapter 19.

Email and Gmail

After selecting one or more images or videos, choose Email or Gmail from the Share menu to send the media files from your Galaxy Tab as a message attachment. Fill in the To, Subject, and Message text boxes as necessary. Touch the Send button to send the media.

 ✔ See Chapter 7 for more information on Email and Gmail on the Galaxy Tab.

 ✔ You may not be able to send video files as email attachments. That's probably because some video files are humongous. They would not only take too long to send but also might be too big for the recipient's inbox.

 ✔ As an alternative to sending large video files, consider uploading them to YouTube instead. See the later section "Posting your video to YouTube."

Facebook

To upload a mobile image to Facebook, choose the Facebook command from the Share menu. Optionally, type (or dictate) a caption. Touch the Upload button. Eventually, the media makes its way to Facebook, for all your friends to enjoy and make rude comments about.

See Chapter 9 for more information about Facebook.

Messaging

Media can be attached to a text message, which then becomes the famous MMS, or multimedia message, that I write about in Chapter 6. After choosing the Messaging sharing option, input the contact name or phone number to which you want to send the media. Optionally, type a brief message. Touch the Send button to send the message.

- ✔ Some images and videos may be too large to send as multimedia text messages.

- ✔ The Galaxy Tab may prompt you to resize an image to properly send it as an MMS.

- ✔ Not every cell phone can receive multimedia text messages.

Picasa

Perhaps the sanest way to share photos is to upload them to Google's Picasa photo-sharing site. Heck, you probably already have a Picasa account synced with your Galaxy Tab, so this option is perhaps the easiest and most obvious to use. Here's how it works:

1. **View a picture in the Gallery.**

2. **Choose Picasa from the Share menu (refer to Figure 14-8).**

3. **Type a caption.**

4. **Optionally, choose your Google account (if you have more than one).**

5. **Choose a Picasa album.**

   You may need to scroll up the top part of the screen a bit to see the Album item, which might be hidden behind the onscreen keyboard.

6. **Touch the Upload button to send the images.**

Because Picasa may automatically sync certain albums with your Galaxy Tab, you can end up with two copies of the image. If so, you can delete the non-Picasa version of the image from its original gallery.

✔ Picasa is for sharing images only, not video.

✔ Your Google account automatically comes with access to Picasa. If you haven't yet set things up, visit `picasaweb.google.com` to get started.

✔ You can share images stored on the Picasa Web site by clicking the Share button found above each photo album.

✔ To make a Picasa album public, on the Internet (preferably using your computer) choose the Edit⇨Album Properties command, found just above the album. Choose Public from the pop-up menu, by the Visibility command in the Edit Album Information window.

✔ Other photo-sharing Web sites are available on the Internet, including Flikr, Image Shack, Photobucket, and more. None of these, however, synchronizes as well with the Galaxy Tab as Picasa.

Twitter

Images are shared on the popular Twitter social networking site by saving the image on a Twitter image-sharing Web site and then tweeting the image's link. You should have the Twitter app installed on your Galaxy Tab and be logged in to that account before you use Twitter to share an image.

The Twitter app uses the TwitPic Web site to share images. After choosing the Twitter option for sharing, you see the TwitPic link in your tweet message. Type additional text (whatever will fit) and then touch the Update button to tweet the pic's link.

YouTube

The YouTube sharing option appears when you've chosen to share a video from the Gallery. See the next section.

Posting your video to YouTube

The best way to share a video is to upload it to YouTube. As a Google account holder, you also have a YouTube account. You can use the YouTube app on the Galaxy Tab along with your account to upload your videos to the Internet, where everyone can see them and make rude comments about them. Here's how:

1. **Ensure that the Wi-Fi connection is activated.**

   The best — the only — way to upload a video is to turn on the Wi-Fi connection, which is oodles faster than using the digital cellular network. See Chapter 18 for information on how to turn on the Wi-Fi connection.

2. **Start the Gallery app.**

3. **View the video you want to upload.**

   Or, simply have the video displayed on the screen: Touch the screen to display the onscreen menu and then touch the Pause button.

4. **Press the Menu soft button.**

5. **Choose the Share Via command.**

6. **Choose YouTube.**

7. **Type the video's title.**

8. **Touch the More Details button.**

9. **Optionally, type a description, specify whether to make the video public or private, add tags, or change other settings.**

10. **Touch the Upload button.**

    You return to the Gallery and the video is uploaded. It continues to upload, even if the Galaxy Tab falls asleep.

To view your video, open the YouTube app. It's found on the main Home screen or, as always, on the Applications screen. Press the Menu soft button and choose the My Account command. If you don't see your recently uploaded video in the My Videos list, choose the command View All My Videos and you'll find it there.

You can share your video by long-pressing it in the My Videos list. Choose a sharing method from the list, such as email or a text message, and you can share the YouTube video link with all your friends in the world.

✔ YouTube often takes awhile to process a video after it's uploaded. Allow a few minutes to pass (longer for larger videos) before the video becomes available for viewing.

✔ *Upload* is the official term to describe sending a file from the Galaxy Tab to the Internet.

✔ See Chapter 16 for more information on using YouTube.

15

The Galaxy Is Alive with the Sound of Music

In This Chapter

▶ Finding music on the Galaxy Tab

▶ Enjoying a tune

▶ Turning the Tab into a deejay

▶ Transferring music from your computer to the Tab

▶ Buying music online

▶ Organizing your tunes into a playlist

▶ Listening to streaming music

Going along with the one-less-thing-to-carry school of thought, the Galaxy Tab saves you the drudgery of having to lug around an MP3 player. The MP3 player is the digital version of the old, portable cassette player, popularized by the Sony Walkman. And the Sony Walkman came around because people experienced too many back injuries from carrying around gramophones. So be thankful that you can employ the Galaxy Tab as your primary, portable music-playing gizmo.

Your Hit Parade

I'll bet you didn't know that your Galaxy Tab is eager to entertain you. For music, you'll probably want a nice pair of earphones or a headset. Oh, and it helps to use the Music Player app, as covered in this section.

Browsing your music library

The music-playing duties of your Galaxy Tab are deftly handled by an app named Music Player. The app can be found on the Applications screen, or you may find a copy adorning one of the Home screen panels.

After you start the Music Player, you see a screen similar to Figure 15-1. You may not see any music on your Galaxy Tab just yet. That's okay; the later section "Put Some Music in Your Life" explains how to add music.

Music in the library

Categories for presenting your music

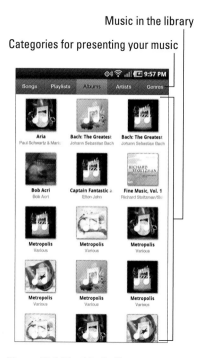

Figure 15-1: The Music library.

The music stored on your Galaxy Tab is presented in the Music Player app by category. Figure 15-1 shows the Albums category. Here are all five categories:

Songs: All music (songs and audio), listed individually in alphabetical order.

Playlists: Music you've organized into playlists that you create. Choose a playlist name to view songs organized in that playlist. Included are recently played songs, favorites, and other preset categories.

Albums: Music is organized by album. Choose an album to list its songs.

Artists: Songs are listed by recording artist or group. Choose Artist to see those songs organized by album.

Genres: Audio is organized by categories such as Rock, Vocal, and Classical.

These categories are merely ways the music is organized — ways to make the music easier to find when you may know an artist's name but not an album title. The Genres category is for those times when you're in a mood for a certain type of music but don't know or don't mind who recorded it.

A *playlist* is a list you create yourself to organize songs by favorite, theme, or mood or whatever other characteristic you want. The section "Organize Your Music," later in this chapter, discusses playlists.

- ✔ Music is stored on the Galaxy Tab's MicroSD card.

- ✔ The size of the MicroSD card limits the total amount of music that can be stored on your Tab. Also, consider that storing pictures and videos horns in on some of the space that can be used to store music.

- ✔ Two types of album artwork are used by the Music Player app. For purchased music, the album artwork represents the original album. That may also happen for music copied (imported) from your computer. Otherwise, the Music Player slaps down a generic album cover.

- ✔ There's no easy or obvious way to apply album cover artwork to music with a generic album cover.

- ✔ When the Galaxy Tab can't recognize an artist, it uses the title Unknown Artist. It usually happens with music you copy manually to your Tab, but it can also apply to audio recordings you make yourself. Music you purchase, or import or synchronize with a computer, generally retains its artist and album information. (Well, the information is retained as long as it was supplied on the original source.)

Playing a tune

To listen to music by locating a song in your music library, as described in the preceding section, touch the song title, and the song plays as shown in Figure 15-2.

While the song plays, you're free to do anything else on the Galaxy Tab. In fact, the song continues to play even when the Tab goes to sleep.

After the song is done playing, the next song in the list plays. Touch the Song List button (refer to Figure 15-2) to review the songs in the list; you can even rearrange songs by dragging them in the list.

Figure 15-2: A song is playing.

The next song doesn't play if you have the Shuffle button activated (refer to Figure 15-2). In that case, the Music Player app randomly chooses another song from the list. Who knows which one is next?

The next song also might not play when you have the Repeat option on: The three repeat settings are illustrated in Table 15-1, along with the Shuffle settings. To change settings, simply touch either the Shuffle or Repeat button.

Table 15-1	Shuffle and Repeat Button Icons	
Icon	***Setting***	***What Happens When You Touch the Icon***
	No Shuffle	Songs play one after the other
	Shuffle	Songs are played in random order
	No Repeat	Songs don't repeat
	Single Repeat	The same song plays over and over
	List Repeat	All songs in the list play over and over

To stop the song from playing, touch the Pause button (refer to Figure 15-2).

A notification icon appears while music is playing on the Galaxy Tab, as shown in the margin. To quickly summon the Music Player app and see which song is playing, or to pause the song, pull down the notifications and choose the first item, which is the name of the song that's playing.

- You may not see the screen shown in Figure 15-2 when a song plays. In that case, choose the song again from the list to see the screen.

- The volume can always be set by using the Volume switch on the side of the Galaxy Tab: Up is louder, down is quieter.

- When you're browsing your music library, you may see a blue Play icon, similar to the one shown in the margin. This icon flags any song that's playing or paused.

- While browsing the music library, you also see the currently playing song displayed at the bottom of the screen, along with the Rewind, Pause/Play, and Next controls.

- Determining which song plays next depends on how you chose the song that's playing. If you choose a song by artist, all songs from that artist play, one after the other. When you choose a song by album, that album plays. Choosing a song from the entire song list causes all songs in the Music Player's library to play.

🖝 To choose which songs play after each other, create a playlist. See the section "Organize Your Music," later in this chapter.

🖝 After the last song in the list plays, the Music Player app stops playing songs — unless you have the List Repeat option set, in which case the list plays again.

🖝 You can use the Galaxy Tab's search abilities to help locate tunes in your music library. You can search by artist name, song title, or album. The key is to press the Search soft button when you're using the Music Player app. Type all or part of the text you're searching for and touch the Search button on the onscreen keyboard. Choose the song you want to hear from the list that's displayed.

Being the life of the party

You need to do four things to make your Galaxy Tab the soul of your next shindig or soirée:

🖝 Connect it to a stereo.

🖝 Use the Shuffle command.

🖝 Set the Repeat command.

🖝 Provide plenty of drinks and snacks.

Hook the Galaxy Tab into any stereo that has a standard line input. You need, on one end, an audio cable that has a mini-headphone jack and, on the other end, an audio input that matches your stereo. Look for such a cable at Radio Shack or any stereo store.

After your Tab is connected, start the Music Player app and choose the party playlist you've created. If you want the songs to play in random order, touch the Shuffle button.

You might also consider choosing the List Repeat command (see Table 15-1) so that all songs in the playlist repeat.

To play all songs saved on your Galaxy Tab, choose the Songs category and touch the first song in the list.

Enjoy your party, and please drink responsibly.

Put Some Music in Your Life

Odds are good that your Galaxy Tab came with no music preinstalled. It might have: Some cellular providers may have preinstalled a smattering of tunes, which merely lets you know how out of touch they are musically. Regardless, you can add music to your Galaxy Tab in a number of ways, as covered in this section.

Borrowing music from your computer

Your computer is the equivalent of the 20th century stereo system — a combination tuner, amplifier, and turntable, plus all your records and CDs. If you've already copied your music collection to your computer, or if you use your computer as your main music storage system, you can share that music with your Galaxy Tab.

Many music-playing, or jukebox, programs are available. On Windows, the most common program is Windows Media Player. You can use this program to synchronize music between your PC and the Galaxy Tab. Here's how it works:

1. **Connect the Galaxy Tab to your PC.**

   Use the USB cable that comes with the Tab.

 2. **If necessary, pull down the USB notification.**

   The Galaxy Tab may automatically display the USB Connected screen. If not, pull down the notifications and choose USB Connected.

3. **Touch the Mount button.**

4. **Touch OK.**

   An AutoPlay dialog box appears in Windows, prompting you to choose how best to mount the Galaxy Tab into the Windows storage system.

5. **Close the AutoPlay dialog box.**

6. **Start Windows Media Player.**

7. **Click the Sync tab or Sync toolbar button.**

   The Galaxy Tab appears in the Sync list on the right side of the Windows Media Player, as shown in Figure 15-3.

8. **Drag to the Sync Area the music you want to transfer to your Tab (refer to Figure 15-3).**

Sync tab

Music on your PC   Start sync   Galaxy Tab

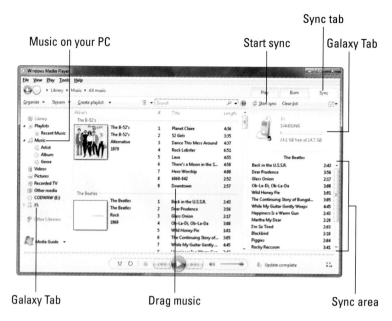

Galaxy Tab   Drag music   Sync area

Figure 15-3: Windows Media Player meets Galaxy Tab.

9. **Click the Start Sync button to transfer the music from your PC to the Galaxy Tab.**

   The Sync button may be located atop the list, as shown in Figure 15-3, or it might be found on the bottom.

10. **Close the Windows Media Player when you're done transferring music.**

    Or, you can keep it open — whatever.

11. **On your Galaxy Tab, touch the Turn Off button.**

    You may need to wake up and unlock the Tab, if it has snoozed while the music was being transferred.

12. **Unplug the USB cable.**

    Or, you can leave the Tab plugged in.

When you have a Macintosh, or you detest Windows Media Player, you can use the doubleTwist program to synchronize music between your Galaxy Tab and your computer. Refer to the section about synchronizing with doubleTwist in Chapter 19 for more information.

✔ Chapter 19 not only contains information about making the USB connection between the Galaxy Tab and your computer but also offers instructions on synchronizing files and information other than music.

✔ You must mount the Galaxy Tab — specifically, its MicroSD card — into your computer's storage system before you can synchronize music.

✔ The Galaxy Tab can store only so much music! Don't be overzealous when copying your tunes. In Windows Media Player (refer to Figure 15-3), a capacity thermometer-thing shows you how much storage space is used and how much is available on your Tab. Pay heed to the indicator!

✔ Windows Media Player complains when you try to sync the Galaxy Tab to more than one PC. If you do, you're warned after Step 6 in this section. It's not a big issue: Just inform Windows Media Player that you intend to sync with the computer for only this session.

✔ You cannot use iTunes to synchronize music with the Galaxy Tab.

✔ Okay, I lied in the preceding point: You *can* synchronize music using iTunes but only when you install the *iTunes Agent* program on your PC. You then need to configure the iTunes Agent program to use your Galaxy Tab with iTunes. After you do that, iTunes recognizes the Galaxy Tab and lets you synchronize your music. Yes, it's technical; hence the icon in the margin.

✔ When the USB connection is on and the Galaxy Tab's MicroSD card is mounted into the computer's storage system, you cannot access certain information stored on your Tab: You cannot play music, look at photos, or access contacts while the MicroSD card is mounted.

Getting music from your cellular provider

Another way to get music is to buy it, and your Galaxy Tab's cellular service provider is more than happy to comply! Most likely, your Tab came with preinstalled music-buying software. You can use this software to browse for music and to purchase and download those tunes right into your Tab.

I don't have all the apps from all the cellular providers, so I can't be specific about how they work or what's good or evil in any particular app. Basically, you start the app, browse for music, and preview songs and then download them for the prices listed. Ho-hum.

✔ The music-buying service provided on the Verizon Galaxy Tab is Rhapsody, also known as V CAST Music.

✔ Your Sprint Galaxy Tab probably has access to the Sprint Music Store.

✔ On T-Mobile, the music-purchasing service is Dash, which works with Yahoo! Music.

✔ AT&T Tabs can take advantage of AT&T Mobile Music.

Buying music at the Amazon MP3 store

A more specific solution for buying music for the Galaxy Tab is to use the Amazon MP3 store. It's a universal approach, which works on just about every Android device, including the Galaxy Tab.

The best way to use the Amazon MP3 store is to have an Amazon account. If you don't have one set up, use your computer to visit www.amazon.com and create one. You also need to keep a credit card on file for the account, which makes purchasing music with the Galaxy Tab work O so well.

You also need to download the Amazon MP3 app for your Tab. Scan the barcode in the margin, and refer to Chapter 17 for information on obtaining new apps.

Follow these steps to buy music from the Amazon MP3 store:

1. **Start the Amazon MP3 app.**

   The Amazon MP3 app connects you with the online Amazon music store, where you can search or browse for tunes to preview and purchase for your Galaxy Tab.

2. **Touch the Search button to begin your music quest.**

   Or, you can browse the top-selling songs and albums or browse by genre.

3. **Type some search words, such as an album name, a song title, or an artist name.**

   You can also dictate the search text. See Chapter 4 for more dictation information.

   Your search results appear, if any matches are found, as shown in Figure 15-4.

4. **Touch a result.**

   If the result is an album, you see the contents of the album. Otherwise, a brief audio preview plays.

   When the result is an album, choose a song from the album to hear the preview.

   Touch the song again to stop the preview.

5. **To purchase the song, touch the big, orange button with the amount in it.**

   For example, the big, orange button at the top of the list (refer to Figure 15-4) specifies $16.99.

   Touching the button changes the price into the word *BUY*.

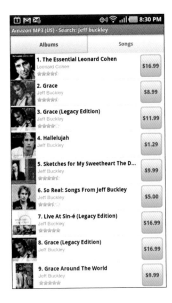

Figure 15-4: Songs found at the Amazon MP3 store.

6. **Touch the word** *BUY.*

7. **If necessary, you may need to accept the license agreement.**

   This step happens the first time you buy something from the Amazon MP3 store.

8. **Log in to your Amazon.com account: Type your account name or email address and password.**

   Your purchase is registered, account authorized, and download started. If not, touch the Retry button to try again.

9. **Wait while the music downloads.**

   Well, actually, you don't have to wait: The music continues to download while you do other things with your Galaxy Tab.

No notification icon appears when the song or album has finished downloading. The MP3 Store downloading icon, however, vanishes from the notification part of the screen. That's your clue that the new music is in the Tab and ready for your ears.

✔ Amazon emails you a bill for your purchase. That's your purchase record, so I advise you to be a good accountant and print it and then input it into your bookkeeping program or personal finance program at once!

✓ You can review your Amazon MP3 store purchases by pressing the Menu soft button in the Amazon MP3 app and choosing the Downloads command.

✓ If possible, try to use Wi-Fi when downloading your purchased music. That way, you don't rack up digital cellular fees.

Organize Your Music

The Music Player app categorizes your music by album, artist, song, and so forth, but unless you have only one album and enjoy all the songs on it, that situation probably won't do. To better organize your music, you can create *playlists*. That way, you can hear the music you want to hear, in the order you want, for whatever mood hits you.

Reviewing your playlists

Any playlists you've already created, or that have been preset on the Tab, appear under the Playlists heading on the Music Player app's main screen. Touching the Playlists heading displays playlists, similar to the ones shown in Figure 15-5.

To see which songs are in a playlist, touch the playlist name. To play the songs in the playlist, touch the first song in the list.

A playlist is a helpful way to organize music when a song's information may not have been completely imported into the Galaxy Tab. For example, if you're like me, you probably have a lot of songs labeled Unknown. A quick way to remedy that situation is to name a playlist after the artist and then add those unknown songs to the playlist. The next section describes how it's done.

Creating your own playlists

Making a new playlist is easy, and adding songs to the playlist is even easier. Follow these steps:

1. **Choose the Playlist heading in the Music Player app.**

   You see a screen similar to Figure 15-5.

2. **Press the Menu soft button and choose the command New Playlist.**

3. **Type a name for your playlist.**

   Short and descriptive names are best.

Preset playlists   Song that's playing now

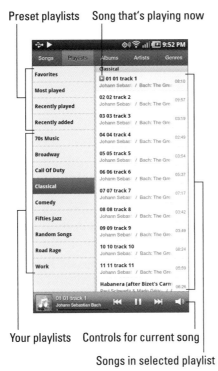

Your playlists   Controls for current song

Songs in selected playlist

Figure 15-5: Playlists in the Music Player app.

4. Touch the Done button to create the playlist.

The playlist is empty, so the next step is to add songs. Preferably, you'll add songs that match the theme or mood of the playlist you're trying to create.

5. Touch the Add Music button.

The list of songs stored on your Galaxy Tab is displayed. You can choose albums or artists or another heading to select music from those categories, which might be easier than plowing through a long Songs list.

6. Touch a green check mark to select songs for your playlist.

Select as many as fit the playlist.

7. Touch the Add button.

The songs are placed into the playlist.

You can have as many playlists as you like on the Galaxy Tab and stick as many songs as you like into them. Adding songs to a playlist doesn't noticeably affect the storage capacity of the MicroSD card.

- ✏ You can add songs to a playlist after it's created: Choose the playlist and press the Menu soft button. Choose the Add Music command to choose more music for the playlist.

- ✏ To remove a song from a playlist, open the playlist and long-press the song. Choose the Remove command and then touch the Remove button to confirm.

- ✏ Removing a song from a playlist doesn't delete the song from the Galaxy Tab's music library.

- ✏ Songs in a playlist can be rearranged: While viewing the playlist, press the Menu soft button. Choose More and then Change Order. Use the tab on the far right end of a song title to drag that song up or down in the list.

- ✏ To delete a playlist, long-press its name in the list of playlists. Choose the Delete command. Touch the Delete button to confirm.

Deleting unwanted music

To purge music from your Galaxy, follow these brief, painless steps:

1. **Locate the music that offends you.**

   You can choose any music category except Playlist; deleting music from a playlist doesn't permanently remove it from the Tab. I recommend using the Songs heading.

2. **Long-press the musical entry.**

3. **Choose Delete.**

   A warning message appears.

4. **Touch the Delete button to confirm.**

   The music is gone. La, la, la, la: The music is gone.

The music is deleted permanently from the MicroSD card.

By deleting music, you free up storage space, though you cannot recover any music you delete. If you want the song back, you have to reinstall it, sync it, or buy it again, as described elsewhere in this chapter.

Soap, No Soap, Galaxy Radio

Though they're not broadcast radio stations, some sources on the Internet — *Internet radio* sites — play music. You can listen to this Internet music using the Slacker Personal Radio app that comes with your Galaxy Tab.

Start Slacker from the Applications screen. You need to create an account, if you don't already have one. Otherwise, log in to your account and then peruse the various available stations. From that point on, Slacker works just like listening to a portable radio.

Beyond Slacker, you can get other apps on your Galaxy Tab for listening to music as though the Tab were a radio:

- ✔ Pandora Radio
- ✔ StreamFurious

 Pandora Radio lets you select music based on your mood and customizes, according to your feedback, the tunes you listen to. The app works like the Internet site `www.pandora.com`, in case you're familiar with it.

 StreamFurious streams music from various radio stations on the Internet. Though not as customizable as Pandora, StreamFurious uses less bandwidth.

Both apps are available at the Android Market. They're free, though a paid, pro version of StreamFurious exists.

- ✔ Various apps also available at the Android Market claim to turn your Galaxy Tab into an FM radio. I have nothing specific to recommend, mostly because the good apps aren't free. But keep your eyes peeled for FM radio apps for your Galaxy Tab.

 - ✔ Always listen to Internet radio when your Tab is connected to the Internet via a Wi-Fi connection. Streaming music can use a lot of your cellular data plan's data allotment.

- ✔ See Chapter 17 for more information about the Android Market.

 - ✔ Internet music of the type delivered by Slacker Personal Radio is referred to by the nerds as *streaming music*. That's because the music arrives on your Galaxy Tab as a continuous download from the source. Unlike music you download and save, streaming music is played as it comes in and not stored long-term.

16

What Else Does It Do?

In This Chapter

▶ Waking up to your Galaxy Tab

▶ Keeping your appointments

▶ Scheduling new events

▶ Reading the news

▶ Watching junk on YouTube

▶ Buying or renting films and TV shows

▶ Playing games

*E*very gizmo in your life probably has one purpose. For example, the lawn mower is good at cutting the grass, but terrible at drying your hair. The coffee machine fails utterly at making toast. And you can't iron your clothes with a tuba. That's okay: People accept limitations on a device designed with a specific purpose.

The Galaxy Tab is a gizmo without a specific purpose. It can do many things, its abilities limited only by the apps you get for it. To help you grasp this concept, the Tab comes with a slate of apps preinstalled. They can give you an idea of what the Tab is capable of, or you can simply use those apps to make the Galaxy Tab a more versatile and useful device.

It's an Alarm Clock

Your Galaxy Tab keeps constant, accurate track of the time, which is displayed at the top of the Home screen as well as on the lock screen. The display is lovely and informative, but it can't actually wake you up. To have it do that, you need to somehow choose a specific time and apply a noise to that time. This process turns the Galaxy Tab into an alarm clock.

Turn your music into an alarm

You can easily substitute your own music for the Galaxy Tab's preset selection of dreary, boring, or inappropriate alarm clock melodies. To do so, visit the Music Player app (covered in Chapter 15) and display the list of songs stored on your Tab. Long-press a song and choose the Set As command. Choose Alarm Tone. You instantly switch to the Alarm Clock app, where you can choose an existing alarm to which to assign the music.

This music-assignment trick works only when you've already created one or more alarms for your Galaxy Tab.

Alarm clock duties are handled on the Tab by using the aptly named Alarm Clock app, illustrated in Figure 16-1. You start the Alarm Clock app by choosing it from the Applications screen.

Figure 16-1: The Alarm Clock app.

To set an alarm, follow these steps while using the Alarm Clock app:

1. Touch the Add button (refer to Figure 16-1).

The Set Alarm screen appears.

2. **Choose Time and use the pop-up window to configure the hour and minute and to specify either AM or PM; touch the Set button to set the time.**

3. **Choose Alarm Tone to specify which music plays when the alarm sounds.**

4. **If prompted, choose Android System.**

   You can choose the Silent alarm tone, found at the top of the Alarm Tones list, if you prefer not to have the Tab make noise when the alarm goes off.

5. **Optionally, determine whether the Tab will vibrate when the alarm triggers.**

   Obviously, you want vibration on when you've chosen a silent alarm.

6. **Choose Repeat to set whether the alarm happens once, daily, or on specific days.**

7. **Touch Label to give the alarm a name.**

   Figure 16-1 illustrates several examples of alarm names.

8. **Touch the Done button to create the alarm.**

The alarm you create appears on the Alarm Clock app's screen, similar to the one shown in Figure 16-1.

Any new alarm you create is automatically set — it goes off when the proper time approaches. To disable an alarm, touch the Alarm icon shown in Figure 16-1.

The Galaxy Tab alerts you to set alarms by displaying the Alarm Clock status icon, shown in the margin, in the Tab's status area. The icon indicates that an alarm is set and pending.

Alarms must be set or else they don't trigger. To set an alarm, touch its Alarm icon (refer to Figure 16-1).

- Turning off an alarm doesn't delete the alarm.
- To remove an alarm, long-press it and choose the option Delete Alarm from the menu. Touch the OK button to confirm.
- The alarm doesn't work when you turn off the Galaxy Tab. The alarm does, however, go off when the Tab is sleeping.
- A notification icon appears when an alarm has gone off but has been ignored.

It's a Calendar

Feel free to take out any datebook you have and throw it away. You never need to buy another one again. That's because your Galaxy Tab is the ideal datebook and appointment calendar. Thanks to the Calendar app, and the Google Calendar feature on the Internet, you can manage all your scheduling right on your Galaxy Tab. It's almost cinchy.

> ✔ Google Calendar works with your Google account to keep track of your schedule and appointments. You can visit Google Calendar on the Web at
>
>   calendar.google.com

> ✔ You automatically have a Google Calendar; it comes with your Google account.

> ✔ I recommend that you use the Calendar app on your Galaxy Tab to access Google Calendar. It's a better way to access your schedule than using the Browser app to reach Google Calendar on the Web.

> ✔ Before you throw away your datebook, copy into the Calendar app some future appointments and info, such as birthdays and anniversaries.

Browsing your schedule

To see what's happening next, to peruse upcoming important events, or just to know which day of the month it is, summon the Calendar app. It's found on the Applications screen along with all the other apps that dwell on your Galaxy Tab.

Figure 16-2 shows the monthly view. It looks like a typical calendar, with the month and year at the top. Scheduled appointments and events appear on various days.

To view your appointments by week, touch the Week tab. Or, you can touch the Day command to see your daily schedule. The List tab shows you all your events, one after the other, in a long list.

> ✔ See the later section "Creating a new event" for information on reviewing and creating events.

> ✔ Use Month view to see an overview of what's going on, and use Week or Day view to see your appointments.

> ✔ I check Week view at the start of the week to remind me of what's coming up.

 ✒ Different colors flag your events to represent different calendars, or event categories, to which the events are assigned. See the later section "Creating a new event" for information on calendars.

 ✒ Use your finger to flick the calendar displays left or right to see the next or previous day, week, or month.

Figure 16-2: The Calendar's month view.

Reviewing appointments

To see more detail about an event, touch it. When you're using Month view, touch the date with the event on it and then choose the event from the list at the bottom of the screen.

The amount of detail you see depends on how much information was recorded when the event was created. Some events have only a minimum of information; others may have details, such as a location for the event. When the event's location is listed, you can touch that location and the Maps app pops up to show you where the event is being held.

 ✒ A great way to see all upcoming events is to choose the List tab at the top of the screen (refer to Figure 16-2).

 ✒ Birthdays and a few other events on the calendar may be pulled in from your social networking sites. That probably explains why some events are listed twice; they're pulled in from two sources.

It's not a calculator, but it can be

One app that's missing from the list of prein-stalled apps on the Galaxy Tab is a calculator. Honestly, I'm surprised that the Tab doesn't come with its own calculator app. Even so, you can still get one, though you have to go to the Android Market to pick one up.

 Easy Calculator: I like Easy Calculator because it calculates instantly. It also features parenthe-ses, which make typing complex cal-culations a heck of a lot easier. Add the color scheme and, well, it's a handy little app to have.

 RealCalc Scientific Calculator: The inner nerd in me enjoys using the RealCalc Scientific calculator. Some of its advanced functions would frighten anyone trying to add up how much to pay the babysitter or how to split a dinner tab three ways, but for technical stuff, it does the job well.

One common reason for using a calculator app is to calculate the tip due when dining out. Multiple free tip calculators are available at the Android Market. I have no particular one that I like more than the others; simply search for *tip calculator* at the market and you'll see a bunch of them.

Creating a new event

The key to making the calendar work is to add events: appointments, things to do, meetings, or full-day events such as birthdays or colonoscopies. To create a new event, follow these steps in the Calendar app:

1. **Select the day for the event.**

   Or if you like, you can switch to Day view, where you can touch the starting time for the new event.

2. **Touch the Add New Event button (refer to Figure 16-2).**

   The New Event screen appears. Your job now is to fill in the blanks to create the new event.

   The more information you supply, the more detailed the event, and the more you can do with it on your Galaxy Tab as well as on Google Calendar on the Internet.

3. **Type an event title.**

   Sometimes I simply write the name of the person I'm meeting.

4. **Set the meeting duration using the From and To buttons.**

   Because you followed Step 1, you don't have to set the date (unless the event is longer than a day). Touch the time buttons, if necessary, to adjust when the event starts and stops.

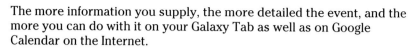

   When the event lasts all day, such as a birthday or your mother-in-law's visit that was supposed to last for an hour, touch the All Day check mark.

   Steps 5 through 7 are optional:

5. **Specify whether the event repeats.**

   Touch the Repeat button to set up a recurring schedule.

6. **Choose a calendar category for the event.**

   Calendars are created on the Google Calendar Web site. You can choose which calendar to assign an event to only by using the Galaxy Tab's Calendar app.

7. **Input a location for the meeting.**

8. **Set whether the event has an Alarm reminder.**

   The Calendar app is configured to automatically set a reminder 15 minutes before an event begins. If you prefer not to have a reminder, touch the Alarm item and choose None as the alarm.

9. **Optionally, enter a note.**

   I create events for each leg on an airplane trip, and in the Note field I type the reservation number. That way, I can refer to my Tab when checking in, in case the airline screws up and I need to recall my reservation.

10. **Touch the Done button to create the new event.**

You can change an event at any time: Simply touch the event to bring up more information and then touch the Edit button.

To remove an event, touch the event to bring up more information and touch the Trash Can icon. Touch the OK button to confirm.

✔ Adding an event location not only tells you where the event will be located but also hooks that information into the Maps app. My advice is to type information into the event's Location field just as though you're typing information to search for in the Maps app. When the event is displayed, the location is a clickable link; touch the Location link to see where it is on a map.

✔ Use the Repetition button to create repeating events, such as weekly or monthly meetings, anniversaries, and birthdays.

✔ Reminders can be set so that the Tab alerts you before an event takes place. The alert can show up as a notification icon (shown in the margin), or it can be an audio alert or a vibrating alert. Pull down the notifications and choose the calendar alert. You can then peruse pending events.

✔ To deal with an event notification, pull down the notifications and choose the event.

✔ You can also create events by using the Google Calendar on the Internet. Those events are instantly synced with the calendar on your Galaxy Tab.

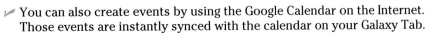

It's Your Newspaper

Newspapers aren't dead; they're merely electronic. Odds are good that the news and weather you read most often comes to you over the Internet in an electronic format. It's perfectly acceptable — cutting edge, in fact — to read your news, sports, and weather on the Galaxy Tab, not on paper. Not only is the news current but reading news on the Tab also negates the frustration of being able to properly fold a newspaper.

The News and Weather app, nestled in the Applications screen, is your daily link to weather and news on the Galaxy Tab.

The Weather tab, shown in Figure 16-3, uses the Tab's GPS abilities to pin-point your local weather. Or, you can change your location by pressing the Menu soft button and choose Settings and then Weather Settings.

Slide to see more categories.

Location information is being used.

Figure 16-3: The News and Weather app.

Tabs to the right of the Weather tab give you Top Stories, U.S., Sports, and Entertainment news.

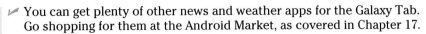

- ✔ You can get plenty of other news and weather apps for the Galaxy Tab. Go shopping for them at the Android Market, as covered in Chapter 17.

- ✔ A great app for sports fans is SportsTap. Use the barcode in the margin to get a copy.

- ✔ In addition to news and weather apps, you can also get news and weather widgets to adorn the Galaxy Tab Home screen. See Chapter 21 for more information on widgets.

It's Your Video Entertainment

It's not possible to watch "real" TV on the Galaxy Tab, but a few apps come close. The YouTube app is handy for watching random, meaningless drivel, which I suppose makes it a lot like TV. And then there's Media Hub, which lets you buy and rent real movies and TV shows.

Enjoying YouTube

YouTube is the Internet phenomenon that proves that real life is indeed too boring and random for television. Or is that the other way around? Regardless, you can view the latest videos on YouTube — or contribute your own — by using the YouTube app on your Galaxy Tab. The main YouTube screen is depicted in Figure 16-4.

To view a video, touch its name or icon in the list.

To search for a video, touch the Search button (refer to Figure 16-4). Type or dictate what you want to search for and then peruse the results.

Videos in the YouTube app play in Landscape mode, so tilt your Galaxy Tab to the left to see videos in their proper orientations. The videos take up the entire screen; touch the screen to see the onscreen video controls.

Press the Back soft button to return to the main YouTube app after watching a video or if you tire of a video and need to return to the main screen out of boredom.

- ✔ Use the YouTube app to view YouTube videos, rather than use the Browser app to visit the YouTube Web site.

- ✔ Because you have a Google account, you also have a YouTube account. I recommend that you log in to your YouTube account when using YouTube on the Galaxy Tab: Press the Menu soft button and choose the command My Account. Log in, if you haven't already. Otherwise, you see your account information, your videos, and any video subscriptions.

Search for videos

Shoot and upload a new video

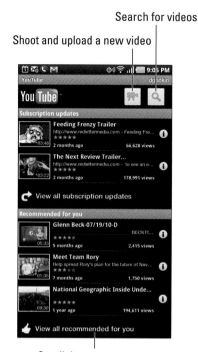

Scroll down to see more.

Figure 16-4: YouTube.

✔ Not all YouTube videos are available for viewing on mobile devices.

✔ You can touch the Record & Upload button (refer to Figure 16-4) to shoot and then immediately send a video to YouTube. Refer to Chapter 13 for information on recording video with your Galaxy Tab.

Buying and renting movies

Two apps that come on the Galaxy Tab allow you to buy or rent films and television shows. They're Media Hub and Blockbuster.

The Media Hub app allows you to buy popular films and television shows, which you can then view on your Galaxy Tab. The TV shows are for purchase, but the films can be either rented or purchased.

The Blockbuster app allows you to rent or purchase mainstream movies to view on the Galaxy Tab. The key is to have an account at Blockbuster. When you do, you can follow the directions on the screen after starting the Blockbuster app and get everything signed up and configured.

It's Your Game Machine

One of the best ways to put expensive, high-tech gizmos to work is to play games. Don't even sweat the thought that you have too much "business" or "work" or other important stuff you can do on a Galaxy Tab. The more advanced the mind, the more the need for play, right? So indulge yourself.

Two sample games come with the Galaxy Tab: Let's Golf, the golfing simulation game shown in Figure 16-5, and N.O.V.A, a first-person shooter game.

Figure 16-5: A sample game on the Galaxy Tab.

Both apps are teasers; neither is the full version of the game. You get just enough to whet your appetite. To get a full version, you have to pay for an upgrade, which each app happily and repeatedly reminds you to do.

Beyond the prepackaged apps is an entire universe of games, available at the Android Market.

See Chapter 17 for information on using the Android Market.

I have a few game suggestions listed in Chapter 25.

17

A Galaxy of Apps

In This Chapter

▶ Shopping at the Android Market

▶ Downloading a free app

▶ Buying an app

▶ Updating your apps

▶ Removing an app

▶ Moving an app to the SD Card

▶ Working with the Task Manager

Your Galaxy Tab is nothing without apps. A whole clutch of apps were preinstalled by Samsung, and probably another few apps were installed by the cellular service. Beyond that, you can add more apps to your Tab, which extends the list of things you can do in the mobile universe. Adding new apps, and managing all your Tab's apps, is the topic of this chapter.

aghetti Marshmallows
Fruxotic Games

 Thumbplay Music
Thumbplay Inc.

 How the Grinch Stole Christmas
Oceanhouse Media, Inc.

 NinJump
Backflip Studios Inc.

Winamp
soft, Inc.

Behold the Android Market

Everyone loves to shop when they're buying something they want, or when they're spending someone else's money. You can go shopping for your Galaxy Tab, and I'm not talking about going back to your local Phone Store to buy overpriced accessories. I'm talking about software, programs, applications — or just plain old apps.

The Android Market may sound like the place where you can go buy an R2-D2 or a Robby the Robot. Instead, it's an online place where you go to pick up new apps for your Galaxy Tab. You can browse, you can get free apps, or you can pay. It all happens at the Android Market.

✔ *App* is short for application. It's a program, or software, you can add to your Galaxy Tab to make it do new, wondrous, or useful things.

✔ Because the Galaxy Tab uses the Android operating system, it can run nearly all applications written for Android.

✔ You can be assured that all apps that appear in the Android Market can be used with the Galaxy Tab. There's no way to download or buy something that's incompatible with your Tab.

✔ You obtain software from the Android Market by *downloading* it into your Galaxy Tab. That file transfer works best at top speeds; therefore:

✔ I highly recommend that you connect to a Wi-Fi network if you plan to purchase software at the Android Market. See Chapter 18 for details on connecting the Galaxy Tab to a Wi-Fi network.

Visiting the Market

You access the Android Market by opening the Market app, found on the Applications screen. After opening the Market app, you see the main screen, similar to the one shown in Figure 17-1. You can browse for apps or games or for special apps from your cellular provider, by touching the appropriate doodad, as shown in the figure.

Figure 17-1: The Android Market.

Find apps by browsing the lists: Choose Apps (refer to Figure 17-1). Then choose a specific category to browse. You can view apps by their price (paid or free) or find those that are "just in."

When you know an app's name or an app's category or even what the app does, searching for the app works fastest: Touch the Search button at the top of the Market screen (refer to Figure 17-1). Type all or part of the app's name or perhaps a description. Touch the Search button (the Magnifying Glass icon, to the right of the Search Android Market text box) to begin your search.

To see more information about an app, touch it. Touching the app doesn't buy it, but instead displays a more detailed description, screen shots, and comments, plus links to see additional apps or contact the developer.

Return to the main Android Market screen at any time by pressing the Menu soft button and choosing the Home command.

- ✒ The first time you enter the Android Market, you have to accept the terms of service: Touch the Accept button.

- ✒ Pay attention to an app's ratings. Ratings are added by people who use the apps, like you and me. Having more stars is better. You can see additional information, including individual user reviews, by choosing the app.

- ✒ In addition to getting apps, you can download widgets for the Home screen as well as wallpapers for the Galaxy Tab. Just search the Android Market for *widget* or *live wallpaper*.

- ✒ See Chapter 21 for more information on widgets and live wallpapers.

Getting a free app

After you locate an app you want, the next step is to download it. Follow these steps:

1. **If possible, activate the Wi-Fi connection.**

   Downloads may complete much faster over the Wi-Fi connection than when using the digital cellular connection. Also, you don't incur any data usage charges when using Wi-Fi. See Chapter 18 for information on connecting to a Wi-Fi network.

2. **Open the Market app.**

3. **Locate the app you want and open its description.**

   Refer to the preceding section for details. Notice that many apps are free, especially those from your cellular provider.

4. **Touch the Free button.**

   The Free button is at the top of the screen, beneath the word *Install*.

5. **Touch the OK button to begin the download.**

   You return to the main Market screen as the app downloads. It continues to download while you do other things on your Galaxy Tab.

   After the download is successful, the status bar shows a new icon, as shown in the margin. That's the Successful Install notification.

6. **Pull down the notifications.**

   See Chapter 3 for details, in case you've never pulled down notifications.

7. **Choose the app from the list of notifications.**

   The app is listed by its app name, with the text `Successfully Installed` beneath it.

At this point, what happens next depends on the app you've downloaded. For example, you may have to agree to a license agreement. If so, touch the I Agree button. Additional setup may involve signing in to an account or creating a profile, for example.

After the initial setup is complete, or if no setup is necessary, you can start using the app.

- The new app's icon can be found on the Applications screen, along with all the other apps on your Galaxy Tab.

- Newly installed apps are placed at the end of the Applications screen, on the last (far right) panel. When the last panel is full, a new panel is added and new apps are placed on that new panel.

- You can also place a shortcut icon for the app on the Home screen. See Chapter 21.

- The Android Market has many wonderful apps you can download. Chapter 25 lists some that I recommend, all of which are free.

Buying an app

Some great free apps are available, but many of the apps you dearly want probably cost money. It's not a lot of money, especially compared to the price of computer software. In fact, it seems odd to sit and stew over whether paying 99 cents for a game is "worth it."

I recommend that you download a free app first, to familiarize yourself with the process.

When you're ready to pay for an app, follow these steps:

1. **Activate the Galaxy Tab's Wi-Fi connection.**

2. **Open the Market app.**

3. **Browse or search for the app you want, and choose the app to display its description.**

   Review the app's price. It's priced in dollars, or whatever the local currency happens to be. Apps sold in a foreign currency show an approximate cost, as illustrated in Figure 17-1.

4. **Touch the button that lists the app's cost.**

   For example, the button may show US$0.99 as the cost. The button is found beneath the word *Buy*.

5. **Touch OK.**

   If you don't have a Google Checkout account, you're prompted to set one up. Follow the directions on the screen.

6. **Choose the payment method.**

   You can choose to use an existing credit card, add a new card, or — most conveniently — add the purchase to your cellular bill.

   If you choose to add a new card, you're required to fill in all information about the card, including the billing address.

7. **Touch the Buy Now button.**

   The Buy Now button has the app's price listed.

   After you touch the Buy button, the app is downloaded. You can wait or do something else with the Tab while the app is downloading.

The app may require additional setup steps, confirmation information, or other options.

The app can be accessed from the Applications screen, just like all other apps on your Galaxy Tab.

Eventually, you receive an email message from Google Checkout, confirming your purchase. The message explains how you can get a refund from your purchase within 24 hours. The section "Removing apps," later in this chapter, discusses how it's done.

App Management for Normal People

There's more to your Galaxy Tab apps than just running them. Beyond getting and installing new apps, you're occasionally asked to install an update. Or, maybe you want to remove an app. If so, keep reading.

Reviewing installed apps

To peruse the apps you've installed on your Galaxy Tab, follow these steps:

1. **Start the Market app.**
2. **Press the Menu soft button.**
3. **Choose My Apps.**
4. **Scroll your downloaded apps.**

The list of downloaded apps should look similar to the one shown in Figure 17-2. Instantly, you can see any apps that are in need of a manual update, as shown in the figure.

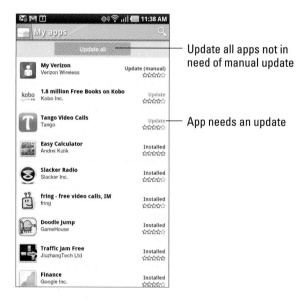

Figure 17-2: Downloaded apps.

Touch an app to see the app's information screen (see Figure 17-3, later in this chapter). On that screen, you can read more about the app, open the app, uninstall the app, or configure automatic updating options. Later sections in this chapter describe the details.

- The list of installed apps shows all the apps you've downloaded on your Galaxy Tab.

- Some apps on the My Apps screen might not be installed on your Galaxy Tab. For example, they could have been downloaded and then removed. They remain in the list because you did, at one time, download the app.

✔ You may also see apps in the list that you have purchased or down-loaded for other Android devices you might own. Look for those apps at the bottom of the list.

✔ To install on your Galaxy Tab an app you've previously purchased or downloaded for another Android device, choose the app from the My Apps list and touch the Purchase or Install button.

✔ Older versions of the Market app use the Downloads command instead of My Apps in Step 3.

Updating your apps

One nice thing about using the Android Market to get apps is that the market also notifies you of new versions of those programs that are available: You see the Updates Available notification icon, shown in the margin.

Locate apps that need updating by pulling down the notifications and choosing Updates Available. Or, you can visit the My Apps list, as described in the preceding section.

When several apps require updating, you see an Update All button. Touch that button, and all apps in the list that need updating are updated, one after the other. (Apps that require manual updating need to be updated one at a time.)

To update individual apps, or apps that require manual updating, follow these steps:

1. **Open the Market app.**

2. **Press the Menu soft button and choose My Apps.**

3. **Choose the app that needs to be updated.**

   In Figure 17-2, the My Verizon app requires a manual update, but the Kobo and Tango apps can be updated all at once:

4a. **When multiple apps need updating, touch the Update All button.**

4b. **When only one app needs updating, or for a manual update, choose that app and then touch the Update button; touch the OK button that replaces the Update button.**

5. **Touch the OK button in the warning dialog box to continue.**

   The app update is downloaded.

As when you initially install the app, you're free to do other things while your Galaxy Tab apps are being updated.

When downloading is complete, the Successful Install notification appears, as shown in the margin. When updating multiple apps, you see multiple Successful Install notification icons. Choose each notification to run the updated app, or touch the Clear button on the notifications panel to dismiss all Successful Install notifications.

- ✓ Just as when you first installed some apps, you may be prompted to agree (again) to the app's terms of services or licensing agreement, or you may be required to sign in to your account.

- ✓ Some apps update themselves automatically. Refer to the next section.

- ✓ When updating an app, the app is completely replaced by a new version. The original settings are retained, but an entirely new app is downloaded and installed.

- ✓ The Android operating system itself gets updated every so often. When an update is available, you see a message appear. You can choose to install the update now or later. I recommend installing all Android operating system updates as soon as you receive the notification.

Configuring automatic updating

Most of the time, you'll probably accept all updates offered by the Android Market. Rather than review the notifications every time, you can configure an app to be updated automatically. Here's how:

1. **Start the Market app.**

 2. **Press the Menu soft button and choose the My Apps command.**

3. **Touch the app you want to configure.**

    The app's information screen appears.

4. **Touch the box by Allow Automatic Updating.**

    The box shows a green check mark when automatic updating is enabled, as shown in Figure 17-3.

5. **Press the Back soft button to return to the My Apps list, where you can configure automatic updating for other apps.**

Some apps require manual updating. It says so right beneath the Allow Automatic Updating prompt (refer to Figure 17-3). For example, on my Galaxy Tab, the My Verizon app requires manual updating.

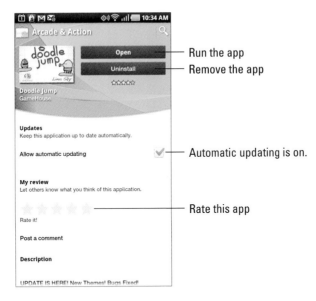

Run the app
Remove the app
Automatic updating is on.
Rate this app

Figure 17-3: An app's info screen.

Uninstalling an update

Occasionally, you can uninstall an update. That might happen when you notice that the new version of an app doesn't seem to work right or you dislike the changes or improvements that come with the new version.

To uninstall an update, display the app's info screen (see Figure 17-3) and look for the Uninstall Updates button near the top part of the screen. Touch the Uninstall Updates button to remove the app's most recent update.

- Removing an app's updates sometimes removes the app itself.
- Not every app has the Uninstall Updates button available.

Removing apps

I can think of a few reasons to remove an app. It's with eager relish that I remove apps that don't work or somehow annoy me. It's also perfectly okay to remove redundant apps, such as when you may have multiple eBook readers that you don't use. Finally, removing apps frees up a modicum of storage in the Galaxy Tab's internal storage area or the MicroSD card.

Whatever the reason, remove an app by following these directions:

1. **Start the Market app.**

2. **Press the Menu soft button.**

3. **Choose the My Apps command.**

4. **Touch the app that offends you.**

5. **Touch the Uninstall button.**

6. **Touch the OK button to confirm.**

   The app is uninstalled.

7. **Fill in the survey to specify why you removed the app.**

   Be honest, or be as honest as you can, given the short list of reasons.

8. **Touch OK.**

   The app is gone!

The app continues to appear on the My Apps list even after it's been removed. After all, you downloaded it once. That doesn't mean the app is installed on your Galaxy Tab — merely that at one time you had it installed.

 ✔ In most cases, if you uninstall a paid app before 24 hours has passed, your credit card or account is fully refunded.

 ✔ You can always reinstall paid apps that you've uninstalled. You aren't charged twice for doing so.

 ✔ You cannot remove apps that are preinstalled on the Tab, by either Samsung or your cellular service provider. I'm sure there's probably a technical way to uninstall the apps, but seriously: Just don't use the apps if you want to remove them and discover that you can't.

App Management for Nerds

There are some areas beyond where the mere mortal Galaxy Tab user would dare tread. Trust me, you can safely use your Galaxy Tab, install and manage your apps, without having to read this section. Still, you may be one of those few readers who finds this information useful.

Moving an app

Beyond the My Apps list in the Market app lies a more technical place you can visit to monitor all apps on the Galaxy Tab, as well as control a few more esoteric aspects of your apps. It's the Manage Applications screen, shown in Figure 17-4.

Apps that are running now   All installed apps

Apps you've installed   Apps installed on MicroSD card

Figure 17-4: The Manage Applications screen.

To get to the Manage Applications screen, heed these directions:

1. **At the Home screen, touch the Menu soft button.**

2. **Choose Settings.**

3. **Choose Applications.**

4. **Choose Manage Applications.**

   You see a screen similar to the one shown in Figure 17-4.

5. **Touch an application to see its Application Info screen.**

   The Application Info screen is shown in Figure 17-5.

App name and version

Stop app

Remove app

Move app

Trivia

Figure 17-5: The Application Info screen.

6. Press the Back soft button to return to the Manage Applications screen.

Or, you can press the Home soft button to go directly to the Home screen.

One of the more popular things you can do at the Application Info screen is move an app from the Galaxy Tab's internal storage area to the MicroSD card: Touch the Move to SD Card button. The app is moved.

Conversely, you can move an app back to the Galaxy Tab's main storage area by touching the Move to Device button, which replaces the Move to SD Card button (shown in Figure 17-5) for apps already installed on the MicroSD card.

Touch the Uninstall button on the Application Info screen to uninstall an app, similar to the steps described in the section "Removing apps," earlier in this chapter. This technique works for those rare Android apps that don't appear on the My Apps list.

The Force Stop button is used to halt a program that runs amok. For example, I had to stop an older Android app that continually made noise and offered no option to exit. It was a relieving experience. See Chapter 22 for more details on shutting down apps run amok.

✏ Refer to the information in the Storage section (see Figure 17-5) to determine how much space the app is using in the Galaxy Tab's internal storage area or MicroSD card.

✏ When an app is consuming a huge amount of space compared with other apps and you seldom use the app, consider it a candidate for deletion.

✏ Some apps automatically install themselves on the MicroSD card. You can determine which apps are installed there by touching the On SD Card tab in the Manage Applications window (see Figure 17-4).

✏ Moving an app is a hot topic on the various Android support forums on the Internet. I feel that you should keep apps in the Galaxy Tab's main storage area as much as possible. One reason:

✏ If an app is placed on the MicroSD card, mounting the MicroSD card to your computer's storage system removes that app's shortcut from the Home screen. Refer to Chapter 19 for information on mounting the MicroSD card on your computer's storage system. See Chapter 21 for information on Home screen shortcuts.

Using the Task Manager

It's possible to view all apps running on the Galaxy Tab — even the apps used by the Android operating system — by touching the Running tab in the Manage Applications window (refer to Figure 17-4). A better, and not so technical way, is to use the Task Manager.

To start the Task Manager, touch its icon, found on the Applications screen. You see the Task Manager screen, shown in Figure 17-6. The Active Applications tab lists all (if any) apps you've started.

Running apps   Odd trivia

Uninstall apps   Battery tips

Active applications: 4   End all — Kill off all apps

Kindle
RAM: 13.20MB, CPU: 0.00%   End

Facebook
RAM: 11.40MB, CPU: 0.00%   End — Quit this app

Email
RAM: 15.18MB, CPU: 0.00%   End

Gallery
RAM: 7.46MB, CPU: 0.00%   End

Figure 17-6: Task Manager.

To end an app, touch the End button. Or, to end all apps you've started, touch the End All button.

- The only time I've ended an app as described in this section is when the app kept popping up notifications and I saw no other way to quit the app.

- You can force-close stubborn apps that may not appear on the Task Manager's Active Applications list. Refer to the preceding section, "Moving an app," about using the Force Stop button.

- A few apps include either an Exit or Sign Out command, though you can always stop them by using the End button, as described in this section.

- You can also start the Task Manager by touching the Task Manager button, displayed at the bottom of the Recently Used Apps window. Press and hold the Home soft button to see the Recently Used Apps window. See Chapter 3 for information on this window.

Customizing the Applications screen

It's probably a safe thing to leave the Applications screen alone: New apps are installed at the end of the list, and new panels appear as you need them. I'm okay with that. If you find yourself frustrated with that situation and you prefer a more organized method of keeping your apps, you can freely mess with and rearrange the app icons on the Applications screen.

To modify the Applications screen, heed these steps:

1. **Touch the Applications button on the Home screen to summon forth the Applications screen.**

2. **Press the Menu soft button.**

3. **Choose the Edit command.**

   You may not notice anything on the first few panels. That's because they contain built-in apps that cannot be removed. But if you look at a panel that contains apps you've installed, you see something like Figure 17-7.

Preinstalled apps cannot be removed.

New panel is added.

Long-press to move the app.

Delete app

Figure 17-7: Changing the Applications screen.

4. **Long-press an app to move it.**

   You feel a slight vibration after you've long-pressed the app. It's a tactile clue that you can drag the app around, shuffling its position with another app or dragging it to another panel.

5. **Touch the Red Circle icon to delete an app; touch the OK button to confirm.**

   Deleting an app is the same thing as uninstalling it.

6. **To save your changes, touch the Home button.**

   You can also press the Menu soft button and choose the Save command.

When you enter the Applications screen editing mode, an extra panel appears, as shown in Figure 17-7. You can drag an app to that new panel, in which case another new panel is added.

You can move preinstalled apps the same way you move apps you've installed yourself.

If you make a boo-boo while moving app icons around, press the Menu soft button and choose the Cancel command. Touch the OK button, and any icons you've moved are restored to their original locations.

Choosing the Cancel command doesn't undelete any app icons you've removed (uninstalled).

Deleting an app from the Applications screen uninstalls that app from your Galaxy Tab. It doesn't merely remove it from the Applications screen.

Part IV
A Well-Connected Tab

The 5th Wave

By Rich Tennant

RICHTENNANT

"Frankly, the idea of an entirely wireless future
scares me to death."

In this part . . .

Your Galaxy Tab isn't the only gizmo in the universe, but it could be the loneliest. Even with all its fun and useful apps, the Galaxy Tab needs to communicate to be useful. It wants to talk to something else — a digital dude, a binary buddy. Together, the Galaxy Tab and the other gizmos can exchange information, share resources, or keep things synchronized.

To get your Galaxy Tab to digitally converse, you must connect it to something else. That connection can be wireless or wired, and it can be done in a variety of ways to meet a variety of needs. The specifics of making the connections and of finding what you can do after you're connected are covered in this part of the book.

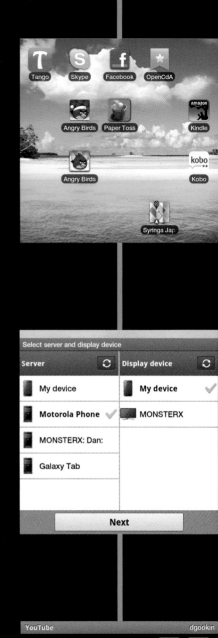

18

It's a Wireless Life

In This Chapter

▷ Using the cellular data network

▷ Accessing a Wi-Fi network

▷ Using the Galaxy Tab as a mobile hotspot

▷ Tethering the Galaxy Tab connection

▷ Using Bluetooth

A great mythology surrounds the concept of what exactly it means to be *portable*. Back in the old days, something was portable when the marketing geniuses bolted on a handle. I remember having a "portable" TV that weighed about 50 pounds, but it had a handle on it, so it was portable. The true measure of portability, in my opinion, isn't a handle, but whether a device is wired to other things.

You couldn't get far with a wired Galaxy Tab. Even if the thing sported a 2,000-foot-long spool extension cord, a wired-only Galaxy Tab would be doomed to failure. Be thankful that your Tab can communicate with the Internet and other gizmos without a wire in site.

Wireless Networking Wizardry

You know that wireless networking has hit the big-time when you see people asking Santa Claus for a wireless router at Christmas. Such a thing would have been unheard of years ago because routers were used primarily for woodworking back then. Today, wireless networking is what keeps gizmos like the Galaxy Tab connected to the Internet.

The primary reason for wireless networking on the Galaxy Tab is to connect to the Internet. For exchanging and synchronizing files, refer to Chapter 19.

Understanding the cellular data network

The Galaxy Tab can connect to the Internet by using the digital cellular network. This signal is the same type used by cell phones and cellular modems to wirelessly connect to the Internet.

Several types of digital cellular networks are available:

4G: The fourth generation of wide-area data network is as much as ten times faster than the 3G network, and is the latest craze in cellular networking. Not every gizmo is capable of 4G network access, nor is the 4G signal available in every location.

3G: The third generation of wide-area data networks is several times faster than the previous generation of data networks. This type of wireless signal is the most popular in the United States.

EDGE: The best of the second generation of cellular technologies allows for wide-area communications with the Internet but is also significantly slower than 3G.

GPRS: This second-generation (2G) network is fine for transmitting data, though it isn't as fast as EDGE.

Your Galaxy Tab always uses the best network available. So, if the 3G network is within reach, that network is used for Internet communications. Otherwise, the 2G (GPRS or EDGE) network is chosen.

A notification icon for the type of network being used appears in the status area, right next to the Signal Strength icon. When digital information is being transmitted, the arrows in the Network icon become animated, indicating that data is being sent or received or both.

✔ Accessing the digital cellular network isn't free. Your Galaxy Tab most likely has some form of subscription plan for a certain quantity of data. When you exceed that quantity, the costs can become prohibitive.

✔ See Chapter 20 for information on how to avoid cellular data overcharges when taking your Galaxy Tab out and about.

✔ A better way to connect your Galaxy Tab to the Internet is to use the Wi-Fi signal, covered in the next section. The digital cellular network signal makes for a great fallback because it's available in more places than Wi-Fi is.

✔ Wi-Fi-only Galaxy Tabs cannot access the digital cellular network.

✔ The Galaxy Tab isn't designed to communicate with 4G networks, though that situation may change in the future.

Activating Wi-Fi

The digital cellular connection is nice, and available pretty much all over, but it will cost you moolah. A better option, and one you should seek out when it's available, is *Wi-Fi,* or the same wireless networking standard used by computers for communicating with each other and the Internet.

To make Wi-Fi work on the Galaxy Tab requires two steps. First, you must activate Wi-Fi, by turning on the Tab's wireless radio. The second step, covered in the following section, is connecting to a specific wireless network.

Follow these carefully written directions to activate Wi-Fi networking on your Galaxy Tab:

1. **On the Home screen, press the Menu soft button.**

2. **Choose Settings.**

3. **Choose Wireless & Network.**

4. **Choose Wi-Fi Settings.**

    The Wi-Fi Settings screen shows up.

5. **Touch the square by Wi-Fi to place a green check mark by that option.**

On the Wi-Fi Settings screen, you may see a list of available wireless networks. Connecting with a specific network is covered in the next section.

From the And-Now-He-Tells-Us Department, you can quickly activate the Tab's Wi-Fi radio by pulling down the notifications and touching the Wi-Fi button in the Quick Actions area, as shown in Figure 18-1. Chapter 3 has more information on the quick-actions feature.

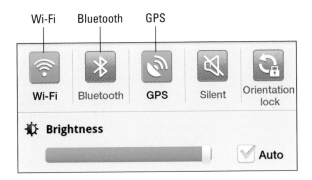

Figure 18-1: Wireless radios in the Quick Actions area.

To turn off Wi-Fi, repeat the steps in this section or touch the Wi-Fi quick-action button on the notification list (refer to Figure 18-1). Turning off Wi-Fi disconnects the Tab from any wireless networks.

- ✔ In some cases, the Wi-Fi connection might be faster than the cellular data connection, but that's not always true.

- ✔ If you place a check mark by the option Network Notification on the Wi-Fi Settings screen, the Tab alerts you to the presence of available Wi-Fi networks whenever you're in range and not connected to a network. This option is a good one to have set when you're frequently on the road. That's because:

- ✔ Using Wi-Fi to connect to the Internet doesn't incur data usage charges.

- ✔ The Galaxy Tab Wi-Fi radio places an extra drain on the battery, but it's truly negligible. If you want to save a modicum of juice, especially if you're out and about and don't plan to be near a Wi-Fi access point for any length of time, turn off the Wi-Fi radio as described in this section.

Connecting to a Wi-Fi network

After you've activated the Galaxy Tab's Wi-Fi radio, you can connect to an available wireless network. Heed these steps:

1. **Press the Menu soft button while viewing the Home screen.**

2. **Choose Settings.**

3. **Choose Wireless & Network.**

4. **Choose Wi-Fi Settings.**

5. **Ensure that Wi-Fi is on.**

   When you see a green check mark next to the Wi-Fi option, Wi-Fi is on.

6. **Choose a wireless network from the list.**

   Available Wi-Fi networks appear at the bottom of the screen, as shown in Figure 18-2. When no wireless networks are listed, you're sort of out of luck regarding wireless access from your current location.

   In Figure 18-2, I chose the Imperial Wambooli network, which is my office network.

7. **Optionally, type the network password.**

   Touch the Password text box to see the onscreen keyboard.

   Touch the Show Password check box so that you can see what you're typing; some of those network passwords can be *long*.

Available Wi-Fi networks

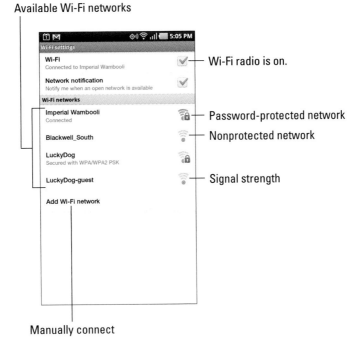

Wi-Fi radio is on.

Password-protected network

Nonprotected network

Signal strength

Manually connect

Figure 18-2: Finding a wireless network.

8. Touch the Connect button.

You should be immediately connected to the network. If not, try the password again.

 When the Galaxy Tab is connected to a wireless network, you see the Wi-Fi status icon, shown in the margin. This icon means that the Tab's Wi-Fi is on and that it's connected and communicating with a Wi-Fi network.

Some wireless networks don't broadcast their names, which adds security but also makes connecting more difficult. In those cases, choose the command Add Wi-Fi Network (refer to Figure 18-2) to manually add the network. You need to input the network name, or *SSID*, and choose the type of security. You also need the password, if one is used. You can obtain this information from the girl with the pink hair who sold you coffee, or from whoever is in charge of the wireless network at your location.

✔ Not every wireless network has a password.

✔ Some public networks are open to anyone, but you have to use the Browser to find a login page that lets you access the network: Simply browse to any page on the Internet and the login page shows up.

✔ The Galaxy Tab automatically remembers every Wi-Fi network it has ever been connected to and automatically reconnects upon finding the same network again.

✔ To disconnect from a Wi-Fi network, simply turn off Wi-Fi. See the preceding section.

✔ Unlike a cellular data network, a Wi-Fi network's broadcast signal goes only so far. My advice is to use Wi-Fi whenever you plan to remain in one location for a while. If you wander too far away, your Tab loses the signal and is disconnected.

A Connection Shared

Your Galaxy Tab has no trouble sniffing out a digital cellular signal, so it can access the Internet just about anywhere. Your laptop might not be so lucky. Because you're already paying for the digital cellular signal, why should you bother getting a second digital cellular modem, or buying into another cellular contract, when you could just use the Galaxy Tab as a portable modem?

Sharing the Galaxy Tab's Internet connection is not only possible but also relatively easy. You can go about sharing in one of two ways: The wireless way is to create a mobile hotspot; the wired way is to use the *tethering* technique. Both methods are covered in this section.

Creating a mobile hotspot

You can direct the Galaxy Tab to share its digital cellular connection with as many as five other wireless gizmos. This process is referred to as *creating a mobile, wireless hotspot,* though no heat or fire is involved.

To set up a mobile hotspot with your Galaxy Tab, heed these steps:

1. **Disable the Galaxy Tab's Wi-Fi radio.**

   You cannot be using a Wi-Fi connection when you create a Wi-Fi hotspot. Actually, the notion is kind of silly: If the Galaxy Tab can get a Wi-Fi signal, then other gizmos can too, so why bother creating a Wi-Fi hotspot in the first place?

2. **If you can, plug in the Galaxy Tab.**

   It's okay if you don't find a power outlet, but running a mobile hotspot draws a lot of power. The Tab's battery power drains quickly if you can't plug in.

3. **From the Applications Tray, open the 3G Mobile Hotspot app.**

4. **Touch the box to place a green check mark by 3G Mobile Hotspot.**

   See Figure 18-3 for the location of the check mark.

Digital cellular signal

Mobile hotspot service | Galaxy Tab is plugged in.

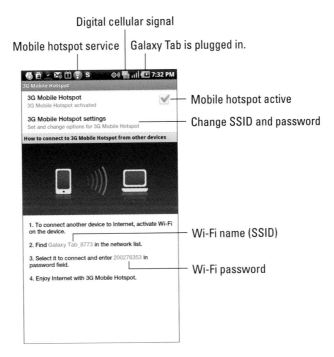

Mobile hotspot active

Change SSID and password

Wi-Fi name (SSID)

Wi-Fi password

Figure 18-3: Configuring a mobile hotspot.

5. **Touch the Continue button in the Attention dialog box.**

6. **Touch the button labeled Turn On Mobile Hotspot.**

   Directions on the screen explain how others can connect to your Galaxy Tab's mobile hotspot, illustrated in Figure 18-3. That's the information you use to connect to the mobile hotspot from another Wi-Fi gizmo — a computer or cell phone.

You can continue to use the Galaxy Tab while it's sharing the digital cellular connection.

 When the 3G hotspot is active, you see the Mobile Hotspot Service status icon appear, as shown in the margin.

To turn off the mobile hotspot, pull down the Mobile Hotspot Service notification and remove the green check mark by 3G Mobile Hotspot (refer to Figure 18-3).

- One of the easiest ways to disable the Wi-Fi radio is to use the quick-actions on the notification panel. Refer to Figure 18-2.

- You can change the mobile hotspot configuration by touching the 3G Mobile Hotspot Settings command (refer to Figure 18-3). On the screen that appears, you can change the Wi-Fi network name (SSID) and set a new password, if you like.

- The range for the mobile hotspot is about 30 feet.

- Some cellular providers may not allow you to create a mobile hotspot and, of course, you cannot create a mobile hotspot when your Galaxy Tab doesn't use the cellular data network.

- Don't forget to turn off the mobile hotspot when you're done using it. Those data rates can certainly add up!

Sharing your Internet via tethering

Another, more personal way to share your Galaxy Tab's digital cellular connection, and to get one more device on the Internet, is *tethering*. This operation is carried out by connecting the Tab to another gizmo, such as a laptop computer, via the USB cable. Then you activate USB tethering, and the other gizmo is suddenly using the Galaxy Tab like a modem.

To set up tethering on your Galaxy Tab, heed these directions:

1. **Turn off the Tab's Wi-Fi radio.**

   You cannot share a connection with the Wi-Fi radio on; you can share only the digital cellular connection.

2. **Connect the Tab to a PC using its USB cable.**

   Specifically, the PC must be running Windows 7 or Windows Vista or another flavor of the Linux operating system.

3. **At the Home screen, press the Menu soft button.**

4. **Choose Settings.**

5. **Choose Wireless and Network.**

6. **Choose Tethering.**

7. **Place a green check mark by the option USB Tethering.**

    The option is disabled when you're using a Wi-Fi connection, which means that you ignored Step 1, or when the Galaxy Tab isn't connected to a PC via the USB cable, which means that you ignored Step 2.

8. **On the PC, choose Public when prompted to specify the type of network you've just connected to.**

Though the Galaxy Tab's digital cellular network is being shared, you see the USB Tethering notification, shown in the margin. You can pull down the notification to turn off tethering: Simply remove the check mark by the USB Tethering option.

    ✔ Sharing the digital network connection incurs data usage charges against your cellular data plan. Be careful with your data usage when you're sharing a connection.

    ✔ You may be prompted on the PC to locate and install software for the Galaxy Tab. Do so: Accept the installation of new software when prompted by Windows.

The Bluetooth Thing

Computer nerds have long had the desire to connect high-tech gizmos to one another. The Bluetooth standard was developed to sate this desire in a wireless way. Though Bluetooth is wireless communication, it's not the same as wireless networking. It's more about connecting peripheral devices, such as keyboards, mice, printers, headphones, and other gear. It all happens in a wireless way, as described in this section.

Understanding Bluetooth

Bluetooth is a peculiar name for a wireless communications standard. Unlike Wi-Fi networking, with Bluetooth you simply connect two gizmos. Here's how the operation works:

1. **Turn on the Bluetooth wireless radio on each gizmo.**

    There are two Bluetooth gizmos: the peripheral and the main device to which you're connecting the gizmo, such as the Galaxy Tab.

2. **Make the gizmo you're trying to connect to discoverable.**

    By making a device discoverable, you're telling it to send a signal to other Bluetooth gizmos, saying, "Here I am!"

3. **On the main device, choose the peripheral gizmo from the list of Bluetooth devices.**

    This action is known as *pairing* the devices.

4. **Optionally, confirm the connection on the peripheral device.**

    For example, you may be asked to input a code or press a button.

5. **Use the device.**

    What you can do with the device depends on what it does.

When you're done using the device, you simply turn it off. Because the Bluetooth gizmo is paired with the Galaxy Tab, it's automatically reconnected the next time you turn it on (that is, if you have Bluetooth activated on the Tab).

Bluetooth devices are marked with the Bluetooth icon, shown in the margin. It's your assurance that the gizmo can work with other Bluetooth devices.

Bluetooth was developed as a wireless version of the old RS-232 standard, the serial port on early personal computers. Essentially, Bluetooth is wireless RS-232, and the variety of devices you can connect to, as well as the things you can do with Bluetooth, are similar to what you could do with the old serial port standard.

Turning on the Bluetooth

To make the Bluetooth connection, you turn on the Galaxy Tab's Bluetooth radio. Obey these directions:

1. **From the Applications screen, open the Settings icon.**

2. **Choose Wireless and Network.**

3. **Choose Bluetooth Settings.**

4. **Place a green check mark by the Bluetooth option.**

The easier way, of course, is to use the Quick Actions area in the notification panel, shown in Figure 18-1. Simply touch the Bluetooth button to activate Bluetooth on the Galaxy Tab.

When Bluetooth is on, the Bluetooth status icon appears, as shown in the margin.

To turn off Bluetooth, repeat the steps in this section: Remove the check mark or touch the Bluetooth button in the Quick Actions area.

Connecting to a Bluetooth device

To make the Bluetooth connection between the Galaxy Tab and some other gizmo, follow these steps:

1. **Ensure that Bluetooth is on.**

   Refer to the preceding section.

2. **Turn on the Bluetooth gizmo and ensure that its Bluetooth radio is on.**

   Some Bluetooth devices have separate power and Bluetooth switches.

3. **On the Galaxy Tab, press the Menu soft button from the Home screen and choose the Settings command.**

4. **Choose Wireless and Network.**

5. **Choose Bluetooth Settings.**

6. **If the other device has an option to become visible, select it.**

   For example, some Bluetooth gizmos have a tiny button to press that makes the device visible to other Bluetooth gizmos. (You don't need to make the Galaxy Tab visible unless you're accessing it from another Bluetooth gizmo.)

7. **Choose Scan Devices.**

   Eventually, the device should appear on the Bluetooth Settings screen, in the Bluetooth Devices area, as shown in Figure 18-4.

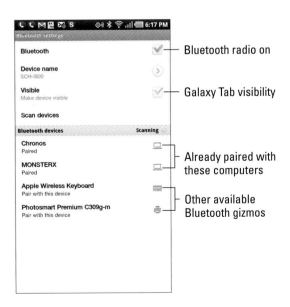

Figure 18-4: Finding Bluetooth gizmos.

8. **Choose the device.**

9. **If necessary, input the device's passcode or otherwise acknowledge the connection.**

    Not every device has a passcode. If prompted, acknowledge the passcode on either the Galaxy Tab or the other device.

After you acknowledge the passcode (or not), the Bluetooth gizmo and your Galaxy Tab are connected and communicating. You can begin using the device.

To break the connection, you can either turn off the gizmo or disable the Bluetooth radio on your Galaxy Tab. Because the devices are paired, when you turn on Bluetooth and reactivate the device, the connection is instantly reestablished.

- ✔ How you use the device depends on what it does. For example, the computer shown in Figure 18-4 can be accessed for sharing files, which is covered in Chapter 19.

- ✔ You can unpair a device by long-pressing it on the Bluetooth Settings screen (refer to Figure 18-4) and choosing the Unpair command from the menu that pops up.

- ✔ Bluetooth can use a lot of power. Especially for battery-powered devices, don't forget to turn them off when you're no longer using them with the Galaxy Tab.

Connect and Share

*B*eyond the Internet, there are a number of useful things to which you can connect the Galaxy Tab. Some things are more useful than others. For example, you can plug the Galaxy Tab into a couch, but the connection is very slow and, honestly, there's little information in the couch worth accessing. A more useful thing to connect the Galaxy Tab to is your computer.

It's possible to connect your Galaxy Tab to your computer, whether it's a PC or a Mac. You can use this connection to share files, by transferring or synchronizing them between the Tab and your computer. Beyond your PC are other interesting, non-Internet connections you can make on the Tab. This chapter covers the lot.

USB connected

You have connected your phone to your com... B. Select Mount if you want to copy files your computer and your phones SD ca...

The USB Connection

The most direct way to connect a Galaxy Tab to a computer is by using a wire — specifically, the wire nestled cozily in the heart of a USB cable. There are lots of things you can do after the USB connection is made. Before doing those things, you need to connect the cable.

Yeah, it may seem excessive to write an entire section on what's apparently a simple operation. But if you've used the Galaxy Tab and already tried to make a USB connection, you probably discovered that it's not really so simple.

Configuring the Tab's USB connection

Perhaps you've already discovered this, but it's entirely possible to connect the Galaxy Tab to a computer's USB port and have absolutely nothing happen. The battery indicator shows that the Tab is being charged, but you can't seem to locate the Tab using any of the computer's features.

The reason the Tab might be having difficulty connecting is that you haven't yet set the USB connection. In some cases, the Galaxy Tab may prompt you to configure the USB connection the first time it's connected to a computer. If not, follow these steps:

1. **Unplug the Galaxy Tab's USB cable.**

   You can't complete these steps when the USB cable is plugged in.

2. **At the Home screen, press the Menu soft button.**

3. **Choose Settings.**

4. **Choose Wireless and Network.**

5. **Choose USB Settings.**

   Three options are available:

   Media Player: The Galaxy Tab mounts itself as though it were a portable MP3 player. This option is best for synchronizing files with a music jukebox player, such as Windows Media Player.

   Mass Storage: The Galaxy Tab mounts itself as though it were a removable storage device, such as a thumb drive or an external hard drive. Choose this option if you have a Macintosh; the Media Player option doesn't work on the Mac.

   Ask On Connection: A prompt appears, asking whether you want to choose Media Player or Mass Storage as the connection option.

6. **Choose an option for the Galaxy Tab's USB connection.**

   I chose the Mass Storage setting, though the Ask On Connection setting is good when you simply just don't know.

After making the USB connection setting, your next step is to plug the Galaxy Tab into your computer, which is covered in the next section.

 When the Galaxy Tab is configured as USB mass storage, connecting the Tab to a computer causes the USB connection notification icon to appear.

When the Galaxy Tab is configured as a media player, connecting the Tab to a computer causes the Media Sync notification icon to appear.

Connecting the Galaxy Tab to your computer

The USB connection between the Galaxy Tab and your computer works fastest when both devices are physically connected. This connection happens by using the USB cable that comes with the Tab. Like nearly every computer cable in the Third Dimension, the USB cable has two ends:

- The A end of the USB cable plugs into the computer.
- The other end of the cable plugs into the bottom of the Galaxy Tab.

The connectors are shaped differently and cannot be plugged in either backward or upside down. (The end that inserts into the Galaxy Tab has the *SAMSUNG* text facing you when you plug it in.)

After you understand how the cable works, plug the USB cable into one of the computer's USB ports. Then plug the USB cable into the Galaxy Tab.

Depending on how you've configured the USB connection (refer to the preceding section), one of three things will happen, as described in the following three subsections.

- See the sidebar "Stuff that happens when you plug the Tab into a PC for the first time" for stuff that can happen the first time you plug the Galaxy Tab into a PC.
- No matter which USB connection option you've chosen, the Galaxy Tab's battery charges when it's connected to a computer's USB port — as long as the computer is turned on, of course.
- If you have a Macintosh, use the mass storage USB option only.

 - You cannot access the Tab's MicroSD card while the Galaxy Tab is mounted into a computer storage system. Items such as your music and photos are unavailable until you unmount the MicroSD card the from the computer.

The Select USB Mode screen

If you're prompted to Select USB mode, choose either Media Player or Mass Storage. Based on your selection, read the later sections "The Media Sync USB connection" or "The Mass Storage USB connection."

The Media Sync USB connection

 For the Media Player connection, you see the Media Sync icon displayed in the notification area. There's nothing else you need to do on your Galaxy

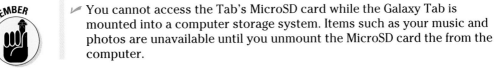

Tab, but on a Windows PC, you have to deal with the AutoPlay dialog box, similar to the one shown in Figure 19-1.

Figure 19-1: The AutoPlay dialog box, for media syncing.

Choose an option from the AutoPlay dialog box, such as Sync Digital Media Files to This Device. From that point on, you'll use Windows or a program on your computer to work with the files on your Galaxy Tab.

The Mass Storage USB connection

 For the Mass Storage connection, you see the USB Connected screen with the Jolly Green Android, shown in Figure 19-2. The USB Connected icon appears in the notification area.

If you don't see the USB Connected screen (see Figure 19-2), pull down the notifications and choose USB Connected.

Touch the Mount button, and then touch the OK button after ignoring the warning.

Stuff that happens when you plug the Tab into a PC for the first time

The very, very first time you plug the Galaxy Tab into a Windows PC, you may see a lot of activity. Notifications might pop up about new software that's installed, or you may see the AutoPlay dialog box. If you do, run the suggested program. The program copies software to your PC that allows it to more easily communicate with the Tab.

The software may also attempt to install other software specific to the Galaxy Tab's cellular carrier. For example, the Verizon Galaxy Tab may try to install the V CAST Media Manager. That choice is optional, though you may be harassed by a prompt time and time again if you elect not to install the software.

Figure 19-2: The USB Mass Storage connection screen.

The AutoPlay dialog box, similar to the one shown earlier, in Figure 19-1, appears. Choose an option for mounting the Galaxy Tab. From that point on, you use Windows or a program on your computer to access information on the Tab.

- ✔ After the Galaxy Tab is mounted into the computer's storage system, the android icon on the USB Mass Storage screen turns orange.

- ✔ It's actually the Galaxy Tab's MicroSD card that's mounted into your computer's storage system.

> ✔ The AutoPlay dialog box may not appear if you've configured Windows to automatically recognize the Galaxy Tab. Choosing the option Always Do This for This Device (refer to Figure 19-1) means that you won't see the AutoPlay dialog box again.

Disconnecting the Tab from your computer

You don't just yank out the USB cable when you're done using the Galaxy Tab with your computer. That would be a Bad Thing. I'm serious: Unplugging a USB cable without properly unmounting the Galaxy Tab can damage the Tab's MicroSD card. Rather than risk such a thing, follow my advice in the following sections, depending on how you've made the USB connection.

Media Sync

To disconnect from the Media Player connection, follow these steps:

1. **Quit the program you're using to access the Galaxy Tab's media.**

   For example, quit the Windows Media Player.

2. **On the Tab, pull down the notifications and choose Media Sync: Connected.**

3. **Touch the Yes button to disable Media Sync mode, and unmount the Galaxy Tab from the computer.**

4. **Unplug the USB cable.**

USB mass storage

Follow these steps to end a USB storage session with a computer:

1. **If you're using a Macintosh, drag the Galaxy Tab's Disk icon to the Trash.**

   You must eject the Galaxy Tab first or else the Macintosh will be very cross with you.

2. **On the Galaxy Tab, touch the Turn Off button on the USB Mass Storage screen.**

   If you don't see the USB Mass Storage screen, pull down the notifications and choose Turn Off USB Storage.

   The MicroSD card is unmounted from the computer's storage system.

3. **Unplug the USB cable.**

   You can safely disconnect the USB cable after the Galaxy Tab's MicroSD card has been unmounted.

After you unmount the MicroSD card, it once again becomes available to the apps on your Galaxy Tab.

Files from Here, Files to There

The point of making the USB connection between your Galaxy Tab and the computer is to exchange files. You can't just wish the files over. Instead, I recommend following the advice in this section, which also covers transferring files using Bluetooth.

A good understanding of basic file operations is necessary before you attempt file transfers between your computer and the Galaxy Tab. You need to know how to copy, move, rename, and delete files. It also helps to be familiar with what folders are and how they work. The good news is that you don't need to manually calculate a 64-bit cyclical redundancy check on the data, nor do you need to know what a parity bit is.

Transferring files to the Galaxy Tab

There are plenty of reasons you would want to copy a file from your computer to the Galaxy Tab. You can copy over your pictures and videos, and you can copy over music or audio files. You can even copy vCards that you export from your email program, which helps you build your Contacts list.

Follow these steps to copy a file from your computer to the Galaxy Tab:

1. **Connect the Galaxy Tab to the computer by using the USB cable.**

   Specific directions are offered elsewhere in this chapter.

   Mount the Galaxy Tab as a mass storage device.

2a. **On a PC, in the AutoPlay dialog box, choose the option Open Folder to View Files.**

   The option might also read Open Device to View Files.

   You see a folder window appear, which looks like any other folder in Windows. The difference is that the files and folders in that window are on the Galaxy Tab, not on your computer.

2b. **On a Macintosh, open the Removable Drive icon that appears.**

   The Galaxy Tab is assigned a generic, removable drive icon when it's mounted on a Macintosh. Most likely, it's given the name NONAME, unless you renamed it to something else.

3. **Locate the files you can to copy to the Galaxy Tab.**

   Open the folder that contains the files, or somehow have the file icons visible on the screen.

4. **Drag the File icon from its folder on your computer to the Galaxy Tab window.**

If you want to be specific, drag the file to the download folder; otherwise, you can place the file into the Galaxy Tab's root folder, as shown in Figure 19-3. Try to avoid dragging the file into other, specific folders, which would make the file more difficult to locate in the future.

Drag files to here to copy to the root.

Specific folders on the Galaxy Tab

Galaxy Tab is drive N on this PC.

Files on your computer

Files on the Galaxy Tab

Figure 19-3: Copying files to the Galaxy Tab.

5. **Properly unmount the Galaxy Tab from your computer's storage system and disconnect the USB cable when you're done.**

Refer to specific instructions earlier in this chapter.

You must eject the Galaxy Tab's Disk icon from the Macintosh computer before you can turn off USB storage on the Tab.

Any files you've copied are now stored on the Galaxy Tab's MicroSD card. What you do with them next depends on the reasons you copied the files: to view pictures, use the Gallery, import vCards, use the Contacts app, listen to music, or use the Music Player, for example.

  ✔ The best way to move music and pictures over to your Galaxy Tab from the computer is to synchronize them. See the later section "Synchronize with doubleTwist."

> ✓ Alas, doubleTwist doesn't help you copy over files individually, which is what you need to do when copying contact pictures or vCard files.

> ✓ The name of the Galaxy Tab device is SCH-I800. You may see this name when mounting the Tab into your computer's storage system.

Copying files to your computer

After you've survived the ordeal of copying files from your computer to the Galaxy Tab, copying files in the other direction is a cinch: Follow the steps in the preceding section, but in Steps 3 and 4 you're dragging the File icons from the Galaxy Tab folder window to your computer.

My advice is to drag the files to your computer's desktop, unless you know of another location where you want the files copied.

> ✓ Files you've downloaded on the Galaxy Tab are stored in the `download` folder.

> ✓ Pictures and videos on the Galaxy Tab are stored in the `DCIM/Camera` folder.

> ✓ Music on the Galaxy Tab is stored in the `Music` folder, organized by artist.

> ✓ Files transferred via Bluetooth are stored in the `bluetooth` folder. See the next section.

> ✓ Quite a few files can be found in the *root folder,* the main folder on the Galaxy Tab's MicroSD card, which you see when the Tab is mounted into your computer's storage system and you open its folder.

Using Bluetooth to copy a file

Another way to copy files between your computer and the Galaxy Tab is to pair the two using Bluetooth. After pairing them, you can copy files, but only if the Galaxy Tab has been added to the computer as a device capable of receiving files. Your Windows PC, for example, may let you access the Galaxy Tab hardware only to use as a speaker or microphone and not to transfer files.

On a Macintosh, to copy a file to the Galaxy Tab by using Bluetooth, follow these steps:

1. **Pair the Galaxy Tab with the Macintosh.**

2. **Ensure that the Bluetooth wireless radio is on for both the Galaxy Tab and the Mac.**

3. From the Bluetooth menu, choose the Galaxy Tab and then Send File.

The Bluetooth menu appears at the far right end of the menu bar, as shown in Figure 19-4. The Galaxy Tab is probably named SCH-I800.

Bluetooth menu item

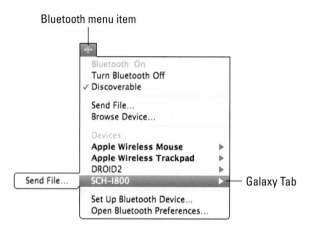

Figure 19-4: Copying a file using Bluetooth on the Mac.

4. Use the Select File to Send dialog box to locate the file you want to beam to the Galaxy Tab.

5. Click to select the file.

6. Click the Send button.

On the Tab you see an alert, explaining that the Mac is attempting to send a file.

7. Touch the Accept button on the Tab to accept the file from the Mac.

The file is transferred.

You find the file located in the bluetooth folder on the Tab.

Files transfer only one at a time between the Mac and the Galaxy Tab. Further, you can copy the files only one way — from the computer to the Mac. That limitation makes this method of file transfer rather inefficient when compared with the USB method, described earlier in this chapter.

✔ You can review any Bluetooth file received by pulling down the Download notification and choosing the Bluetooth Share: Received item. You see the Inbound Transfers screen, which lists files received via Bluetooth on the Galaxy Tab.

✔ See Chapter 18 for information on pairing the Galaxy Tab with your Bluetooth-capable computer, as well as how to activate Bluetooth on the Tab.

✔ Not all PCs are equipped with Bluetooth. To add Bluetooth to a PC, you need a Bluetooth adapter. Inexpensive USB Bluetooth adapters are available at most computer and office supply stores.

✔ Hopefully, Bluetooth on the PC will improve in the future, to allow file transfers. Even so, being able to transfer only one file at a time seriously limits the ability of Bluetooth as an effective way to share files between a computer and the Galaxy Tab.

Synchronize with doubleTwist

Perhaps the most effective and easy way to move information between the Galaxy Tab and your computer is to use a synchronization utility. One of the most popular is the free program doubleTwist, available at `www.double twist.com`.

doubleTwist isn't an Android app. You use it on your computer. It helps you synchronize picture, music, videos, and Web page subscriptions between your computer and its media libraries and any portable device, such as the Galaxy Tab. Additionally, doubleTwist gives you the ability to search the Android Market and obtain new apps for your phone.

To use doubleTwist, connect the Galaxy Tab to your computer as described earlier in this chapter. Mount the Tab as a USB mass storage device to copy over pictures and videos; mount the Tab using Media Sync to synchronize your computer's music.

If the doubleTwist program doesn't start automatically after you connect the Tab, start it manually. The doubleTwist interface is illustrated in Figure 19-5.

To best use doubleTwist, place a check mark by the items you want to sync on the General tab (refer to Figure 19-5). Or, you can choose a tab, such as Videos or Pictures, as shown in Figure 19-5, to select specific items to synchronize. Click the Sync button to copy those files to the Galaxy Tab.

Another way to use doubleTwist is to copy media items to the Galaxy Tab by selecting and then dragging their icons. Choose a media category on your computer, as shown on the left side of the doubleTwist window in Figure 19-5. Drag media from your computer to the Galaxy Tab's icon to copy over those files.

✔ Versions of doubleTwist are available for both the PC and the Mac.

✔ doubleTwist doesn't synchronize contact information.

View local media

Look for apps

Choose items to sync.

Items to sync

Sync button

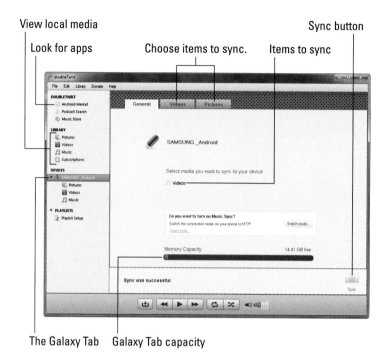

The Galaxy Tab   Galaxy Tab capacity

Figure 19-5: The doubleTwist synchronization utility.

- Some media organization programs on your computer, such as Windows Music Player or Windows Photo Gallery, may allow you to synchronize your media with the Galaxy Tab just as well as or perhaps better than doubleTwist.

- I'm not exactly pleased that you need to connect the Galaxy Tab in two different ways to effectively use doubleTwist. That limitation doesn't apply to other Android devices. Hopefully, doubleTwist will fix that issue in the future, which would make the program far more useful to Galaxy Tab owners.

Life on the MicroSD card

Storage on the Galaxy Tab is all about the MicroSD card. It's a removable memory card on which your stuff is stored. Oh, and regular memory is inside the Galaxy Tab as well, but for file transfer and synchronization, the storage being used is found on the MicroSD card.

- The Galaxy Tab ships with a 16GB MicroSD card.

- The MicroSD card is removable, as described in Chapter 1.

> ✔ You can remove the MicroSD card to replace it with a second MicroSD card, if you like. I recommend getting a higher-capacity MicroSD card, which can be found at any office-supply or computer store. (The cards aren't cheap.)

> ✔ Adding a higher-capacity MicroSD card is the best way to increase storage on your Galaxy Tab.

> ✔ You can read the MicroSD card on your computer, but you need a MicroSD card adapter; most computers read the Secure Digital (SD) card, which is larger than the MicroSD card.

Formatting a MicroSD card

You don't need to format the MicroSD card — unless you buy a newer, higher-capacity card. When that happens, follow these steps:

1. **At the Home screen, press the Menu soft button and choose Settings.**

2. **Choose SD Card and Device Storage.**

3. **Choose Unmount SD Card for Safe Removal.**

4. **Touch the OK button to confirm.**

   The SD card is unmounted from the Galaxy Tab storage system.

5. **Remove the old MicroSD card.**

   Specific directions are found in Chapter 1.

   Don't remove the MicroSD card unless it's been unmounted. Doing so can damage the MicroSD card, rendering it unreadable.

6. **Insert the new MicroSD card.**

7. **Choose Format SD Card.**

   The warning is clear and to the point: Formatting erases all data on the MicroSD card. Format only a new card or a card that doesn't hold important information.

8. **Touch the Format SD Card button.**

   You see another warning.

9. **Touch the Erase Everything button.**

   The MicroSD card is formatted.

After formatting, the MicroSD card is mounted into the Galaxy Tab. It comes instantly available for use.

✔ You can follow Steps 1 through 6 to simply remove one MicroSD card and replace it with another. In that case, you wouldn't want to format the second MicroSD card. Upon inserting the second MicroSD card, it's mounted and available almost instantly.

✔ It's always safe to remove the MicroSD card when the Galaxy Tab has been turned off.

Reviewing storage stats

You can see how much storage space is available on your Galaxy Tab's MicroSD card by following these steps:

1. **From the Home screen, press the Menu soft button.**

2. **Choose Settings and then SD Card and Device Storage.**

   You see a screen similar to Figure 19-6. It details information about storage space on the MicroSD card as well as the Galaxy Tab's internal storage.

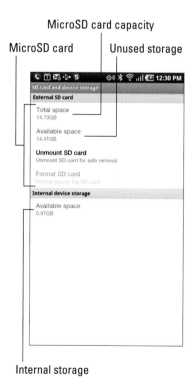

Figure 19-6: Galaxy Tab storage information.

There isn't much you can do with the information presented on the SD Card and Device Storage screen (see Figure 19-6). You can always buy a larger capacity MicroSD card. And, if apps are being installed on the MicroSD card, you can move them to the Tab's internal storage. Refer to Chapter 17.

✔ Things that consume storage on the MicroSD card are videos, music, and pictures, in that order.

✔ To see how much room is left on the MicroSD card, refer to the Available Space item.

✔ The SD Card and Device Storage screen is used to unmount the MicroSD card as well as to format a new MicroSD card. Refer to the preceding section.

✔ Don't complain that the Total Space value is far less than the number stamped on the MicroSD card. In Figure 19-6, it shows 14.73GB total space, even though the Galaxy Tab features a 16GB MicroSD card. The missing space is considered overhead, as are several megabytes taken by the government for tax purposes.

Managing files on the MicroSD card

You probably didn't get a Galaxy Tab because you enjoy managing files on a computer and wanted another gizmo to hone your skills. Even so, you can practice the same type of file manipulation on the Tab as you would on a computer. The secret is to use the My Files app, which I consider one of the nerdiest of all Tab apps.

Starting the My Files app displays a list of files and folders on the Galaxy Tab, as shown in Figure 19-7. The display is similar to the programs you avoid using on your computer that manage files: You can get lost in folder icons, file icons, and lots of text and statistics.

The My Files app allows for very primitive file management: Touch the Manage File buttons to see the file manipulation commands, shown in Figure 19-7. You can copy, cut, and delete files, and you can share files as email attachments. Some files can be viewed by touching them. You cannot rename files.

✔ When the Galaxy Tab is mounted into your computer's storage system, you can manipulate its files just as you can on any other storage device. In fact, using your computer is easier because it most likely has file management features that the My Files app lacks.

✔ You can't manage your apps using the My Files app; that's because apps are installed in a folder that doesn't appear in the window. Manage your apps using the Android Market app, discussed in Chapter 17.

File

Select all files and folders

Selected file

Commands affecting
selected files

Folder

Figure 19-7: The My Files app.

- ✒ Review the stuff you've downloaded from the Internet or saved as email attachments by opening the `download` folder.

- ✒ The Galaxy Tab ships with the ThinkFree Office app. You've probably used it to preview downloads and files on Web sites, such as Microsoft Office or PDF files. The app can also be used to browse files on the MicroSD card, though it's not intended as a file management app.

Options for Viewing Media

It may not be the same thing as sharing media, but it's possible to use the Galaxy Tab to play media on another gizmo, or to have another gizmo's media play on the Galaxy Tab. Yeah, I suppose that's the definition of sharing, but it's not exactly straightforward, which is why I tucked away the information in this section.

The HDMI connection

Tired of that boring 7-inch screen on the Galaxy Tab? How large a screen do you want to have? The answer depends on how large of a television set is available. As long as the TV has an HDMI input, you can connect your Galaxy Tab to see the Big Picture.

To make the HDMI connection, you need the multimedia dock and an HDMI cable that connects to the dock on one end and a standard HDMI adapter on the other end. I'm certain that the friendly folks at your local Phone Store would be happy to sell you this type of cable.

Connect the HDMI cable to the multimedia dock and plug it into the TV. Plug the multimedia dock into a power source and then attach the Galaxy Tab. Tune the TV to the proper HDMI input, and everything displayed on the Tab — YouTube, videos, slide shows, Internet, books — appears on the TV, larger than life.

- The multimedia dock must be connected to a power source for HDMI output to work.

- You can also view the Galaxy Tab on a computer monitor that features HDMI input.

- Though this trick is certainly fun, it's not cheap. The multimedia dock and HDMI cable are costly items, both of which are required to pull off the TV trick.

Using AllShare

On the surface, the idea behind AllShare seems brilliant: You can view media stored on one gizmo by using another gizmo. For example, you can view pictures and videos stored on your computer using your Galaxy Tab, or vice versa. The problem isn't in the concept — it's in the execution.

On the Galaxy Tab, a program named AllShare is used to connect the Galaxy Tab to another Wi-Fi device, such as another phone, a mobile gizmo, a computer, or even a DLNA-compliant TV.

DLNA stands for the Digital Living Networking Alliance. It's a set of rules for connecting gizmos to share media.

After starting AllShare, you see the main screen, similar to Figure 19-8. The left side lists DLNA-aware devices. You start by choosing a device from the left side of the window, which is the device that will share its media. Then choose a device on the right side of the window, which is the device that will host the media.

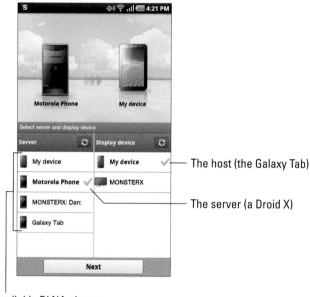

The host (the Galaxy Tab)

The server (a Droid X)

Available DLNA gizmos

Figure 19-8: AllShare in action.

If you're just starting out, it's easiest to use the Galaxy Tab, named My Device in Figure 19-8, as the display device. Choose another source (Server) from the list, and then choose your Galaxy Tab (My Device) and touch the Next button. You can then browse media from the other device on the next screen.

- Yeah, all this is probably too much of an ordeal simply to watch media from another device, especially when the other device is generally just a few feet away.

- AllShare requires that your Galaxy Tab be connected to a Wi-Fi network. See Chapter 18.

- The devices you connect to must have DLNA configured. On most Android phones, that process is done by running the DLNA app.

Part V
Your Personal Galaxy

The 5th Wave — By Rich Tennant

"Okay, antidote, antidote, what would an antidote app look like?"

In this part . . .

1 believe that people have a tendency to be possessive of familiar things. For example, I refer to the street on which I live as "my street." The television programs I watch are "my shows." Even the letter carrier is "my mailman." I don't claim to own any of those things, particularly the mailman, but people commonly refer in a selfish way to the things that are near and recognizable. Your Galaxy Tab is no different.

Because it's *your* Galaxy Tab, you're free to do an amazing number of things with it. You can take it just about anywhere. You can also customize the way the thing looks and sounds, truly making it your own, personal Galaxy Tab. Also covered in this part are routine maintenance and troubleshooting information.

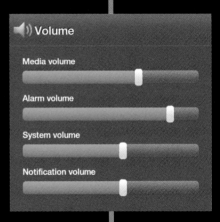

Taking Your Tab with You

Well, of course you can take the Galaxy Tab with you. It's a *mobile* device. It's wireless. It runs on battery power. You can take the Galaxy Tab with you everywhere you go and not get those peculiar looks you get when you take the washing machine with you.

How far can you go with the Galaxy Tab? As far as you want. As long as you can carry the Tab with you, it goes where you go. How it functions may change depending on your environment, and you can do a few things to prepare before you go, which are all covered in this chapter.

Before You Go

Unless the house is on fire, you should prepare several things before leaving on a trip with your Galaxy Tab. First and most important, of course, is to charge the thing. I plug my Tab in overnight before I leave the next day.

Another good thing to do is synchronize media with your computer. This operation isn't so much for taking media with you, but, rather, to ensure that you have a backup of the Tab's media on your computer. See Chapter 19 for synchronization information.

04:20 AM Catch plane

07:10 AM Get up and go to w
Mon, Tue, Wed, Thu, Fri

03:00 PM Wake up from nap

Consider getting some eBooks for the road. I prefer to sit and stew over the Kindle online library before I leave, as opposed to wandering aimlessly in some airport sundry store, trying hard to focus on the good books rather than on the salty snacks. Chapter 11 covers reading eBooks on your Galaxy Tab.

Another nifty thing to do is save some Web pages for later reading. I usually start my day by perusing online articles and angry editorials in the local paper. Because I don't have time to read that stuff before I leave, and I do have time on the plane, and I'm extremely unwilling to pay for in-flight Wi-Fi, I save my favorite Web sites for later reading. Here's how to save a Web page by using the Browser app:

1. **Locate the link to the page you want to save.**

   It has to be a link. The Tab has no obvious way to save the page you're viewing.

2. **Long-press the link.**

3. **From the pop-up menu, choose the command Save Link.**

   The Web page is downloaded, saved to the MicroSD card.

Repeat these steps for each Web page you want to read when offline.

To view the Web page, press the Menu soft button in the Browser app. Choose Download Manager and then select the Web page from the list displayed in the Download Manager. Unfortunately, Web pages are saved using a generic name, something like `downloadfile-12.htm`. Even so, simply touch a saved Web page to view it.

The Web pages will be missing some information; only the text and formatting are saved; pictures are missing. Though this arrangement may not look pretty, at least you'll have some reading material on the plane — specifically, stuff you're used to reading that day anyway.

   ✔ Web pages you download are saved in the `download` folder. See Chapter 19 for information on browsing the download folder using the My Files app.

   ✔ See Chapter 8 for more information on the Browser app and browsing the Web on the Galaxy Tab.

Galaxy Tab Travel Tips

I'm not a frequent flier, but I am a nerd. The most amount of junk I've carried with me on a flight is two laptop computers and three cell phones. I know that's not a record, but it's enough to warrant my list of travel tips, all of which apply to taking the Galaxy Tab with you on an extended journey:

✓ Take the Galaxy Tab's AC adapter and USB cable with you. Put them in your carry-on luggage. Many airports feature USB chargers, so you can charge the Tab in an airport, if you need to.

✓ At the security checkpoint, place your Galaxy Tab in a bin by itself or with other electronics.

✓ Use the Calendar app to keep track of your flights. The event title serves as the airline and flight number. For the event time, use the takeoff and landing schedules. For the location, list the origin and destination airport codes. And, in the Notes field, put the flight reservation number. If you're using separate calendars (categories), specify the Travel calendar for your flight.

✓ See Chapter 16 for more information on the Calendar.

✓ Some airlines feature Android apps you can use while traveling. At the time this book went to press, both Southwest Airlines and Continental Airlines featured apps. You can use the apps to not only keep track of flights but also to check in: Eventually, printed tickets will disappear and you'll merely show your "ticket" on the Galaxy Tab screen, which is then scanned at the gate.

✓ Some apps you can use to organize your travel details are similar to, but more sophisticated than, using the Calendar app. Visit the Android Market and search for *travel* or *airlines* to find a host of apps.

Into the Wild Blue Yonder

It truly is the most trendy of things to be aloft with the latest mobile gizmo. Like taking a cell phone on a plane, however, you have to follow some rules. Though you can't make phone calls on the Galaxy Tab, you have to heed the flight crew's warnings regarding cell phones.

First and foremost, turn off the Galaxy Tab when instructed to do so. This direction is given before takeoff and landing, so be prepared.

Before takeoff, you'll most likely want to put the Tab into Airplane mode. Yep, it's the same Airplane mode you see on a cell phone: The various scary and dangerous wireless radios on the Tab are disabled in Airplane mode. With Airplane mode active, you're free to use the Tab in-flight, and you can rest assured that with Airplane mode active, you face little risk of the Galaxy Tab causing the plane's navigational equipment to fail and the entire flight to end as a fireball over Wyoming.

To enter Airplane mode on the Galaxy Tab, follow these steps just before takeoff:

1. **At the Home screen, press the Menu soft button.**
2. **Choose Settings.**
3. **Choose Wireless and Network.**
4. **Touch the square by Airplane Mode to set the green check mark.**

   When the green check mark is visible, Airplane mode is active.

 When the Galaxy Tab is in Airplane mode, a special icon appears in the status area, as shown in the margin. You might also see the text No Service appear on the lock screen.

And now, for the quick shortcut: To put the Galaxy Tab into Airplane mode, press and hold the Power button and choose the Airplane Mode command.

 To exit Airplane mode, repeat the steps in this section but remove the green check mark by touching the square next to Airplane Mode.

- ✓ Officially, the Galaxy Tab must be powered off when the plane is taking off or landing. See Chapter 2 for information on turning off the Tab.

- ✓ You can compose email while the Tab is in Airplane mode. The messages aren't sent until you disable Airplane mode and connect again with a data network.

- ✓ Bluetooth networking is disabled in Airplane mode. Even so:

- ✓ Many airlines now feature wireless networking onboard, which you can use with the Galaxy Tab — if you're willing to pay for the service. Simply activate Wi-Fi on the Tab, per the directions in Chapter 18, and then connect to the in-flight wireless network when it's available.

The Galaxy Tab Goes Abroad

Like a cell phone, the Galaxy Tab hones in on the digital cellular service offered in whichever country in which you and the Tab happen to be loitering. You see the foreign cellular service listed on the Tab's lock screen. And, unless you want to incur data roaming charges in *zloty* or *pengö*, you should heed the advice in this section.

Traveling overseas with the Tab

The Tab works overseas. The two resources you need to heed are a way to recharge the battery and access Wi-Fi. As long as you have both of them, you're pretty much set. (Data roaming is covered in the next section.)

The Tab's AC plug can easily plug into a foreign AC adapter, which allows you to charge the Tab in outer Wamboolistan.

Wi-Fi is pretty universal, and as long as your location offers this service, you can connect the Tab and pick up your email, browse the Web, or do whatever other Internet activities you desire. Even if you have to pay for Wi-Fi access, I believe that you'll find it less expensive than paying a data roaming charge.

- ✔ Another important point to consider is security. See Chapter 21 for information on security options for your Galaxy Tab.

- ✔ Even when you have Wi-Fi, you need to set up international credit on Skype. See Chapter 10 for more information on making Skype calls.

Disabling data roaming

The way I've used the Galaxy Tab abroad is simply to keep it in Airplane mode. That way, there's no chance of data roaming charges, and you can still enable Wi-Fi. Even so, and just to be sure, you can disable data roaming on the Galaxy Tab by obeying these steps:

1. **On the Home screen, press the Menu soft button and choose Settings.**

2. **Choose Wireless and Network.**

3. **Choose Mobile Networks.**

4. **Ensure that the Data Roaming option isn't selected.**

   Remove the green check mark by the Data Roaming option.

Another place to check for data roaming has to do with text messaging. Follow these steps:

1. **Open the Messaging app.**

2. **If you're viewing a specific conversation, press the Back soft button to return to the main messaging screen.**

3. **Touch the Menu soft button and choose Settings.**

4. **Remove the green check mark by Roaming Auto-Retrieve.**

   Or, if the item isn't selected, you're good to go — literally.

Of course, you don't need to disable data roaming, and you don't need to keep the Tab stuck in Airplane mode, if you simply want to use your Tab overseas and see what comes in the mail regarding a data bill. I prefer not to have such a surprise.

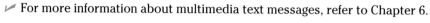

- For more information about multimedia text messages, refer to Chapter 6.

- Contact your digital cellular provider to tell them where you're traveling and to ask about overseas data roaming. A subscription service or other options may even be available, especially when you plan to stay overseas for an extended length of time.

- You can determine whether the Tab is roaming by looking at the Status screen: Run the Settings app, choose About Device, and then choose Status. A Roaming item in the list describes whether the Tab is data roaming.

- The Mobile Network Settings screen, where you disable data roaming (the first set of steps in this section), also contains the Use Packet Data option. This option is normally activated, and it's what enables the Galaxy Tab to read digital information from the cellular network. If you disable the Use Packet Data option, the Galaxy Tab cannot read the digital cellular network at home or abroad.

Customize Your Galaxy Tab

In This Chapter

▶ Changing the background image

▶ Putting apps and widgets on the Home screen

▶ Using folders for Home screen organization

▶ Adding and removing Home screens

▶ Rearranging things on the Home screen

▶ Adding a pattern lock, PIN, or password

▶ Changing the notification ringtone

There is a desire in many people to customize the things they own, to make them their own. Nothing symbolized that ideal in our culture more than the salad bar craze of the 1980s. Why bother having a professional chef make your salad, and the wait staff deliver it to your table, when you can pile as much stuff as you like on a chilled plate, bury it in dressing, toss on a fistful of bacon bits, and bring it back to your seat yourself? Now, *that* was living!

The Galaxy Tab isn't a salad bar, and it's difficult to see the screen through a fistful of bacon, but you can customize the thing, if you so desire. Most of the things you see or sounds you hear can be changed, modified, or tailored to suit your mood or whim. After all, it's *your* Galaxy Tab.

Home Screen Decorating

Lots of interesting doodads are on the Galaxy Tab Home screen. Items such as icons, widgets, and shortcuts adorn the Home screen like freckles on some cute kid. All that stuff can change, even the background images.

The key is the long-press: Press and hold your finger on a blank part of the Home screen (not on an icon). A pop-up menu appears, as shown in Figure 21-1. From that menu, you can begin your Home screen decorating adventure, as discussed in this section.

> **Add to Home screen**
>
> Widgets
>
> Shortcuts
>
> Folders
>
> Wallpapers

Figure 21-1: The Add to Home Screen menu.

Hanging new wallpaper

The Home screen has two types of backgrounds, or *wallpapers:* traditional and live. A *live* wallpaper is animated. A not-so-live *(traditional)* wallpaper can be any image, such as a picture you've taken and stored in the Gallery.

To set a new wallpaper for the Home screen, obey these steps:

1. **Long-press the Home screen.**

   The Add to Home Screen menu appears, as shown in Figure 21-1.

2. **Choose Wallpapers.**

   Another menu appears, with these three options:

   Gallery: Choose a still image from those you've taken, stored in the Gallery app.

   Live Wallpapers: Choose an animated or interactive wallpaper from a list.

   Wallpaper Gallery: Choose a wallpaper from a range of images preinstalled on the Galaxy Tab.

3. **Select a wallpaper option type.**

4. **Choose the wallpaper you want from the list.**

   For the Media Gallery option, you see a preview of the wallpaper where you can select and crop part of the image.

   For certain live wallpapers, a Settings button may appear. The settings let you customize certain aspects of the interactive wallpaper.

5. **Touch the Save or Set Wallpaper button to confirm your selection.**

   The new wallpaper takes over the Home screen.

Live wallpaper features some form of animation, which can often be interactive. Otherwise, the wallpaper image scrolls slightly as you swipe from one Home screen panel to another.

   ✎ The Zedge app has some interesting wallpaper available. It's an über-repository of wallpaper images, collected from Android users all over the world. Check out Zedge at the Android Market; see Chapter 17.

   ✎ See Chapter 14 for more information about the Gallery, including information on how cropping an image works.

   ✎ Be careful when using certain live wallpapers. The animation consumes processor power, which can affect the performance of other apps on the Tab.

Adding apps to the Home screen

The first thing I did on my Galaxy Tab was to place my most favorite apps on the Home screen. Here's how that works:

1. **Touch the Applications button to hunt down the app you want to add to the Home screen.**

2. **Press — and keep pressing— an app's icon.**

   After a moment, you return to the Home screen with the app's icon still stuck under your finger.

3. **If necessary, slide your finger (and the icon still attached) left or right to go to another Home screen panel.**

   As you move your finger to the left or right edge of the screen, the Home screen slides in that direction.

4. **Position your finger — still pressed down — on the spot where you want the app's icon to be placed.**

5. **Release your finger.**

   A copy of the app's icon is tacked to the Home screen. There's no need to clean your fingertip after completing these steps.

The app hasn't moved: What you see is a copy. You can still find the app on the Applications Tray, but now the app is — more conveniently — available on the Home screen.

- ✔ A second procedure that goes along with adding apps to the Home screen is removing apps and widgets already affixed to the Home screen. See the section "Moving and removing icons and widgets," later in this chapter.

- ✔ Keep your favorite apps, those you use most often, on the Home screen.

- ✔ Icons on the Home screen are aligned to a grid. You can't stuff more icons on the Home screen than will fit in the grid, so when a Home screen is full of icons (or widgets), use another Home screen.

- ✔ You can add more Home screens if you run out. See the later section "Making more Home screens."

Slapping down widgets

A *widget* works like a tiny, interactive or informative window, often providing a gateway into another app on the Galaxy Tab. Just as you can add apps to the Home screen, you can also add widgets.

The Galaxy Tab comes with a smattering of widgets preaffixed to the Home screen, possibly just to show you how they can be used. You can place even more widgets on the Home screen by following these steps:

1. **Long-press the Home screen.**

2. **Choose Widgets from the Add to Home Screen menu.**

3. **From the list, choose the widget you want to add.**

   The widget is plopped on the Home screen.

The variety of available widgets depends on the applications you have installed. Some applications come with widgets, some don't. Some widgets come independently of any application.

- ✔ More widgets are available at the Android Market. See Chapter 17.

- ✔ You cannot install a widget when the Home screen has no room for it. Choose another panel, or remove icons or widgets to make room.

- ✔ To remove a widget, see the later section "Moving and removing icons and widgets."

Creating shortcuts

A *shortcut* is a doodad you can place on the Home screen that's neither an app nor a widget. Instead, a shortcut is a handy way to get at a feature or an informational tidbit stored in the Galaxy Tab without having to endure complex gyrations.

For example, I have a shortcut on my Home screen that uses the Maps app Navigation feature to help me return to my house. I have the shortcut there in case of a zombie attack so that I can return home to my hardy stock of power tools.

To add a shortcut, long-press the Home screen and choose the Shortcuts command from the Add to Home Screen menu (refer to Figure 21-1). What happens next depends on which shortcut you choose.

For example, when you choose a bookmark, you add a Web page bookmark to the Home screen. Touch that shortcut to open the Browser app and pluck the Web page from your list of bookmarks.

Choose a Contact shortcut to display contact information for a specific person.

A nerdy shortcut to add is the Settings shortcut. After choosing this item, you can select from a number of on–off options or status items that can appear on the Home screen as widgets.

 The Any Cut app is useful for creating certain shortcuts that the Galaxy Tab cannot create by itself, such as a shortcut to direct-dial a contact. Check out Any Cut at the Android Market; see Chapter 17.

Organizing apps into folders

Another item you can stick on the Home screen is a folder. It's an option available on the Add to Home Screen menu (refer to Figure 21-1), so I'm compelled by the Technology Authors Brotherhood International to write about it here.

Folders are used for organization. They allow you to stuff a bunch of apps — preferably, similar apps, such as games — into a single container. The concept makes sense, but it's not something I see people doing often. Even so, if you feel compelled to create a folder, you can conjure one up by following these steps:

1. **Long-press the Home screen.**

2. **Choose the Folders command.**

   A list of different types of folders appears. The variety depends on the various apps you have installed and whether the app allows you to create handy Home screen folders.

3. **Choose New Folder from the list.**

   The new folder icon appears on the Home screen.

4. **Touch the folder icon to open it and show its contents.**

   New folders are empty, of course. Figure 21-2 shows a folder into which I've copied various game apps.

5. **Long-press the folder window's title.**

   Refer to Figure 21-2 for the location. When you press too briefly, the folder closes. Start over again in Step 4.

App icons in the folder

Close folder window

Long-press to change the folder name.

Figure 21-2: A folder for games.

6. **Type or dictate a new folder name.**

   Touch the folder's Name field to summon the onscreen keyboard.

7. **Touch the OK button to lock in the new name.**

   Optionally, close the folder by touching its X button. Refer to Figure 21-2 for the location of the X button.

You place app icons into the folder by dragging and dropping with your finger. See the later section "Moving and removing icons and widgets" for information on dragging icons around the Home screen.

Icons can also be dragged from the Applications screen directly into the folder.

To move an icon out of a folder, long-press the icon. The folder closes, and then you can drag the icon to a new position on the Home screen or drag it to the Trash, as covered in the later section "Moving and removing icons and widgets."

Delete folders by dragging them to the Trash.

Home Screen Modification

There are many interesting and useful things you can do to the Galaxy Tab's Home screen, none of which requires that you rent an industrial sander. Beyond adding new things to the Home screen, and changing the wallpaper, you can add more Home screens, modify primary shortcuts, and move things around. This section tells you how.

Making more Home screens

The Galaxy Tab ships with five Home screens. The main Home screen is in the center, and then two bonus Home screen panels are to the left and right. This setup can change so that you can add or remove Home screen panels. You can even set which Home screen panel is the main Home screen.

The action starts by pinching your fingers on the Home screen: Start with two fingers touching the Home screen and then bring your fingers together — a pinch. You see a screen similar to Figure 21-3.

You can do several things when viewing the screen shown in Figure 21-3:

To quickly visit any specific Home screen panel, touch it.

Touch to make this the main Home screen.

Current main Home screen panel

Drag a panel around to rearrange. | Touch to add a new panel.

Drag a panel here to delete.

Figure 21-3: Manipulating Home screen panels.

To add a new Home screen panel, touch the Plus button, shown in Figure 21-3. You can have as many as nine Home screen panels.

Remove a Home screen by dragging its panel to the Trash icon. Removing a Home screen panel gets rid of not only the panel but also any apps, widgets, folders, or other items stuck to the panel.

Rearrange the order in which the Home screen panels appear by dragging one panel to another location. The remaining panels reshuffle to make room for the new panel.

Finally, to set the main Home screen, touch the Set As Home button. The current, main Home screen has the Home button beneath it, as illustrated in Figure 21-3.

✓ The main Home screen is the one you see when you press the Home soft
    button twice.

  ✓ Dragging panels around is accomplished by long-pressing a panel. When
    you've "grabbed" one, the Set As Home buttons disappear and you can
    then move the panel around, as long as you keep your finger in contact
    with the touchscreen.

Moving and removing icons and widgets

Icons and widgets are fastened to the Home screen by something akin to
the same glue they use on sticky notes. You can easily pick up an icon or a
widget, move it around, and then restick it. Unlike sticky notes, the icons and
widgets never just fall off, or so I'm told.

To move an icon or a widget, long-press it. Eventually, the icon seems to lift
and break free, as shown in Figure 21-4.

Long-press an icon.

Drag the icon to the trash.

Figure 21-4: Moving an icon about.

You can drag a free icon to another position on the Home screen or to another Home screen panel, or you can drag it to the Remove (trash can) icon that appears at the bottom of the Home screen, which replaces the Applications button (refer to Figure 21-4).

Widgets can be moved around or deleted in the same manner as icons.

✔ Dragging a Home screen icon or widget to the Trash removes the icon or widget from the Home screen. It doesn't remove the application, which is still found on the Applications screen, or the widget, which you can add to the Home screen again, as described earlier in this chapter.

✔ When an icon hovers over the Remove icon, ready to be deleted, its color changes to red.

✔ See Chapter 17 for information on uninstalling applications.

✔ Your clue that an icon or widget is free and clear to navigate is that the Launcher button changes to the Remove icon (refer to Figure 21-4).

Changing the primary shortcuts

The *primary* shortcuts are the two app icons that appear to the left and right of the Applications button at the bottom of every Home screen. The Galaxy Tab ships with the Browser and Email apps preset in the left and right primary shortcut positions, respectively. To change this setup, follow these steps:

1. **Long-press the primary shortcut you want to change.**

2. **Drag the shortcut icon to the trash icon.**

   The trash icon replaces the Applications button, so you just need to swipe the old primary shortcut to the left or right to remove it.

   After removing a primary shortcut, the place where it was is blank — empty.

3. **Drag another app to the blank primary shortcut.**

   You can drag the app from the Applications screen or from the Home screen.

The new app takes over as a primary shortcut, appearing at the bottom of every Home screen.

✔ You can leave either one or both primary shortcuts blank. That would, however, be a waste.

✔ Rather than delete a primary shortcut, simply drag its icon to a Home screen.

>   ✔ You can place just about anything as a primary shortcut, including a
>   contact icon or navigation shortcut or just about any icon.
>
>   ✔ You cannot use a widget as a primary shortcut.

Lock Your Galaxy Tab

The Galaxy Tab features a basic lock screen: Simply slide the Padlock
button to the right and the Tab is unlocked and ready to use. If you prefer
to have a lock that's not so easy to pick, you can choose from one of three
different types of lock screens: Pattern, PIN, and Password, as described in
this section.

Finding the locks

Lock screen security is set on the Set Screen Lock screen. Here's how to get
there:

1. **From the Home screen, press the Menu soft button.**

2. **Choose Settings.**

3. **Choose Location & Security.**

4. **Choose Set Screen Lock.**

5. **If a screen lock is already set, you must trace the pattern or input the
   PIN or password to continue.**

   The Set Screen Lock screen lists four types of locks:

   None: Rather than no lock, the Tab simply uses the standard locking
   screen: Slide the Padlock button to the right and the Tab is unlocked.
   Choosing this option disables the other three options.

   Pattern: To unlock the Tab, you must trace a pattern on the touchscreen.

   PIN: The Tab is unlocked by typing a personal identification number (PIN).

   Password: You must type a password to unlock the Galaxy Tab.

6. **To set a lock, refer to the following sections, or to remove any existing
   lock, choose None.**

When you choose None to remove another type of lock, you're asked to
unlock the Tab one more time, tracing the pattern or typing the PIN or password to remove that type of lock.

> ✔ The security you add affects the way you turn on and wake up your Galaxy Tab. See Chapter 2 for details.

> ✔ The security lock can be overridden when USB Debugging is enabled. Unless you're writing software for the Galaxy Tab, however, odds are good that you'll never have USB Debugging turned on.

Creating an unlock pattern

One of the most common ways to lock the Tab is to apply an *unlock pattern:* The pattern must be traced exactly as it was created to unlock the device and get access to your apps and other Galaxy Tab features.

To set the unlock pattern, summon the Set Screen Lock screen as described in the preceding section. Choose Pattern.

If you've not yet set a pattern lock, you may see a text screen describing the process; touch the Next button to page through the dreary directions.

Trace an unlock pattern, as shown in Figure 21-5. You can trace over the dots in any order, but you can trace over a dot only once. The pattern must cover at least four dots.

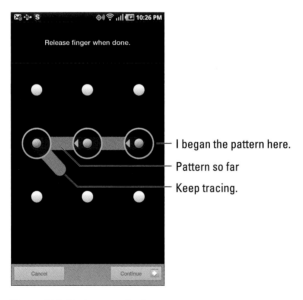

I began the pattern here.

Pattern so far

Keep tracing.

Figure 21-5: Setting an unlock pattern.

Touch the Continue button and redraw the pattern again, just to prove to the doubtful Galaxy Tab that you know the pattern.

Touch the Confirm button and the pattern lock is set.

Ensure that a check mark appears by Use Visible Pattern on the Location and Security screen. The check mark ensures that the pattern shows up. For even more security, you can disable the option, but you have to be sure to remember how — and where — the pattern goes.

- ✔ To remove the pattern lock, set None as the type of lock, as described in the preceding section.
- ✔ The unlock pattern can be as simple or complex as you like. I'm a big fan of simple.
- ✔ Wash your hands! Smudge marks on the display can betray your pattern.

Setting a PIN

I suppose that using a PIN, or personal identification number, is more left-brained than using a pattern lock. What's yet another number to memorize?

A *PIN lock* is a code between 4 and 16 numbers long. It contains only numbers, 0 through 9. To set a PIN lock for your Galaxy Tab, follow the directions in the earlier section "Finding the locks" to reach the Set Screen Lock screen. Choose PIN from the list of locks.

Input your PIN twice to confirm that you know it. The next time you need to unlock your Tab, you see a keypad similar to Figure 21-6. Type your PIN and touch the OK button to proceed.

To disable the PIN, reset the Galaxy Tab security level to None, as described in the section "Finding the locks," earlier in this chapter.

Assigning a password

The most secure way to lock the Galaxy Tab is to apply a full-on password. Unlike a PIN (refer to the preceding section), a *password* can contain numbers, symbols, and both upper- and lowercase letters.

Set a password by choosing Password from the Set Screen Lock screen; refer to the earlier section "Finding the locks" for information on getting to that screen. The password you select must be at least four characters long. Longer passwords are more secure.

You're prompted to type the password whenever you unlock the Galaxy Tab or whenever you try to change the screen lock. Touch the OK button to accept the password you've typed.

To remove the password lock, choose None after following the steps in the section "Finding the locks," earlier in this chapter.

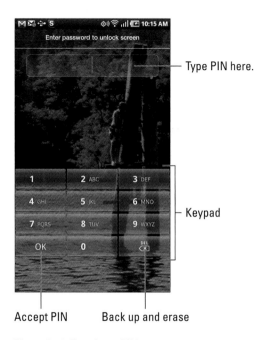

Type PIN here.

Keypad

Accept PIN   Back up and erase

Figure 21-6: Entering a PIN.

Various Galaxy Tab Adjustments

You have plenty of things to adjust, tune, and tweak on the Galaxy Tab. The Settings screen is the gateway to all those options, and I'm sure you could waste hours there, if you had hours to waste. My guess is that your time is precious; therefore, this section highlights some of the more worthy options and settings.

Singing a different tune

The Sound Settings screen is where you control which sound the Galaxy Tab plays as a ringtone, but also where you can set volume and vibration options.

To display the Sound Settings screen, press the Menu soft button when viewing the Home screen and choose Settings. Choose Sound.

Here are the worthy options on the Sound Settings screen:

Silent Mode: Place the Tab into Silent mode by putting a green check mark by that option. In Silent mode, the Galaxy Tab makes no sound, though it may vibrate, depending on the Vibrate setting, covered next.

Vibrate: Choose the Vibrate item to see the Vibrate menu. You have four options for vibrating the Galaxy Tab:

> *Always:* The Tab always vibrates when it issues an alert.
>
> *Never:* The Tab never vibrates.
>
> *Only in Silent Mode:* The Tab vibrates when you activate Silent mode.
>
> *Only When Not in Silent Mode:* The Tab vibrates all the time unless Silent Mode is activated.

Volume: Though you can set the Galaxy Tab volume using the Volume buttons on the side of the gizmo, the Volume command on the Sound Settings screen lets you set the volume for a number of sound events, as shown in Figure 21-7. Table 21-1 describes what the various volume items control.

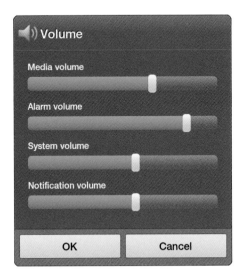

Figure 21-7: Various volume settings.

Table 21-1	Various Noisy Things
Volume Setting	*Sounds It Controls*
Media	Music, videos, YouTube, Internet, games, and others
Alarm	Warnings set by the Alarm Clock app, and other alerts
System	Sounds generated by the Android operating system, such as when locking the screen or connecting the dock or USB cable
Notification	New notifications, such as new email messages, calendar appointments, or whatever else produces an alert

For example, if you want the alarms to be loud, and all those notification sounds to be rather mute, adjust the sliders (refer to Figure 21-7) accordingly.

Notification Ringtone: Choose which sound you want to hear for a notification alert. The list of preset sounds for the Galaxy Tab is shown on the Alarm Tones menu. Choose a sound or choose Silent (at the top of the list) for no sound.

Haptic Feedback: Though the Haptic Feedback item doesn't make noise, you can activate it to have the Galaxy Tab vibrate slightly as you manipulate items on the touchscreen.

When the Haptic Feedback option is set, the Vibration Intensity option becomes available, where you can set how strongly the Tab vibrates for haptic feedback.

- You can put the Galaxy Tab in Silent mode from the lock screen: Slide the Silence tab to the left, as illustrated in Figure 2-1 (refer to Chapter 2).
- Unlike on a cell phone, you cannot assign music or your own audio to a Galaxy Tab ringtone.
- You can assign music or audio to an alarm, which is covered in Chapter 16.

Changing visual settings

Probably the key thing you want to adjust visually on the Galaxy Tab is screen brightness. This task is deftly handled by the notification panel: Pull down the notifications and you see the Brightness slider, along with the Auto check mark item, which automatically adjusts screen brightness based on ambient light.

Beyond the Brightness setting on the notification panel, the remainder of the Galaxy Tab's visual settings and options are kept on the Display

Settings screen. From the Home screen, press the Menu soft button and choose Settings. Choose Display to see the Display Settings screen.

The Brightness item on the Display Settings screen duplicates the settings you can make on the notification panel.

Another item worthy of note is the Screen Timeout setting. Choose this option to see the Screen Timeout menu, from which you can set the inactivity duration, after which the Galaxy Tab touchscreen turns itself off. I prefer a value of 1 Minute, though the Tab is initially set with a 30-second screen timeout.

    ✓ The Screen Timeout setting is the setting that the Galaxy Tab uses to put itself into Sleep mode.

    ✓ See Chapter 3 for more information on the notification panel.

Adjusting the onscreen keyboards

The Galaxy Tab features two onscreen keyboards. Selecting which keyboard you want to use on the Tab is done on the Language and Keyboard screen.

To visit the Language and Keyboard screen, from the Home screen press the Menu soft button and choose Settings. Choose Language and Keyboard.

The Select Input Method item is used to switch between the Swype and Samsung keypad onscreen keyboards.

You can also switch keyboards by long-pressing any text box and choosing the Input Method command from the Edit Text menu.

On the Language and Keyboard screen, you can choose either the Swype or Samsung Keypad items to make various adjustments to the way the onscreen keyboards behave.

The Swype Settings screen features some options, initially disabled, that might help your Swype typing. The Word Prediction setting can come in handy, though you might find it annoying. Another fun option is Show Complete Trace, which can help you train yourself to be a better Swyper.

The Samsung Keypad Settings screen has only a handful of options, most notably the XT9 predictive-text option, which I recommended setting over in Chapter 4.

See Chapter 4 for additional help and information on using the onscreen keyboards.

Galaxy Tab Health, Happiness, and Maintenance

In This Chapter

▷ Cleaning the Galaxy Tab
▷ Checking on the battery
▷ Saving battery power
▷ Finding help on the Tab
▷ Searching for support
▷ Troubleshooting minor problems
▷ Getting answers to common issues

The Great Pyramid of Giza is still with us, for one reason: maintenance. The lesson to be learned is that when you take care of your stuff, primarily by doing routine maintenance, you always have your stuff with you and in a usable condition. It's no secret.

Your Galaxy Tab is similar to the pyramids of Egypt in that you need to take care of your Tab if you plan on keeping it for 6,000 years. The task of maintaining the Galaxy Tab isn't that involved. For example, cleaning a pyramid can take months; cleaning the Tab takes moments. Before covering maintenance, this chapter covers suggestions for using the battery, plus gives you some helpful tips and Q&A.

Regular Galactic Maintenance

Relax. Maintenance of the Galaxy Tab is simple and quick. Basically, I can summarize it in three words: Keep it clean. Beyond that, another maintenance task worthy of attention is backing up the information stored on your Tab.

Keeping it clean

You probably already keep your Galaxy Tab clean. Perhaps you're one of those people who uses their sleeve to wipe the touchscreen. Of course, better than your sleeve is something called a *microfiber cloth*. This item can be found at any computer- or office-supply store.

 ✔ Never use any liquid to clean the touchscreen — especially ammonia or alcohol. Those substances damage the touchscreen, rendering it unable to read your input. Further, such harsh chemicals can smudge the display, making it more difficult to see.

 ✔ If the screen keeps getting dirty, consider adding a screen protector. This specially designed cover prevents the screen from getting scratched or dirty but also lets you use your finger on the touchscreen. Be sure that the screen protector is designed for use with the Galaxy Tab.

 ✔ The screen protectors I picked up at the Verizon Store also came with a handy microfiber cloth.

Backing up your stuff

A *backup* is a safety copy of information. For your Galaxy Tab, the backup copy includes contact information, music, photos, video, and apps you've installed, plus any settings you've made to customize your Tab. Copying that information to another source is one way to keep the information safe, in case anything happens to your Galaxy Tab.

Yes, a backup is a good thing. Lamentably, there's no universal method of backing up the stuff on your Galaxy Tab.

Your Google account information is backed up automatically. That information includes your Contacts list, Gmail inbox, and Calendar app appointments. Because that information automatically syncs with the Internet, a backup is always present.

To confirm that your Google account information is being backed up, heed these steps:

1. **From the Home screen, press the Menu soft button.**

2. **Choose Settings.**

3. **Choose Accounts and Sync.**

4. **Touch the green Sync button by your Google account name.**

5. **Ensure that check marks appear by every item in the list.**

   On my Galaxy Tab, the list includes Books, Contacts, Gmail, Picasa Web Albums, and Calendar.

6. **Press the Back soft button.**

7. **Optionally, ensure that your other accounts are being synchronized as well.**

   When you have more than one Google account synchronized with your Galaxy Tab, repeat Steps 1 through 6 for each account.

8. **Press the Back soft button to return to the main Settings screen.**

9. **Choose Privacy.**

10. **Ensure that a check mark appears by the item Back Up My Settings.**

    You should see a check mark there. If not, touch the square to add one.

Beyond your Google account, which is automatically backed up, the rest of the information can be manually backed up. You can choose to either synchronize information on the Galaxy Tab with your computer or manually copy files from the Tab's MicroSD card to the computer as a form of backup.

Yes, I agree: Manual backup isn't an example of technology making your life easier.

- See Chapter 19 for information about exchanging files between your computer and the Galaxy Tab.

- The Lookout Mobile Security app features a backup option in addition to antivirus protection. Use the barcode in the margin or refer to Chapter 17 for information on obtaining Lookout Mobile Security from the Android market.

- Your cellular provider may have installed some type of backup software. For example, Verizon installs its Backup Assistant program, though I find it bulky and inefficient.

- A backup of the data stored on the MicroSD card would include all data on your Galaxy Tab, including photos, videos, and music. Specifically, the folders you should copy are DCIM, download, and Music. Additional folders to copy include folders named after apps you've downloaded, such as Aldiko, Kindle, Kobo, layar, and other folders named after the apps that created them.

Updating the system

Every so often, a new version of the Galaxy Tab's operating system becomes available. It's an *Android* update because Android is the name of the operating system, not because the Galaxy Tab thinks that it's some type of robot.

When an automatic update occurs, you see an alert or a message appear, indicating that a system upgrade is available. You usually have three options:

- Install Now
- Install Later
- More Info

My advice is to choose Install Now and get it over with — unless you're doing something urgent, in which case you can put off the update until later by choosing Install Later.

- You can manually check for updates: From the Settings screen, choose About Device and then choose System Updates. When your system is up-to-date, the screen tells you so. Otherwise, you find directions for updating the Android operating system.

- Non-Android system updates might also be issued. For example, Samsung may send out an update to the Galaxy Tab's guts. This type of update is often called a *firmware* update. As with Android updates, my advice is to accept all firmware updates.

Battery Care and Feeding

Perhaps the most important item you can monitor and maintain on your Galaxy Tab is its battery. The battery supplies the necessary electrical juice by which the device operates. Without battery power, your Tab is basically a side-view mirror popped off a 1971 Ford F150 truck. Keep an eye on the battery.

Monitoring the battery

You can find information about the Galaxy Tab's battery status at the top of the screen, in the status area, next to the time. The icons used to display battery status are shown in Figure 22-1.

You might also see an icon for a dead battery, but for some reason I can't get my Galaxy Tab to turn on and display that icon.

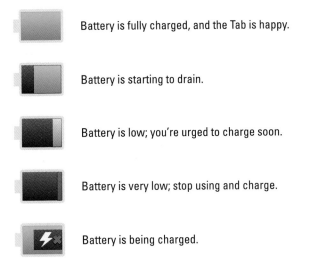

Battery is fully charged, and the Tab is happy.

Battery is starting to drain.

Battery is low; you're urged to charge soon.

Battery is very low; stop using and charge.

Battery is being charged.

Figure 22-1: Battery status icons.

When you find the teensy battery icons (refer to Figure 22-1) too vague, you can check the specific battery level by following these steps:

1. **From the Home screen, touch the Menu button.**
2. **Choose Settings.**
3. **Choose About Device.**
4. **Choose Status.**

The top two items on the Status screen offer information about the battery:

Battery Status: This setting explains what's going on with the battery. It might say Not Charging when the battery is being used or Charging when the battery is being charged, or you might see other text, depending on how desperate the Galaxy Tab is for power.

Battery Level: This setting reveals a percentage value describing how much of the battery is charged. A value of 100 percent indicates a fully charged battery. A value of 110 percent means that someone can't do math.

The next section describes features that consume battery power and how to deal with battery issues.

Heed those low-battery warnings! The Galaxy Tab alerts you whenever the battery level gets low, as shown in Figure 22-2.

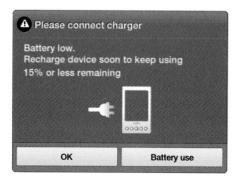

Figure 22-2: A low-battery warning.

Another warning shows up when the battery level gets seriously low, though I've never seen that warning because I find the message in Figure 22-2 serious enough to move me to action: I either plug in the Tab or turn it off.

✔ When the battery level is too low, the Galaxy Tab shuts itself off.

✔ The best way to deal with low battery power is to connect the Tab to a power source: Either plug it into a wall socket or connect it to a computer by using a USB cable. The Galaxy Tab charges itself immediately; plus, you can use the device while it's charging.

✔ You don't have to fully charge the Galaxy Tab to use it. If you have only 20 minutes to charge and you get only a 70 percent battery level, that's great. Well, it's not great, but it's far better than a 20 percent battery level.

✔ Battery percentage values are best-guess estimates. The Galaxy Tab has a hearty battery that can last for hours. But when the battery meter gets low, the battery drains faster. So, if you get 8 hours of use from the Tab and the battery meter shows 20 percent left, those numbers don't imply that 20 percent equals two more hours of use. In practice, the amount of time you have left is much less than that. As a rule, when the battery percentage value gets low, the battery appears to drain faster.

Determining what is sucking up power

A nifty screen that you can visit reviews which activities have been consuming power on the Galaxy Tab. This informative screen is shown in Figure 22-3. To get to that screen, follow these steps:

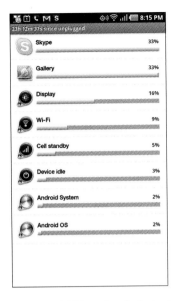

Figure 22-3: Things that drain the battery.

1. **At the Home screen, press the Menu soft button.**
2. **Choose Settings.**
3. **Choose About Device.**
4. **Choose Battery Use.**

   You see a screen similar to the one shown in Figure 22-3.

The number and variety of items listed on the Battery Use screen depend on what you've been doing between charges and how many different apps you're using.

Carefully note which applications consume the most battery power. You can curb your use of these programs to conserve juice — though, honestly, your savings are negligible. See the next section for battery-saving advice.

Not everything you've done shows up on the Battery Use screen (refer to Figure 22-3). For example, even after I read a Kindle book for about half an hour, Kindle didn't show up. Also, I've seen the Gallery app show up from time to time, even though I've not used it.

At the time this book went to press, no feature could control power management on the Galaxy Tab. A future update of the Android operating system may offer this type of management, in which case you can control how the Galaxy Tab uses power, set timeouts, and adjust power-saving features.

Extending battery life

A surefire way to make a battery last a good long time is to never turn on the device in the first place. That's kind of impractical, so rather than let you use your Galaxy Tab as an expensive paperweight, I offer a smattering of suggestions you can follow to help prolong battery life in your Galaxy Tab:

Turn off vibration options: The Tab's vibration is caused by a teensy motor. Though you don't see much battery savings by disabling the vibration options, it's better than no savings. See Chapter 21, the section "Singing a different tune," for information on disabling vibration options.

Lower the volume: Additionally, consider lowering the volume for the various noises the Galaxy Tab makes, especially notifications. Information on setting volume options is also found in Chapter 21.

Dim the screen: If you look at Figure 22-3 (earlier in this chapter), you see that the display sucks down quite a lot of battery power. Though a dim screen can be more difficult to see, especially outdoors, it definitely saves on battery life.

Turn off Bluetooth: When you're not using Bluetooth, turn it off. See Chapter 18 for information on Bluetooth, though you can turn it off easily from the quick actions at the top of the notification panel.

Turn off Wi-Fi: It's a major trade-off, but while Wi-Fi networking keeps the Galaxy Tab on the Internet, it does drain the battery. Because I tend to use Wi-Fi in only one spot, I keep the Tab plugged in. Away from a single location, however, Wi-Fi "wanders" and isn't useful for an Internet connection anyway. So why not turn it off? Refer to Chapter 18 for information on Wi-Fi.

Help and Troubleshooting

Wouldn't it be great if you could have an avuncular, Mr. Wizard-type available at a moment's notice? He could just walk in and, with a happy smile on his face and a reassuring hand on your shoulder, let you know what the problem is and how to fix it. Never mind that such a thing would be creepy — getting helpful advice is worth it.

Getting help

Major electronic gizmos once came with manuals. Though useless, the manual at least provided a jumping-off point for general help information. These days, devices such as the Galaxy Tab come with only a smattering of helpful info, *if* you know where to find it.

There are two places on the Galaxy Tab where you can find help. Well, I should restate: There are two places on the Galaxy Tab where information is offered under the guise of "help."

To view the System Tutorial, follow these steps:

1. **At the Home screen, press the Menu soft button.**

2. **Choose Settings.**

3. **Choose About Device.**

4. **Choose System Tutorial.**

   The text you see on the touchscreen explains that you need to under-stand some important things in order to use the "phone," but only one item is listed: using the onscreen keyboard.

5. **Touch the Begin button.**

   A Swype tutorial starts.

6. **Press the Back soft button to back out of the Swype tutorial.**

My hope is that future updates to the Galaxy Tab include more than just a Swype tutorial on the *Learn How to Use Your SCH-I800* page.

The other place you can find quasi-helpful information is in the Task Manager: Start the Task Manager app from the Applications screen.

From the list of tabs at the top of the Task Manager app's window, choose the one on the far right end: Help. You see a screen titled To Extend Battery Life. It lists five things you can do to help prolong battery life on the Galaxy Tab, though they aren't as well-written as the suggestions I offer earlier in this chapter.

Yes, I must confess: This dearth of helpful information kind of makes me long for the days of the dratted manual.

Fixing random and annoying problems

Here are some typical problems you may encounter on the Galaxy Tab and my suggestions for a solution:

General trouble: For just about any problem or minor quirk, consider restarting the Galaxy Tab: Turn it off and then turn it on again. This procedure will most likely fix a majority of the annoying and quirky problems you encounter.

Check the cellular data connection: As you move about, the cellular signal can change. In fact, you may observe the status bar icon change from 3G to E, indicating that you're in an area that doesn't offer full 3G wireless service. And, sometimes the signal goes away altogether.

My advice for random signal weirdness is to wait. Oftentimes, the signal comes back after a few minutes. If it doesn't, the cellular data network might be down or you may just be in an area with lousy service. Consider changing your location.

As a desperate move, you can try reactivating the Galaxy Tab for the cellular network. Obey these steps:

1. **From the Home screen, press the Menu soft button.**
2. **Choose Settings.**
3. **Choose Wireless and Network.**
4. **Choose Roaming Capability Update.**
5. **Touch the Activate button.**
6. **Heed further directions either on the screen or over the Tab's speaker.**

By following these steps, you can reactivate the cellular data service if something weird has happened. There's no harm in running the steps, so it's worth a try.

Check the Wi-Fi connection: For Wi-Fi connections, you have to ensure that the Wi-Fi is set up properly and working. This process usually involves pestering the person who configured the Wi-Fi signal or made it available, such as the cheerful person with the bad haircut who serves you coffee.

Music is playing and you want it to stop: It's awesome that the Galaxy Tab continues to play music while you do other things. Getting the music to stop quickly, however, requires some skill. Primarily, you need skill at pulling down the notifications and choosing the song that's playing from the top of the Ongoing list. Touch the Pause button to silence the tune.

The MicroSD card is busy: Most often, the MicroSD card is busy because you've mounted it on your computer's storage system. To unbusy the MicroSD card, unmount the MicroSD card by turning off USB storage. See Chapter 19.

When the MicroSD card remains busy, consider restarting the Galaxy Tab, as described earlier in this section.

An app has run amok: Sometimes, apps that misbehave let you know. You see a warning on the screen announcing the app's stubborn disposition. Touch the Force Close button to shut down the errant app.

When you don't see a warning or when an app appears to be unduly obstinate, you can shut 'er down the manual way, by following these steps:

1. **From the Applications Tray, choose the Settings icon.**

2. **Choose Applications.**

3. **Choose Manage Applications.**

   If you choose the Running tab from the top of the Manage Applications screen, you see a list of only the apps that are running. That helps narrow the list.

4. **Choose the application that's causing you distress.**

   For example, a program doesn't start or says that it's busy or has another issue.

5. **Touch the Force Stop button.**

   The program stops.

After stopping the program, try opening it again to see whether it works. If the program continues to run amok, contact its developer: Open the Market app, press the Menu soft button, and choose My Apps. Choose the app you're having trouble with, scroll to the bottom of the app's main screen, and choose Send Email to Developer. Send the developer a message describing the problem.

Reset the Galaxy Tab software: When all else fails, you can do the drastic thing and reset all Tab software, essentially returning it to the state it was in when it first arrived. Obviously, you need not perform this step lightly. In fact, consider finding support (see the next section) before you start:

1. **From the Home screen, touch the Menu soft button.**

2. **Choose Settings.**

3. **Choose Privacy.**

4. **Choose Factory Data Reset.**

5. **Touch the Reset Device button.**

6. **Touch the Erase Everything button to confirm.**

   All the information you've set or stored on the Galaxy Tab is purged.

Again, do not follow these steps unless you're certain that they will fix the problem or you're under orders to do so from someone in Tech Support.

Getting support

You can use two sources for support for your Galaxy Tab. The first is your cellular provider; the second is Samsung. The cellular provider can assist you with data connection issues, but you have to contact Samsung for hardware or other issues. (I can see the potential for major corporation finger-pointing here.)

Before you contact your cellular provider, you need to know the device's phone number:

1. **From the Home screen, touch the Menu soft button.**
2. **Choose Settings.**
3. **Choose About Device.**
4. **Choose Status.**

    The Galaxy Tab's phone number is specified beneath Device Number.

Jot down that phone number! Do it right here:

Table 22-1 lists the support numbers of Galaxy Tab cellular carriers in the United States.

Table 22-1	Cellular Service Support Information	
Carrier	*Number*	*Web Site*
AT&T	(800) 331-0500	http://www.wireless.att.com/support
Sprint	(800) 639-6111	http://support.sprint.com
T-Mobile	(800) 937-8997	http://support.t-mobile.com
US Cellular	(800) 944-9400	http://www.uscellular.com/support
Verizon	(800) 922-0204	http://support.vzw.com

For hardware and other issues, you have to contact Samsung. The support number is (800) 726-7864.

Samsung doesn't have a specific Galaxy Tab support site. Instead, the support is linked to the cellular provider. You can, however, look for support at the Samsung Web site:

```
www.samsung.com/us/support
```

 No one likes wading through bottomless automatic customer support systems. Odds are good that you merely want to speak to a human. I've found that the fastest way to do that is to keep pressing the Zero key after you phone into their system. This process eventually turns you over to a live person, who, hopefully, can either deal with your problem or connect you with someone who can.

Valuable Galaxy Tab Q&A

I love Q&A! That's because not only is it an effective way to express certain problems and solutions but some of the questions might also cover things I've been wanting to ask.

"I can't turn the Tab on (or off)!"

Yes, sometimes the Galaxy Tab locks up. I even asked Samsung about this issue specifically, and they told me it's impossible for the Galaxy Tab to seize. Despite this denial, I've discovered that if you press and hold the Power button for about 8 seconds, the Tab turns either off or on, depending on which state it's in.

I've had a program lock the Galaxy Tab tight when the 8-second Power switch trick didn't work. In that case, I waited 12 minutes or so, just letting the Tab sit there and do nothing. Then I pressed and held the Power button for about 8 seconds, and it turned itself back on.

"My Home screen app shortcuts disappear!"

Your app shortcuts should stay affixed to the Home screen, even after you've turned the Tab off and then on again. The only time they disappear is when the apps are installed on the MicroSD card rather than in the Galaxy Tab's main memory. In that situation, apps you've placed on the Home screen disappear whenever you mount the MicroSD card into your computer's storage system.

The solution is to move the app from the MicroSD card to the Tab's main storage. See Chapter 17 for information.

"The touchscreen doesn't work!"

A touchscreen, such as the one used on the Galaxy Tab, requires a human finger for proper interaction. The Tab interprets the static potential between the human finger and the device to determine where the touchscreen is being touched.

You cannot use the touchscreen when you're wearing gloves, unless they're specially designed, static-carrying gloves that claim to work on touchscreens.

The touchscreen might also fail when the battery power is low or when the Galaxy Tab has been physically damaged.

"The onscreen keyboard is too small!"

Consider yourself lucky: The onscreen keyboard on the Galaxy Tab is, at minimum, two sizes larger than the typical cell phone. Even so, it's not a full-size keyboard.

You can rotate the Tab to landscape orientation to see a larger onscreen keyboard. Not every app may feature a landscape-orientation keyboard. When one does, you'll find typing on the wider onscreen keyboard much easier than normal.

The Tab also has the keyboard dock, which lets you plug the Tab into a laptop-size keyboard that your fingers will probably enjoy more than the onscreen keyboard.

"The battery doesn't charge"

Start from the source: Is the wall socket providing power? Is the cord plugged in? The cable may be damaged, so try another cable.

When charging from a USB port on a computer, ensure that the computer is turned on. Most computers don't provide USB power when they're turned off.

"The Tab gets so hot that it turns itself off!"

Yikes! An overheating gadget can be a nasty problem. Judge how hot the Galaxy Tab is by seeing whether you can hold it in your hand: When it's too hot to hold, it's too hot. If you're using the Galaxy Tab to cook an egg, it's too hot.

Turn off the Galaxy Tab and let the battery cool.

If the overheating problem continues, have the Galaxy Tab looked at for potential repair. The battery might need to be replaced, and, as far as I can tell, there's no way to remove and replace the Galaxy Tab battery by yourself.

Do not continue to use any gizmo that's too hot! The heat damages the electronics. It can also start a fire.

"The Tab doesn't do Landscape mode!"

Not every app takes advantage of the Galaxy Tab's ability to orient itself in Landscape mode, or even upside-down mode. For example, many games set their orientations one way and refuse to change, no matter how you hold the Tab. So, just because the app doesn't go into Landscape mode doesn't mean that anything is broken.

Confirm that the orientation lock isn't on: Pull down the notifications and check the quick actions at the top of the notification panel. Orientation Lock is the last item in the list, on the far right side. If that item is selected, the Galaxy Tab won't do Landscape mode — or upside-down mode.

Part VI

The Part of Tens

The Tab tells you how much memory
services are using.

Camera (40)

qik (2)

H

bluetooth (1)

sdcard (1)

download (3)

Kids (20)

In this part . . .

The caboose on the *For Dummies* book train is The Part of Tens. Here, you'll find a collection of chapters, each of which is packed with ten items. They aren't useless items or trivia. You won't find a chapter here titled Ten Songs You Can't Get Out of Your Head or Ten Creative Decorating Hints Using Only a Weed Whacker or Ten Things You Wouldn't Want to Find in a Jar of Mayonnaise. No, each chapter in this part of the book contains ten items that deal specifically with the Galaxy Tab.

04:20 AM Catch plane

23

Ten Tips, Tricks, and Shortcuts

In This Chapter

▶ Reviewing your recent apps

▶ Halting services

▶ Making the onscreen keyboard vibrate

▶ Taking a screenshot

▶ Removing the vocal dirty word filter

▶ Using contact screen shortcuts

▶ Finding your wayward Galaxy Tab

▶ Setting locations for your schedule

▶ Adding the Active Applications widget

▶ Remembering the Video app

tip is a small suggestion, a word of advice often spoken from experience or knowledge. A *trick,* which is something not many know, usually causes amazement or surprise. A *shortcut* is a quick way to get home, even though it crosses the old graveyard and you never quite know whether Old Man Grumby is the groundskeeper or a zombie.

I'd like to think that just about everything in this book is a tip, trick, or shortcut for using the Galaxy Tab. Even so, I've distilled a list of items in this chapter that are definitely worthy of note.

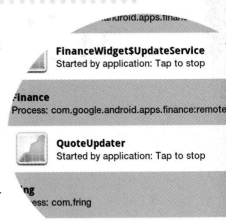

Summon a Recently Opened App

I have to kick myself in the head every time I return to the Applications screen to, once again, page through the panels o' icons to dig up an app I just opened. Why bother? Because I can press and hold the Home soft button to instantly see a list of recently opened apps.

Pressing and holding the Home soft button works no matter what you're doing on the Galaxy Tab; you don't necessarily have to view the Home screen to see the list of recently opened apps.

Stop Unneeded Services

Some things may be going on in your Galaxy Tab that you don't need or even suspect. These activities include the monitoring of information, apps that update, or tiny programs that check on the device's status. The technical term for these activities is *services*.

When a service has started that you don't want, or have been requested to stop, you can halt the service. Here's how:

1. **While at the Home screen, press the Menu soft button.**

2. **Choose Settings.**

3. **Choose Applications.**

4. **Choose Running Services.**

   You see the Running Services screen, similar to Figure 23-1.

5. **Touch a service to stop it.**

   Most likely, it's a service you recognize that you don't need or a service you've been directed to disable from another source or authority.

   For example, in Figure 23-1, you see the Fring Call Service. I don't plan to use Fring, so I can stop this service by touching it.

6. **Touch the Stop button to halt the service.**

When you stop a service, you free resources used by that service. These resources include memory and processor power. The result of stopping unneeded services can be improved performance.

The service you stopped will most likely start up again the next time you start the Galaxy Tab, or if you run the app. The only way to halt a specific service for all eternity is to uninstall the program associated with that service, which is a drastic step. Even then, not every app can be removed; pre-installed apps and phone company apps are stuck to your Galaxy Tab like August ticks on a hound dog.

✏ Do not randomly disable services. Many of them are required for the Galaxy Tab to do its job, or for the apps you use to carry out their tasks. If you disable a service you don't recognize and the device begins to act funny, turn the Galaxy Tab off and then on again. That should fix the problem.

✔ The colorful bar at the bottom of the Running Services screen (refer to Figure 23-1) illustrates memory usage in your Galaxy Tab. The red area represents services that cannot be stopped or killed. In Figure 23-1, four apps are represented there, which occupy a total of 87MB of storage. The yellow area represents services used by seven apps that occupy 86MB. The green area represents 172MB of free space.

Figure 23-1: Services running on the Galaxy Tab.

Set Keyboard Feedback

Typing on a touchscreen keyboard isn't easy. Along with the screen being tiny (or your fingers being big), it's difficult to tell what you're typing. You can add some feedback to the typing process. Heed these steps:

1. **While at the Home screen, press the Menu soft button.**

2. **Choose Settings.**

3. **Choose Sound Settings.**

4. **Put a check mark by the option Haptic Feedback.**

   This option causes physical feedback when you press a "key" on the onscreen keyboard.

5. **Optionally, choose the item Vibration Intensity.**

   Set how much you want the Tab to vibrate. Some high-vibration settings might also be audible.

Now when you type on the onscreen keyboard, you can feel the keys as you press them.

- Haptic feedback also applies to the soft buttons, as well as to other things you touch in the Galaxy Tab interface.

- These steps affect the Swype keyboard, but only when you use hunt-and-peck to type on it, as opposed to using Swype to rapidly input text.

Take a Picture of the Screen

In the computer world, it's a *screen shot*. What it does is take a picture of the display — everything from corner to corner and from edge to edge. The image is then saved, just like any other picture. It can come in handy for doc-umentation purposes or just about any time you need to record something that's shown on the screen.

To take a screen shot on your Galaxy Tab, press and hold the Back soft button and then press the Power button. You hear a shutter click, just as though you've taken a picture. After a moment, the text `Screen Captured, Saved As Image File` appears. It's your clue that the screen shot was successful.

- You can view your Galaxy Tab screen shots in the Gallery: Choose the ScreenCapture pile to view them.

- As with any image stored in the Gallery, you can use the Share menu to send the image elsewhere. For example, you can attach the image to an email message.

- Screen shots are stored in the `ScreenCapture` folder on the MicroSD card.

- Many of this book's figures were taken by using the screen shot tech-nique described in this section. Even so, not every screen can be cap-tured that way; sometimes, pressing the Back soft button moves you back, which is what the button does. In those cases, taking a screen shot doesn't work. (For this book, I also used a special program to capture particularly stubborn screen images.)

Add Spice to Dictation

I feel that too few people use dictation, despite how handy it can be — especially for text messaging. Anyway, if you've used dictation, you might have noticed that it occasionally censors some of the words you utter. Perhaps you're the kind of person who won't put up with that kind of ####.

Relax, ####. You can lift the vocal censorship ban by following these steps:

1. **At the Home screen, press the Menu soft button.**
2. **Choose Settings.**
3. **Choose Voice Input and Output.**
4. **Choose Voice Recognition Settings.**
5. **Remove the check mark by the option Block Offensive Words.**

And just what are offensive words? I would think that *censorship* would be an offensive word. But no, apparently the words ####, ####, and even innocent little old #### are deemed offensive by Google Voice. What the ####?

Create a Contact Screen Shortcut

The people you contact most often are deserving of their own contact shortcuts on the Home screen. You just don't realize how useful such a thing is until you have one.

To create a contact screen shortcut, follow these steps:

1. **Long-press the Home screen.**
2. **Choose Shortcuts.**
3. **Choose Contact.**
4. **Choose a contact from the Contacts list.**

    Preferably, choose someone whom you frequently and electronically contact.

An icon representing the contact appears on the screen. If the contact has an associated picture, you see the picture. Otherwise, you see a generic contact icon.

The beauty of the contact screen shortcut lies in pressing it: Touching the shortcut displays a pop-up list of quick tasks for the contact, as shown in Figure 23-2.

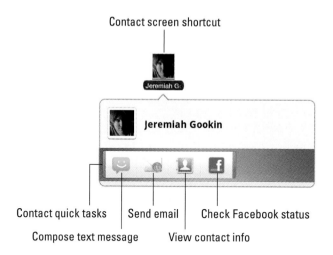

Figure 23-2: Quick tasks for a contact screen shortcut.

Choose a quick task for a contact by touching its icon, as shown in Figure 23-2. For some contacts with lots of quick tasks, you may have to scroll the quick tasks left or right to see them all.

The number of quick task icons that appears for a contact depends on how much information you have available for the contact, such as email address, cell phone number (for texting), or linked contacts for Facebook, Skype, Twitter, and so on.

- ✔ To hide the quick contact information, simply touch another part of the Home screen or press the Back soft button.

- ✔ A contact's Facebook status may appear beneath the name, which isn't shown in Figure 23-2.

- ✔ Just touch the contact screen shortcut to see the quick tasks. When you long-press the shortcut, the Galaxy Tab believes that you want to move or delete the icon.

Find Your Lost Galaxy Tab

Someday you may lose your Galaxy Tab. It might be for a panic-filled few seconds, or it might be for forever. The hardware solution is to weld a heavy object to the Tab, such as a bowling ball or steam shovel, yet that kind of defeats the entire mobile/wireless paradigm. The software solution is to use a cell phone locator service.

Even though the Galaxy Tab isn't a cell phone, you can use the same apps that cell phones use to help find a wayward Galaxy Tab. Those apps use the cellular signal as well as the Tab's GPS to help locate a missing gizmo.

Many apps available on the Android Market can help locate your Galaxy Tab. I've not tried them all. Here are some suggestions:

- Lookout Mobile Security
- LocService
- Mobile Phone Locator

Most of these services require that you set up a Web page account to assist in locating your Galaxy Tab. They also enable services that send updates to the Internet. The updates assist in tracking your Galaxy Tab, in case it becomes lost or is stolen.

Enter Location Information for Your Events

When you create an event for the Calendar app, be sure to enter the event location. You can type either an address (if you know it) or the name of the location. The key is to type the text as you would type it in the Map app when searching for a location. That way, you can touch the event location and the Galaxy Tab displays it on the touchscreen. Finding an appointment couldn't be easier.

- See Chapter 12 for more information about the Maps app.
- See Chapter 16 for details about the Calendar.

Use the Active Applications Widget

The Active Applications widget serves a number of useful purposes: It tells you how many apps are running, how much battery juice is left, whether any apps are drawing a lot of battery power, and more! The Active Applications widget is shown in Figure 23-3.

Touching the Active Applications widget opens the Task Manager window, so in a way it's a shortcut for the Task Manager. Still, the widget is more useful because it lets you know right away how many apps are running.

Figure 23-3: The Active Applications widget.

To install the Active Applications widget, you need to know that its real name is Program Monitor. Follow these steps:

1. **Long-press the Home screen.**

2. **Choose Widgets.**

3. **Choose Program Monitor.**

   The widget is affixed to the Home screen you're viewing.

See Chapter 21 for information on moving the Active Applications widget around, in case you're displeased with its present location. Also see Chapter 17 for more information on Task Manager.

Try the Video App

I keep forgetting that you can get a separate Video app for looking at videos you've shot on the Tab, videos you've downloaded from the Internet, and videos copied to the Galaxy Tab from a computer.

Sure, you can use the Gallery app to view those videos, but they're nestled between all the pictures stored on your Tab — and not exactly easy to find. When you use the Video app, however, all videos show up in one place.

Now if they'd only come up with an app that automatically selects pictures of myself that I like, I'd really be happy.

Ten Things to Remember

*H*ave you ever tried to tie string around your finger to remember something? I've not attempted that technique just yet. The main reason is that I keep forgetting to buy string and have no way to remind myself.

For your Galaxy Tab, some things are definitely worth remembering. Out of the long, long list, I've come up with ten good ones.

...nail...

...: **Barack Obama** potus@whitehouse.go...

message: |

Use Dictation

It's such a handy feature, yet I constantly forget to use it: Rather than type short text messages, use dictation. You can access dictation from any onscreen keyboard by touching the Microphone button. Speak the text; the text appears. Simple.

bcc

You can also use dictation to search for things on the Galaxy Tab: Press and hold the Search soft button. Speak what you're searching for or say a specific command. For example, say "Email Obama." If Mr. Obama is one of your contacts and you have his email input, you see a screen similar to Figure 24-1. Keep dictating the message.

Figure 24-1: Dictating a quick email.

You can utter many other commands using dictation on the Galaxy Tab. Just touch the Help button after summoning the main dictation screen.

Landscape Orientation

I enjoy the occasional widescreen view. Apps such as the Browser, Kindle, and even Email look much better longways than "tallways." Tilting the Galaxy Tab to the side can even help your typing, by presenting a wider version of the onscreen keyboard.

 Not every app supports landscape orientation. Some apps, such as YouTube and a few games, appear only in landscape orientation.

Orientation Lock

The opposite of remembering that the Galaxy Tab has landscape orientation (see the preceding section) is forgetting that it has an orientation lock feature. When engaged, the orientation lock prevents the screen from adjusting between Landscape and Portrait modes: The screen stays fixed in whichever orientation it was in when you set the orientation lock.

To set the orientation lock, pull down the notifications and choose the Notification Lock quick action.

Use the Keyboard Suggestions

Don't forget to take advantage of the suggestions that appear above the onscreen keyboard when you're typing text. In fact, you don't even need to touch a suggestion; to replace your text with the highlighted suggestion, simply touch the onscreen keyboard's space key. Zap! The word appears.

The keyboard suggestions are available only on the Samsung Keypad, not on the Swype keyboard. To ensure that suggestions are enabled, follow these steps:

1. **Start the Settings app.**
2. **Choose Language and Keyboard.**
3. **Choose Samsung Keypad.**
4. **Ensure that a check mark appears by XT9, the predictive text option.**

Also refer to Chapter 4 for additional information on using the keyboard suggestions.

Things That Consume Lots of Battery Juice

Three items on the Galaxy Tab suck down battery power faster than that massive alien fleet is defeated by a plucky antihero who just wants the girl:

- ✔ Wi-Fi networking
- ✔ Bluetooth
- ✔ Navigation

Both Wi-Fi networking and Bluetooth require extra power for their wireless radios. The amount isn't much, but enough that I would consider shutting them down when battery power gets low.

Navigation is certainly handy, but because the Galaxy Tab touchscreen is on the entire time and dictating text to you, the battery drains rapidly. If possible, try to plug the Tab into the car's power socket when you're navigating.

See Chapter 22 for more information on managing the Galaxy Tab's battery.

Use a Docking Stand

I tend to keep my Galaxy Tab in one spot when I'm not on the road. The multimedia dock is a helpful way to hold the Tab, to keep it propped up and easy to use. As its home for the Tab, I always know where it is and, because I don't have the cleanest of desktops, I can always find the Tab despite ominous swells in seas of paper.

Given the choice of multimedia stand or keyboard dock, I prefer the multimedia stand. The keyboard stand is nice, but it takes up some room and I don't do much typing on my Tab. (Refer to the section "Use Dictation," earlier in this chapter.)

The Galaxy Tab Can Make Phone Calls

Yeah, I know: It's not a phone. I wish it were (and I'm sure Samsung does as well), but the Galaxy Tab lacks a native ability to use the cellular system for making phone calls. Even so, with apps like Skype and Tango, you can make phone calls and even video-chat with others. Refer to Chapter 10 for details.

Properly Access the MicroSD Card

The Galaxy Tab's removable storage area, the *MicroSD card,* can be accessed from your computer. To let you do so, the card needs to be mounted into the computer's storage system. That way, all the stuff you have on your Galaxy Tab — music, videos, still pictures, contacts, and other types of information — can be accessed or backed up on the computer. Likewise, you can copy information from your computer to the MicroSD card on the Galaxy Tab.

Oh, the whole accessing-the-MicroSD-card-thing is an old song-and-dance that I go into detail about in Chapter 19. What's important to remember is that when the MicroSD card is mounted on your computer's storage system, the Galaxy Tab cannot access the card. If an attempt is made, a message appears, explaining that the MicroSD card is busy.

When you're done accessing the MicroSD card from your computer, be sure to stop USB storage: Choose the Turn Off button on the USB storage screen. Refer to Chapter 19 for details.

Snap a Pic of That Contact

Here's something I always forget: Whenever you're near one of your contacts, take the person's picture. Sure, some people are bashful, but most folks are flattered. The idea is to build up your Contacts list so that all contacts have photos.

When taking a picture, be sure to show it to the person before you assign it to the contact. Let them decide whether it's good enough. Or, if you just want to be rude, assign a crummy-looking picture. Heck, you don't even have to do that: Just take a random picture of anything and assign it to a contact: A plant. A rock. Your cat. But, seriously, keep in mind that the Tab can take a contact's picture the next time you meet up with that person.

See Chapter 13 for more information on using the Galaxy Tab's camera and assigning a picture to a contact.

The Search Command

Google is known worldwide for its searching abilities. By gum, the word *Google* is now synonymous with searching. So please don't forget that the Galaxy Tab, which uses the Google Android operating system, has a powerful Search command.

The Search command is not only powerful but also available all over. The Search soft button can be pressed at any time, in just about any program, to search for information, locations, people — you name it. It's handy. It's everywhere. Use it.

Ten Great Apps

More than 100,000 apps are at the Android Market — so many that it would take you more than a relaxing evening to discover them all. Rather than list every single app, I've culled from the lot some apps that I find exceptional — that show the diversity of the Android Market but also how well the Galaxy Tab can run Android apps.

Every app listed in this chapter is free; see Chapter 17 for directions on finding them using the Android Market, or scan the barcodes in the margin using your Tab to download the apps quickly. (See the later section "Barcode Scanner" to get started.)

▬pad
.₅KB

Aldiko
1.94MB

 Amazon MP3
1.13MB

 Angry Birds
14.55MB

 Angry Birds
16.04MB

▬rcode Scanner

Angry Birds

 The birds may be angry at the green piggies for stealing eggs, but you'll be crazy for this addictive game. Like most popular games, Angry Birds is simple. It's easy to learn, fun to play. The best part is that on the Galaxy Tab, with its awesome 7-inch display, the Angry Birds game is beautiful.

Barcode Scanner

Many apps from the Android Market can be quickly accessed by scanning their barcode information. Scanning with what? Why, your Galaxy Tab, of course!

By using an app such as Barcode Scanner, you can instantly read in and translate barcodes that open product descriptions, Web page links, or links directly to apps in the Android Market.

Though you can find similar barcode-scanning apps, I find Barcode Scanner the easiest to use: Run the app. Point the Tab's camera at a bar code and, in a few moments, you see a link or an option indicating what to do next. To get an app, choose Open Browser. This option takes you to the Android Market, where obtaining the app is just a few touches away.

Using the Barcode Scanner in this chapter

Throughout this chapter, you find barcode icons. Specifically, they are QR Codes, which is a special square type of barcode. After installing the Barcode Scanner app (or a similar app), use your Galaxy Tab to scan the barcodes. Choose the button Open Browser to download the recommended app from the Android Market.

Additional app recommendations and their barcodes are found all over the Internet, in magazines, and on my Galaxy Tab support page at www.wambooli.com/help/galaxytab.

Dolphin Browser

The Browser app that comes with the Galaxy Tab is despised by many Android users. A better and more popular alternative is Dolphin Browser.

Like many popular computer browsers, Dolphin Browser features a tabbed interface, which works much better than the silly multiple window interface of the standard Browser app.

The Dolphin Browser also sports many handy tools, which you can access by pressing the Menu soft button. Unlike on other Android apps, the tools pop up on a menu you can see on the screen.

Gesture Search

The Gesture Search app provides a new way to find information on your Galaxy Tab. Rather than use a keyboard or dictate, you simply draw on the touchscreen the first letter of whatever you're searching for.

Start the Google Search app to begin a search. Use your finger to draw a big letter on the screen. After you draw a letter, search results appear on the screen. You can continue drawing more letters to refine the search or touch a search result.

Gesture Search can find contacts, music, apps, and bookmarks in the Browser app.

Google Finance

The Google Finance app is an excellent market-tracking tool for folks who are obsessed with the stock market or want to keep an eye on their portfolios. The app offers you an overview of the market and updates to your stocks as well as links to financial news.

To get the most from this app, configure Google Finance on the Web, using your computer. You can create lists of stocks to watch, which are then instantly synchronized with your Galaxy Tab. You can visit Google Finance on the Web at

```
www.google.com/finance
```

As with other Google services, Google Finance is provided to you for free, as part of your Google account.

Google Sky Map

 Ever look up into the sky and say, "What the heck is that?" Unless it's a bird, an airplane, a satellite, or a UFO, the Google Sky Map will help you find what it is. You may learn that a particularly bright star in the sky is, in fact, the planet Jupiter.

The Google Sky Map app is elegant. It basically turns the Galaxy Tab into a window you can look through to identify things in the night sky. Just start the app and hold the Galaxy Tab up to the sky. Pan the Tab to identify planets, stars, and constellations.

 Google Sky Map promotes using the Galaxy Tab without touching it. For this reason, the screen goes blank after a spell, which is merely the Tab's power-saving mode. If you plan extensive stargazing with the Google Sky Map, consider resetting the screen timeout. Refer to Chapter 2 for information on this topic.

Movies

 The Movies app is the Galaxy Tab's gateway to Hollywood. It lists currently running films and films that are opening, and it has links to your local theaters with showtimes and other information. The app is also tied into the popular Rotten Tomatoes Web site for reviews and feedback. If you enjoy going to the movies, you'll find the Movies app a valuable addition to your Galaxy Tab's app library.

SportsTap

 I admit to not being a sports nut, so it's difficult for me to identify with the craving to have the latest scores, news, and schedules. The sports nuts in my life, however, tell me that the very best app for that purpose is a handy thing named SportsTap.

Rather than blather on about something I'm not into, just take my advice and obtain SportsTap. I believe you'll be thrilled.

Voice Recorder

 The Galaxy Tab can record your voice or other sounds, and the Voice Recorder is a good app for performing this task. It has an elegant and simple interface: Touch the big Record button to start recording. Make a note for yourself or record a friend doing his Daffy Duck impression.

Previous recordings are stored in a list on the Voice Recorder's main screen. Each recording is shown with its title, the date and time of the recording, and the recording duration.

Zedge

 The Zedge program is a helpful resource for finding wallpapers and ringtones — millions of them. It's a sharing app, so you can access wallpapers and ringtones created by other Android users as well as share your own. If you're looking for a specific sound, or something special for Home screen wallpaper, Zedge is the best place to start your search.

Index